CULTURE—MEANING—ARCHITECTURE

For my wife, Laura, who carries with her the inquisitive nature of the anthropologist in everything that she does.

Culture—Meaning—Architecture

Critical reflections on the work of Amos Rapoport

Edited by
KEITH DIAZ MOORE
Washington State University at Spokane

Routledge
Taylor & Francis Group
LONDON AND NEW YORK

First published 2000 by Ashgate Publishing

Reissued 2019 by Routledge
2 Park Square, Milton Park, Abingdon, Oxon, OXl 4 4RN
52 Vanderbilt Avenue, New York, NY 10017

Routledge is an imprint of the Taylor & Francis Group, an informa business

A Library of Congress record exists under LC control number:

ISBN 13: 978-1-138-71233-1 (hbk)
ISBN 13: 978-1-138-71232-4 (pbk)
ISBN 13: 978-1-315-20024-8 (ebk)

Contents

List of Contributors

Irwin Altman is a Distinguished Professor of Psychology at the University of Utah. His research examines social and environmental aspects of close, interpersonal relationships from a cross-cultural perspective. A recent publication is: Altman, I. & Ginat, J. (1996). *Polygamous Families in Contemporary Society.* Cambridge: Cambridge University Press.

Robert M. Beckley is currently Professor and Dean Emeritus in the College of Architecture and Urban Planning at the University of Michigan. For more than thirty years, Bob has been engaged in teaching, research and administration related to architectural education and the profession. He is Past President of the Association of Collegiate Schools of Architecture and a Fellow of the American Institute of Architects.

Keith Diaz Moore is a Visiting Associate Professor at the Interdisciplinary Design Institute, Washington State University. Keith is also a registered architect and principal of Place Associates, a development and architectural consultant firm. His current research includes a two-year study funded by the Helen Bader Foundation to develop a planning and design guide for dementia day care facilities.

Francis Duffy is Chairman of the DEGW partnership, a design and consulting firm with offices in Amsterdam, Athens, Berlin, Glasgow, London, Madrid, Milan and Paris. His current research interest is relating changes in organizational situations and information technology to office design. Duffy is the author of *The Changing Workplace* and *The New Office* published by Conran Octopus (1997). Frank is Past President of the Royal Institute of British Architects.

Yasser Elsheshtawy is Assistant Professor in the Department of Architecture, United Arab Emirates University. He received a Ph.D. from the University of Wisconsin - Milwaukee and a B.Arch. from Cairo University. His research has focused primarily on cross-cultural studies of the urban environment.

Charles T. Goodsell received a Ph.D. in Political Science from Harvard University, and for the past twenty years has been Professor in the Center for Public Administration and Policy at the Virginia Polytechnic Institute and State University. He is the author of seventy articles and seven books, his most recent being *The American Statehouse: Political Analysis of a Building Type*, University of Kansas Press.

Linda N. Groat received her Ph.D. in Environmental Psychology from the University of Surrey and is a former Associate Dean and currently Professor in the College of Architecture and Urban Planning, University of Michigan. She was editor of *Giving Places Meaning*, published in 1995 by the Academic Press and her current research focuses on issues of diversity in architectural education.

Wesley Janz is a registered architect who received his Ph.D. in architecture from the University of Michigan and is an Assistant Professor of Architecture at Ball State University, He is a past recipient of fellowships from both the Graham Foundation for the Advancement of the Fine Arts as well as the Institute for the Humanities.

Susan Kent, Professor of Anthropology at Old Dominion University, has conducted ethnographic and ethnoarchaeological research among the Navajo Indians, Tulalip Indians and the Bakgalagadi and Basarwa of the Kalahari Desert. She was editor of *Domestic architecture and the use of space* (1990). Her current research involves a long—term archaeological project in South Africa.

Jon Lang completed his doctoral education at Cornell University working with Barclay Jones and James J. Gibson. Currently he is Head of the School of the Built Environment at the University of New South Wales. He has written numerous publications including *Creating architectural theory: The role of the behavioral sciences in environmental design* (1987), and *Urban Design: The American Experience* (1994). His area of inquiry centers on issues of urban design.

Roderick J. Lawrence received his Doctorate of Science from the Ecole Polytechnique Federale in Lausanne, Switzerland. He currently holds the tenured position of Master of Teaching and Research at the Centre for Human Ecology and Environmental Sciences at the University of Geneva. In 1999 he was appointed Professor in the Faculty of Social and Economic Sciences. He is author of the 1987 publication *Housing, Dwellings and Homes: Design Theory, Research and Practice.*

Setha M. Low received her Ph.D. in Cultural Anthropology from the University of California-Berkeley. She is currently Professor of Environmental Psychology and Anthropology at the Graduate School and University Center of the City University of New York. She is currently finishing two books: *Politics of Public Space: The Culture and History of the Latin American Plaza*, and *Theorizing the City: The New Urban Anthropology Reader*.

Paul Oliver is Director of the Oxford Brookes' Centre for Vernacular Architecture Studies. He is editor of the acclaimed *Encyclopedia of Vernacular Architecture of the World,* published in 1997. Dr. Oliver was instrumental in the establishment of the Graduate Diploma option in International Studies in Vernacular Architecture offered at Oxford Brookes University.

Amos Rapoport is Distinguished Professor of Architecture at the University of Wisconsin-Milwaukee. He is the editor of four books and the author of six others including *House Form and Culture* which has been translated into five other languages. He is Editor-in-Chief of *Urban Ecology*, an Associate Editor of *Environment and Behavior,* and in 1980 was awarded the Distinguished Career Award of the Environmental Design Research Association.

Foreword

Paul Oliver

An Intermittent Memoir

"More in your country than mine" said the author of *Theory and Design in the First Machine Age* (Banham, 1960). Peter Reyner Banham was Professor of History at the Bartlett School of Architecture at University College, London, and in our slightly uneasy relationship, he passed on any contacts that he thought might be of interest to me. "I'm not too sure about him," he added, guardedly. The following day a stocky Australian of about my own age (forty) turned up at my office, squeezed in the second floor of the Architectural Association's School of Architecture down the road in Bedford Square. He introduced himself as Amos Rapoport, doing research in London. We discussed our respective plans - his was a book nearing completion on the importance of culture in defining and shaping house form. Mine was also a book - the first of what I hoped would be a series of several on a related theme, though mine was to be a compilation of case studies. Would Amos Rapoport be interested in contributing to it? He'd think about it, but needed more information.

I explained that mine was to be the first in a series of "New Studies in Vernacular Architecture" but that the publisher, a small but long established firm named Barrie and Rockliff, The Cresset Press, had recommended that I did not use the term "vernacular architecture" (no one would know what it meant). I entitled it *Shelter and Society* (Oliver, 1969). Amos Rapoport agreed to write a chapter with unexpected finality; having made his mind up there was no further hesitation. Soon after he came up with his subject; "The Pueblo and the Hogan" (Rapoport, 1969a). Placing it in the context of the other contributions, I observed in the Introduction that "though similar material resources and similar economies may lead to building types with many elements in common, socio-cultural demands are probably more important in determining the eventual forms employed. Amos Rapoport takes an environment, that of desert regions in New Mexico and Arizona, to show how two North American Indian societies sharing identical climatic conditions and terrain have evolved strikingly dissimilar forms of shelter" (Oliver, 1969: 31).

I was delighted to have his contribution for it challenged two prevalent attitudes to vernacular architecture: climatic determinism and resources determinism. There was a problem: the chapter was illustrated with simplified maps and plans, diagrams and cut-away perspectives. Could he include some photographs? No, he didn't use photographs. But many of our readers would have no idea of what a south-western Pueblo, or a Navajo *hogan* would look like. He promised that he would make an exception, and before publication a sheaf of photographs arrived. "It is likely, and I for one hope, that both life styles and built forms - the future equivalents of the pueblo and the hogan - will preserve their differences and continue to bring richness and beauty to the south-west," (Rapoport, 1969a: 78) Amos wrote, concluding the chapter. Well, that was over thirty years ago. Amos hasn't used photographs much since, and "richness and beauty" seldom appear in his writing.

Amos Rapoport's seminal book, *House Form and Culture* had also been published in 1969 and had rapidly and deservedly become famous. So had its author who, in the intervening years had been writing articles for the *Journal of Aesthetic Education* , the *International Journal of Symbology*, the *International Journal of Environment Studies* and many others. A few years later I invited him to contribute to what was to prove to be the last of the series, *Shelter, Sign and Symbol* (Oliver, 1975). I doubted whether he would have time to write a chapter for, apart from his writing and after a spell as Professor in the University of Sydney, Australia, he had accepted a joint post as professor of Architecture and of Anthropology at the University of Wisconsin, Milwaukee. But he did find the time, and "Australian Aborigines and the Definition of Place" (Rapoport, 1975) was the outcome. It had one photograph - provided by Dr. Stephen Bochner - and a score of lively drawings and diagrams.

The text displayed the breadth of his reading, which had branched into other disciplines, and his propensity for summarising in terms of lists, like "the way in which hunters and gatherers (including aborigines) use space can be expressed in terms of a set of concepts derived from animal studies" (Rapoport, 1975: 39) which included *Home Range; Core areas; Territory* and *Jurisdiction.* While his arguments were persuasive I was never altogether happy with the lists, their reductionism always leaving me aware of the exceptions to their rules. But there were bound to be minor disagreements and differing points of view in our studies, and our respective approaches to research.

House Form and Culture had been in print for six years by the time *Shelter, Sign and Symbol* was published. It was a landmark in writing on vernacular architecture, countering the simplistic aestheticism of Bernard Rudofsky's (1964) *Architecture Without Architects* with clear reasoning and an impressive frame of reference. I placed it on my bibliographies for students, and it has remained there for three decades. Not that I felt that I could recommend it without drawing their attention to some of the points with which I disagreed. For instance, having been interested in issues of cultural change since I first became aware of them in traditional architecture when I lived in West Africa in 1964, I felt that Amos Rapoport understated their importance in his position that "as we have seen, primitive and vernacular buildings are distinguished by lack of change, differing in this respect from the more 'normal' historical material. These buildings are, therefore, basically non-chronological in nature" (Rapoport, 1969: 15). Diverse though they were, the numerous examples cited in his book also appeared to exist in a political vacuum, untouched by economic deprivation, social conflict, or oppression by dominant groups.

There were also problems arising from his diagrams. Deft, spontaneous and often witty, they served his purposes in getting over the point that he wished to communicate in a specific context. But I had already found that students were using them as sources of information and sometimes, from my personal experience, the conclusions drawn from them were erroneous. For example, Fig 4.3 "adapted from a number of sources, primarily Haan" depicted a "Matmata dwelling, Sahara" (Rapoport, 1969: 91). The drawing showed a rectilinear, hollow box, though all such shaft dwellings I had seen and visited in the Matmata region of Tunisia were voids with a circular or elliptical plan, excavated from the desert floor. The next page showed a "cutaway view of Ashanti hut," cylindrical and flat-roofed, with "walls, which in terms of structure are curtain walls and do no bearing, are of extremely heavy, thick mud construction" (Rapoport, 1969: 92). Indeed they are so built, but they are also load bearing. There are no cylindrical buildings in Ashanti and nor are the roofs flat. The mistake came from mis-reading the captions on a page of drawings in a 1954 article by Alan Houghton Brodrick in the *Architectural Review*, unreferenced in Amos's text.

Unfortunately, there were several such instances of confusion arising from the drawings, and I wondered for a long time why this was so. Then I had the opportunity to witness Amos "in action" while he was teaching a class at the University of Wisconsin, Milwaukee. The room was surrounded by clean blackboards when we entered , the students already in their places. By the end of the lecture the boards were all covered with chalk line diagrams and sketches in his truly inimitable style. It was an exhilarating, inspiring performance and the explanatory graphics did their work in highlighting the points made in the course of the lecture. They were essentially transitory, to be wiped off before the next lecture's strip was augmented with line drawings, and so the image was tied to the point in time. But in the book they remain for decades, and no one can tell how students are going to read and interpret them. With many of the sources obscure or unmentioned they were frequently used as information resources in themselves and I felt obliged to urge my students to read the arguments, grasp the theories but be cautious in the importance they placed on the drawings.

Though he used one or two photographs in this book and in others, Amos generally eschewed them as being misleading and carrying much irrelevant material in their single view images; he wanted to convey his ideas precisely through his diagrams. My own view was that their very economy and graphic simplicity could be just as misleading, but on this and a number of other issues we could only agree to differ. I got a clearer impression of the basic differences in our respective approaches to the subject of vernacular architecture when my wife Val and I had the opportunity to stay with Amos and his wife Dorothy in the 1970s. My interest in books is a consuming passion and for nearly four decades I have collected books and other publications on the subject, including anthropological and ethnographical works which include substantial references to dwellings and domesticity. So I was looking forward to spending some of the time going through his library.

Consequently, I was very surprised indeed to find that the Rapoport library did not exist. At least, not in the way I had imagined, with rooms lined with bookshelves and books classified with the precision of his writings. Amos took me to his office and showed me the row of filing cabinets in which he kept, as rigorously classified as I had expected, his collection of off-prints and photo-copied texts. He explained that he used the University library and other sources extensively, copied what he required and filed it in the appropriate category for the work he was undertaking. For me, this would be an impossible method, if only because the reading and handling of books is an important sensual pleasure in itself. But it would also be inappropriate partly because I am not always sure in what way a book may be of use to my work, and also because I often find that a volume purchased for one reason, later becomes more relevant to another undertaking. It made me realise that the intellectual pursuit was what mattered most to Amos, though I found it difficult to imagine myself working in his way.

Wherever we met and stayed together, whether house visiting in Wisconsin, or on one of his visits to England, at one of the houses we have had in London, Devon or now, at Woodstock, Oxfordshire; or for that matter, at conferences in Berkeley, Phoenix, Cincinnati, or elsewhere, Amos was always up and about before us. And not only that - he was in his training kit and out jogging, following a familiar route if he had been there before, or finding a new circuitous route that brought him back to his destination. It wasn't that he ran that fast; Amos was and is a determined and steady jogger, who seems to know the way he has to follow from the start no matter where he finds himself lodged. He jogged to keep himself fit, he explained, as he spent most of the day in the library or at his desk; and no doubt that was the reason. Perhaps it served to calm him too, to prepare him for the day's tasks. It seemed to me that his jogging was a kind of metaphor of his authorial quest: he always knew where he was going and what his destination at any one stage was going to be, and he worked steadily, persistently to reach it. Amos's articles and books were way-markers on the route which accounts, in part, for his predisposition to cite his own writings at length in the text and bibliography of each new publication. Irritating though this is for some readers, it is often because his have been the only previous works to develop the points to which he refers. He is not, to my knowledge, a believer in predestination, and yet there is a certain unwavering sense of direction which seems to lead him on, as if his life's work was already mapped out for him and he was obliged to write it up in stages.

Ever since I first knew him, Amos, a compact and short man, has always seemed to have had more energy and drive within him than his frame could quite contain. Only rarely though, did he lose control of his inner fire: once, rather unexpectedly, when another driver beat us to a parking place in Chicago; and on another occasion, at a party at Victor Papanek's home in Lawrence, Kansas, when Amos unleashed his hitherto suppressed anger over the attitudes of some modernist architects. But this was extremely rare, to my knowledge. Not that Amos suffered fools gladly, but he did not wither difficult questioners at conference plenaries with devastating put-downs; instead, he kept to the theme of his argument, tilting his head back, gesturing broadly, strutting on the platform and drawing his diagrams.

By the 1980s, he was much in demand as a keynote or plenary speaker at the Built Form and Culture Research conferences or those of the international associations for the study of Traditional Environments, or of People and Places. Perhaps it was in acknowledgement of their audiences that he changed the name of his newly defined field of Man-Environment Studies to Behavior-Environment Studies. "Towards a Man-Environment Approach to Urban Form and Design" was the sub-title of his book *Human Aspects of Urban Form* (Rapoport, 1977) which appeared ten years after *House Form and Culture*. With its 400-page discussion of environmental cognition , perception and associational meaning in the urban context, he emphasised the experiential aspects of the city which were largely disregarded in planning theory and practice. Though I was greatly in agreement with the thrust of his argument, my own concerns were for the multitudinous vernacular, popular and naive buildings which constituted then, as they do now, the majority of the world's buildings. If our paths were diverging somewhat we met at intervals, for Pergamon Press who were now his publishers, were located opposite the architecture block of Oxford Polytechnic. Amos didn't like Oxford as much as Cambridge. I preferred Oxford to Cambridge, I explained, because Oxford University was much more a part of its city than was Cambridge, and it had an industrial base, especially in automobile works, which gave it a harder edge. It was also ethnically more mixed than was Cambridge, apart from university students. If Oxford was the city of dreaming spires, Cambridge, I said, was more a city of ivory towers. "Ivory towers are all right with me," Amos replied. No doubt he needed the ivory towers in which to develop his theories.

It was another field in which our directions differed. For me, the challenge posed by the necessity to understand vernacular architecture within its cultural contexts had to be met through field work. For many years I was engaged in research in the field — in Europe, Africa, Asia and the Americas — as opportunities arose. Disaster studies in particular, gave a practical purpose to my research and also demonstrated in these heightened circumstances, the values that different cultures expressed through their buildings. Though Amos travelled extensively, sharply observing all around him, as far as I am aware he did not conduct extensive field work. There was a philosophical difference in our respective positions: coming, I suppose, from the British empirical tradition, I was very reluctant to launch into a theory until I had gathered sufficient data on which to establish a theoretical base. Yet, as every case study added new and sometimes conflicting information, this proved to be an unending task. Amos's fertile intellect, on the other hand, spilled out theories which he advanced and tested continually. Once, at a concluding conference plenary, I made a strong plea for more serious field studies in the vernacular traditions in the many parts of the world where little or nothing had been done. Amos did not argue with me; instead, softly striking one fist in the palm of his other hand to emphasise each syllable he said: "We must have our *theories.*" I asked him Why? Uncharacteristically he made no direct reply, but simply said, "yes, by all means do more research — but, we *must* have our theories."

Theories I believed, should be based on knowledge, and for those with less experience and aptitude for theoretical argument than Amos Rapoport, there was a dearth of information in accessible form on vernacular architecture. When the editorship of an encyclopedia of the subject was mooted I resolved to undertake it, being convinced that as no one else had done so, it was unlikely that anyone else would. An advisory board was necessary for the *Encyclopedia of Vernacular*

Architecture of the World (Oliver, 1997) and I invited Amos to join it, fearing again that he would be too committed to spare the time. But he did so willingly, responding to my questions briskly but valuably in his sprawling italic hand-writing. He also agreed to write entries on the "Behavioural" Approach to the study of vernacular architecture, including 'activity area analysis' which is "not much used in studies of vernacular environments" but which clearly should be (Rapoport, 1997a: 16-18); and an entry on "Meaning" in the section on Culture Traits and Attributes, which he considered was "the most important function of the built environment rather than something added to instrumental function" (Rapoport, 1997b: 92-94).

Eventually, in 1997, the *Encyclopedia* was published, and after coping with its 8.4 kilos as he carried it up to his office, Amos faxed his congratulations. "I could never have done it", he wrote. Fortunately he didn't try, for if he had we would have lost ten years of his ideas and theories, his lectures, articles and books, which together constitute a unique exploration of the relationship between human behaviour and the built environment. And I could never have done *that*, as I am all too well aware. I am proud to have been his friend, to have joined him in many debates and discussions and to have had some of his contributions in works I have edited, even if our relationship has at best been intermittent, as he jogged inexorably along his destined path.

References

Banham, R. (1960). *Theory and Design in the First Machine Age* , London: The Architectural Press.

Brodrick, A. H. (1954). "Grass Roots", *Architectural Review,* London. CXV, No. 686, February. 45-46. This reference is given in *House Form and Culture,* 11.

Oliver, P. (Ed). (1969). *Shelter and Society,* London: Barrie and Rockliff: The Cresset Press.

Oliver, Paul, (Ed). (1975). *Shelter, Sign and Symbol.* London: Barrie and Jenkins.

Oliver, Paul (Ed). (1997). *The Encyclopedia of Vernacular Architecture of the World.* (Three volumes). Cambridge, U.K: Cambridge University Press.

Rapoport, A. (1969a). "The Pueblo and the Hogan. A cross-cultural comparison of two responses to an environment" in P. Oliver (Ed.), *Shelter and Society,* London: Barrie and Rockliff: The Cresset Press. 66-79.

Rapoport, A. (1969b). *House Form and Culture,* Englewood Cliffs, N.J. Prentice-Hall, Inc. (*Foundations of Cultural Geography Series).*

Rapoport, A. (1975). "Australian Aborigines and the Definition of Place" in P. Oliver (Ed.), *Shelter, Sign and Symbol.* London: Barrie and Jenkins. 38-51.

Rapoport, A. (1977). *Human Aspects of Urban Form. Towards a Man-Environment Approach to Urban Form and Design.* Oxford: Pergamon Press.

Rapoport, A. (1997a). "Approaches and Concepts," in P. Oliver (Ed.), *The Encyclopedia of Vernacular Architecture of the World.* (Three volumes). Cambridge, U.K: Cambridge University Press.

Rapoport, A. (1997b). "Cultural Traits and Attributes," in P. Oliver (Ed.), *The Encyclopedia of Vernacular Architecture of the World.* (Three volumes). Cambridge, U.K: Cambridge University Press.

Rudofsky, B. (1964). *Architecture Without Architects. A Short Introduction to Non-Pedigreed Architecture* New York: Museum of Modern Art.

Preface

Francis Duffy

There Were No Architects There

"I saw many huts that the natives had made. They were all alike, and they all worked. There were no architects there. I came back with the impression of how clever was man who solved the problems of sun, rain, wind." Louis Kahn quoted by Amos Rapoport in *House Form and Culture*, 1969.

To explain Amos Rapoport's significance for a British architect of my generation it is necessary to reconstruct another world. Rapoport helped me, among many others, to escape the tyranny of an arid rationalism that denied choice, meaning and diversity in architectural form. Alan Colquhoun, Charles Jencks, George Baird, Charles Moore, Robert Venturi and Denise Scott-Brown, were broadcasting similar messages in the mid-sixties, often with more eloquence that Rapoport. But in my case no other architect besides Amos Rapoport had quite the same effect. No one jerked me out of the prejudices of my design training with such rigor. No one else stimulated my curiosity in quite the same way. This essay is an attempt to explain why.

The intellectual and artistic world that I inhabited at that time was puritanical and severe. The problem for architects today is to remember what buildings are for. The problem for architects in the mid sixties, certainly in welfare state Britain, was to find ways of articulating what buildings could be made to express. Functionalist dogma was so strong that to deviate from the narrow path of the program seemed exotic, dangerous, bound to lead to trouble. The social sciences, which in a largely socialist economy had a lot more sway that they do today, were more often called upon by architects to delimit what had to be done rather than to open up a discourse based upon choice. And of all the social sciences anthropology was the least explored by architects – perhaps because the essence of that discipline is diversity, made inevitable by the comparative study of culture and values.

In 1966 I was the part time editor of the Architectural Association Journal (AAJ). Searching for authors, I came upon Amos Rapoport, then newly arrived in London and teaching temporarily at University College London. My day job in architecture at the time, somewhat typical of what young architects just out of AA then tended to do, was in a government organization, the National Building Agency (NBA) whose task was to promote the rationalization of the production of public housing. How deeply I was involved in variety reduction in design at the NBA will soon become clear. Rapoport had a disturbing impact from the start. He wrote a short piece for my special environmental appraisal issue of the AAJ in January 1967 called, provocatively enough, given the unreflective and *dirigiste* mood of the time, "Some Consumer Comments on a Designed Environment" (Rapoport, 1967). The idea of being a 'consumer' of design is still something that makes older British architects of a certain political persuasion choke. The substance of the article was Rapoport's radical proposal for architects to listen to what users said about the environments that they were expected to inhabit. The piece was illustrated by a series of spontaneous verbal descriptions by students who had suffered certain windowless classrooms in what then seemed to me be the outlandish Tolman Hall on the Berkeley campus of the University of California. The words "sterility, over-simplicity, starkness, monotony, emptiness, isolation from the world, boxed-in quality' recurred again and again. It was over a year later as a graduate student at Berkeley, putting up with those very rooms, that I realized exactly the extent of the 'functionalist' reductionism that Rapoport's respondents had so accurately depicted.

Later in 1967 Amos Rapoport wrote another piece in response to yet another special issue of the AAJ, guest-edited by Charles Jencks and George Baird. This issue, perhaps the best we ever did, was called *Meaning in Architecture*. It was the basis of what was later to become a famous book (Jencks & Baird, 1969). What Rapoport wrote for me this time in response to this new special issue again had that deeply skeptical, slightly querulous, extremely well informed tone that, for me, has characterized all his writing ever since. The point he made, was very cogent in the context of the newly emerging, anti-functionalist discourse, that was already establishing a major part of the case for post-modernism. It was simply that to talk of meaning in architecture was meaningless unless you knew whose meaning you were talking about. Architecture is capable of expressing many meanings. To whom do such multiple meanings belong? Do some belong to an artistic elite and others to ordinary people? And, if they do belong to the people, to which people? Rapoport's comparative anthropological perspective was already the distinguishing feature of his work.

To drive the point home that "the universes of discourse of the designer and the public are totally different" Rapoport used a case study – Saarinen's CBS building in New York. CBS wanted to eliminate clutter, not trusting the taste of the individuals who worked for it. It was the 'designers' meaning, the architects' meaning that was enforced. Rapoport's reaction was to ask whether there was a "way of enabling buildings to have meaning for the people in them – the meaning they would like them to have, and can we have allow buildings to have more than one meaning, and a changing one?'

Rapoport raised another, even more political question in his second *AAJ* piece, written long before the Dutch architect, Hertzberger designed the pluralist interiors of the famous Central Beheer office building in 1973. This was to propose that architects – and their clients – suffer, on the whole, from 'overdesign' rather than 'underdesign' because we tend to treat the public as 'consumers' rather than as 'participants'. It is interesting that a sparkling reprise of this same line of argument has recently appeared, almost exactly thirty years later, in Steward Brand's well known book, *How Buildings Learn* (Brand, S., 1994).

In 1967 what particularly disturbed me about Rapoport's underlying message was this. My chief task for a time at the NBA had been the collation from contemporary architectural practice of the range of public housing plan types, published in 1966 as *Generic Plans* (National Building Agency, 1965). The objective of this exercise for my employers at the NBA was the reduction of variety in housing design in order to promote prefabrication and thus make more likely the achievement of the British government's then hugely ambitious house building program. In the course of selecting and studying and drawing some hundreds of house plans, I realized what huge diversity existed in these plans, despite the severe contemporary financial and dimensional constraints within which the architects of public housing were then used to working. I also had a glimpse of an underlying mathematical order that could be used to classify them and to bind them together within a typological array. So far, so functionalist. For me, at a critical moment in my professional development, Rapoport's relativistic and anthropologically grounded arguments prompted an alternative teleological dimension to the NBA's rationalistic and reductionist analysis. What was variety for? Perhaps the variety I had been so sedulously eliminating from the NBA's typology of house plans wasn't such a bad idea after all.

It was the open-ended, relativistic side of Rapoport's thinking that became particularly relevant to me when I went in September 1967, as a graduate student, to the US, first to Berkeley and then to Princeton. It was my coincidental good fortune that, during my year at Berkeley, Rapoport was also a visiting professor, working on what has been for me his most significant book, *House, Form and Culture* (Rapoport, 1969). My initial intention at Berkeley had been to sit at the feet of Christopher Alexander who was then developing his "Pattern Language' (Alexander, 1977). For Alexander, as is well known, a pattern is an elemental design proposition that links together a problem statement (usually expressed as an apparent sociological or psychological or environmental contradiction) that can be resolved by a particular, generic, physical solution (generally explained by a beautiful image or an apt analogy). The attraction of such a design language formed out of generic patterns to someone who had puzzled for weeks and months over the apparently chaotic variety made evident by *Generic Plans* can hardly be exaggerated. Not only could design insights be codified but they could also be justified in human terms. Both kinds of simplification seemed to me, at least for a moment, to be capable of being achieved within the same elegant, over-arching, watertight, ultimately functionalist framework. "Timelessness' was something Alexander aspired to do. I have to admit that the idea of an architecture without custom or ceremony but simply determined, as it were, by such impersonal forces as the wind and rain appealed very much to me at that time.

Horst Rittel, whose influence as a teacher at Berkeley has probably turned out in the end to be greater than Alexander's, was quick to point out what he thought was the principal weakness in the Pattern Language. Rittel was at once highly suspicious of any approach to design method – design methodology was the air we breathed – that was based upon a single set of values. People were involved in design and people had ideas. Ideas are diverse. People did not always behave in the same predictable way. Alexander's Pattern

Language seemed to Rittel to be an inherently closed, monist system. To the extent that Alexander overestimated the resolution of conflict in the Pattern Language and underestimated continuing conflict and change, his design method was flawed.

Amos Rapoport, visiting Berkeley at that time, was able to help me. He understood my fascination with classification and typology in relation to design. Like Rittel, however, he was more interested in diversity than in closure. In a completely un-Alexandrian way he pointed out to me that, for example, in the semi-Antarctic wastes of Tierra del Fuego elaborate conical huts were used for ritual purposes while mere wind breaks served for dwellings. Conversely in the South Seas, elaborate dwellings are found where, in terms of climate alone, the need for shelter is minimal.

No deterministic explanations, argued Rapoport in *House, Form and Culture,* are ever final in architecture. Neither climate, nor materials and technology, nor site, nor defense, nor even economics provide a complete explanation for architectural forms. "The forms of houses are not determined by physical forces and hence can show great variety because of the relatively low criticality of buildings'. Moreover, house forms are subject to change: 'there may lie the great lesson of vernacular buildings for our day – the value of constraints to establish generalized 'loose' frameworks where the interplay of the constant and the changeable aspects of man can find expression.

The impact of Rapoport's teaching on me has been long lasting. The first symptom was a rapid retreat from Alexander's influence. This is captured in a couple of papers written at that time in which I explored the idea of 'slack' rather than 'fit' in design methodology (Duffy & Torrey, 1970). This was my first attempt to define the legitimate scope for variation – but not for arbitrariness – in architectural form rather than my previous functionalist insistence on the constant, the minimal and the static. Very much in imitation of Rapoport's manner one of these papers (Duffy & Friedman, 1970) was an attempt at a cultural comparison of Japanese and Egyptian houses. More importantly and practically, Rapoport's influence helped me cope with the experience of encountering the North American tradition of office design that became the focus of my doctoral work at Princeton (Duffy, 1974). Late sixties New York was the perfect place for an amateur anthropologist to come to terms with the bewildering variety of interior design forms that continue to be endlessly elaborated inside the tight constraints of developer's architecture.

It was at Princeton that I hit upon the idea of devising typological models that link architectural forms and organizational structures. Inherent in this kind of model – many versions of which have been developed over the last thirty years – are three ideas I owe to Rapoport – the legitimacy of diversity in both architectural and social entities, the potential for exploring such diversity within a disciplined but non-deterministic intellectual framework, and the inevitability of open ended mutation, development and change in such models. The practical and intellectual importance of these ideas about architectural typologies to what became DEGW, the international architectural and consultant practice I helped to found in the early seventies, has been described in a recent book, *Design for Change.*

It also goes without saying the Rapoport's respect for the user has also been an enormous influence. There is an old fashioned, and hence politically incorrect, saying in anthropology: the natives never lie. What this means to an anthropologist is that whatever deliberate fantasies are woven by respondents for the benefit of the humorless field worker, basic truths about values are always embedded in their tales. For the architect, the implication is that however confused, short-termist and even wrong headed users may seem to be, whatever they say is always in some way critically important for design.

Without encountering Rapoport's quizzical, skeptical and well-stocked mind at a critical moment in my own intellectual development, a whole universe of possibilities for developing design ideas would have passed me by. I wouldn't have been able to escape to the extent that I have from the limitations of my early sixties design training. I would have been unable to resist the false certainties of the Pattern Language. I would probably have persisted in the one-track approach to office design that has bedeviled the development of the field in both North America and Europe. I would certainly have failed to understand the relevance and the power of the relativistic and comparative way of thinking of the cultural anthropologist to architecture. I would not have been able to respond to the tremendous changes that Information Technology is currently making possible in my own chosen field of office design. There is a lot that I, and many others, owe to Amos Rapoport.

References

Alexander, C. et al. (1977). *A Pattern Language.* New York: Oxford University Press.

Alexander, C. (1979). *The Timeless Way of Building.* New York: Oxford University Press.

Brand, S. (1994). *How Buildings Learn.* New York: Viking.

DEGW. (1998). *Design for Change, The Architecture of DEGW.* Birkhauser/ Watermark, Basel and Haselmere.

Duffy, F. (1974). *Office Interiors and Organizations.* Ph.D. Dissertation. Princeton University.

Duffy, F & Torrey, J. (1970). A Progress Report on the Pattern Language. In G. T. Moore, (Ed.) *Emerging Methods in Environmental Design and Planning.* Cambridge, MA: The MIT Press.

Duffy, F. & Friedman, J. (1970). Patterns and Semiology. In H. Sanoff, & S. Cohn, (Eds). *EDRA 1: Proceedings of the First Annual Design Research Association Conference.*

Jencks, C & Baird, G. (Eds.) (1969). *Meaning in Architecture.* Barrie & Rockliff: The Crescent Press. London.

National Building Agency. (1965). *Generic Plans.* NBA: London.

Rapoport, A. (1969). House Form and Culture. Prentice Hall: Englewood Cliffs.

Rapoport, A. (1967). Some Consumer Comments on a Designed Environment. *Arena. Architectural Association Journal.* January 1967.

Acknowledgements

The fact that this book is a reality was dependent on the Herculean participation of many individuals. First, many thanks to the contributors to the collection who efficiently produced and refined their works as found herein. Thanks must also be extended to Bob Greenstreet, Dean of the School of Architecture and Urban Planning, University of Wisconsin-Milwaukee whose idea it was to develop such a collection and Gerald Weisman who put in much effort in securing the participation of many of the contributors. Gowri Betrabet served admirably as the copy editor for the collection and deserves much more credit than this acknowledgement could possibly give. Thanks also to the people at Ashgate including David Canter, Anne Keirby, Sonia Hubbard, Tracey Daborn and Pauline Beavers for being patient and supportive throughout the entire process. It has been both an honor and a pleasure to work with all of you and I hope you are as pleased with the result as I am.

Finally, this book would not be complete without acknowledging the contributions to environment-behavior research of Amos Rapoport. He has been and continues to be an inspired scholar and a true friend to the emerging interdisciplinary field of Environment-Behavior Studies. We all look forward to many more years of enlightened research from Amos and all the scholars interested in the nexus between culture, meaning and architecture.

Acknowledgements

1 Introduction

Keith Diaz Moore

As we draw the twentieth century to a close, it seems perfunctory to suggest that culture and architecture are somehow related. This, however, was not always the case. In archaeology, where one would expect this connection to be taken for granted, the cultural implications of architecture went largely ignored until only a couple of decades ago. Historically, architectural theory has tended to discount the importance of culture, seeking universal (i.e. "supra-cultural") truths whether those truths be divine or cosmological (such as in the Renaissance) or mechanistic (as was found during the Modern Movement) (c.f. Groat & Despres, 1991). For both disciplines, as well as others, the issue of culture grew in significance with post-modernism, which raised to the fore the issue of meaning. In so doing, understandings came to be seen as pluralistic and fragmented, and inquiry increasingly focused on such differences. Reified "truths" were to be questioned through critical inquiry and soon crumbled as many such truths were based upon false assumptions.

Disciplinary history had much to do with the manner in which this inquiry was engaged. In the social sciences, empirical studies were used to falsify held truths. In archaeology for instance, Kent (see Chapter 14 in this volume; also 1982) used an empirical study of space use by the Navajo to illustrate the falsity of assuming Western Civilization norms in non-western cultures. Architecture however operated, and continues to operate, in a very different fashion. Within architecture, polemics has traditionally been the means for challenging held beliefs and asserting one's own. This has been true certainly since the days of Alberti (see Rykwert & Tavernor, 1988) and continues to this day (e.g. Jencks, 1997). In parallel with this approach to architectural inquiry must be understood the patronage system in which architects have operated. Architectural inquiry/theory has primarily been trapped by this patronage system, focusing upon building types associated with the *haute couture*: from the palaces and churches of aristocracies to the museums and office towers of the twentieth century. Thus architectural discourse has in general been associated with elitism, far removed from the broad base of society in which architecture takes place. Michael Sorkin identified the link between architectural theory and *haute culture* as resulting in buildings speaking only "to cognoscenti and not at all to passersby. Part of the problem, he said — and it is not a new one — is the arcane language of all elites" (Oppenheimer Dean, 1999, p.73).

This polemical approach to inquiry is deeply embedded within the educational system of architects which Amos Rapoport described this way: "Rather than open my eyes to the built environment, architectural education had tried to close them. It had emphasized a tiny body of work that did not seem to be the most significant" (1990a: 87). Much more meaningful to Rapoport and others like him was the work of people like J.B. Jackson whose pieces such as "Pueblo Architecture and our Own" (Jackson, 1953a) and "The Westward Moving House" (Jackson, 1953b) analyzed built form of a type outside of that of concern of the "architectural cognoscenti." This focus on vernacular architecture provided the perfect challenge to the held truths of the time, as sought by the post-modern zeitgeist of the 1960s. Individuals such as Aldo Rossi (1966), Robert Venturi (1966) and Charles Jencks (e.g. Jencks & Baird, 1970) seized the opportunity for challenging the status quo, but did so in the traditional form of architectural discourse: polemical statements. Others, such as Amos Rapoport, chose a more radical path -- to challenge the traditional approach to architectural inquiry altogether. Rather than looking solely internally to architecture, Rapoport sought to broaden his connections to other disciplines to help understand the complex nexus between culture and architecture. Rather than focusing on the powers of persuasion necessary for polemical debate, Rapoport suggested empirical inquiry would broaden understanding in a much more significant way. For Rapoport, his motivation is summarized in a quote from the molecular biologist Jacques Monod, who lying on his deathbed uttered the phrase, "I want to know..."

While the work of Rossi, Venturi and Jencks are better known within architecture than is Rapoport's, it is Rapoport's work that has extended beyond the confines of architecture to become influential in landscape architecture, urban design, anthropology and beyond. It is

Rapoport's work that was seminal in the formation of the multi-disciplinary field of Environment-Behavior Studies and it is Rapoport's work that Kent (this volume) points out provided archaeologists and anthropologists the means for critically exploring the linkage between culture and architecture.

Because the exploration into the relationship between culture and built form is multi-faceted and is ongoing in multiple disciplines, it makes sense that the work of Amos Rapoport that bridges this multiplicity most effectively serves as the fulcrum around which this volume revolves. The time is right for this type of critical reconsideration. Issues of culture whether they be the implications of a developing cyber-culture, or the impact of globalization on Third World countries are on the rise. This concern for culture has manifested itself within architecture, there being growing recognition

> that the dominant understanding of the relationship between architecture and society propagated throughout the institutions of architecture is long overdue for critical reassessment. How architects construct an understanding of the social world and how that construct affects possibilities for practice are pivotal concerns for architects (Dutton and Hurst Mann, 1996, p.1).

With this as the context for this collection, it is timely to critically reflect upon the work of Amos Rapoport, to reconsider the implications of his work regarding the nexus of person-environment relations, and to project what that work may mean as we move forward in an increasingly pluralistic and diversified world. This was the challenge presented to the eleven contributors to this volume. The essays are organized into three substantive areas: theoretical inquiry; architectural education; and architectural anthropology. Each represents an area that ties directly to Rapoport's body of work and also reflect areas in which the nexus of culture and the built environment should be advanced.

The Layout of the Volume

Each substantive area begins with a reprinted essay written by

Rapoport, that engenders the core concepts of his work relevant to that particular substantive area. The essay immediately following the Rapoport piece in each substantive area is an essay that is self-reflective in nature. Under theoretical inquiry, for instance, the social psychologist Irwin Altman's essay (Chapter 3) reflects on how Amos Rapoport's words have influenced the development of Environment-Behavior Studies as well as his own work. Bob Beckley's chapter (Chapter 7) addresses how Rapoport's pedagogical position regarding architectural education has stimulated his own self-reflection. The last self-reflective statement is Yasser Elsheshtawy's contribution (Chapter 11) in which Amos' role as mentor in shaping culture-environment research is presented.

Theoretical Inquiry

In addition to Altman's essay, two additional chapters address the substantive area of theoretical inquiry and development. The human ecologist Roderick Lawrence's chapter, "House Form and Culture: What have we learnt in 30 years?" extends the theoretical framework presented by Rapoport and posits the need for what he calls an ecological perspective to guide culture-environment studies. "The New Functionalism and Architectural Theory" is the Australian architect Jon Lang's contribution in which he presents a framework that can link Environment-Behavior Research with architectural design through a critical consideration of the concept of function.

Together with Altman's essay, the three emphasize the importance of making linear and lateral connections in the effort of theory-building. Altman reflects the depth and breadth of connections Rapoport has made in his own work, into fields as disparate as physics, biology, anthropology, geography, psychology as well as environmental design. Altman raises the point that such lateral connections must address the variance in underlying assumptions held between researchers and disciplines. These assumptions, shaped by the held world view, influence what research is considered valid, what knowledge is considered significant and other fundamentally important considerations that will impact theoretical development. In light of this analysis, Lawrence's essay focusing on housing studies, is significant for emphasizing the need :

> to develop and apply a holistic, conceptual framework which not only reconciles the divergence between the two classes of housing studies presented earlier, but also accounts for the environmental and societal dimensions of housing as well as the reciprocal relations over time. This approach implies the application of an ecological perspective which is systemic rather than atomistic or hierarchical (this volume, p.65).

Lawrence by asserting this ecological perspective, suggests that housing studies in particular, and culture-environment studies in general, need to agree to a world view in which, among other things, the following is valued: integrative approaches, collaboration rather than disciplinary confinement; conceptual innovation; and multiple methods and measures.

Jon Lang's essay in many ways extends Lawrence's ecological perspective by looking at the issue of praxiology. Lang' model has the implicit assumption that architectural practice takes place within a problem-solving mode of thought. Lang suggests that Environment-Behavior research can possess utility for environmental designers through the acceptance of the assumption that places, as do human actions, have purposes or goals associated with them. As problems and goals are flip sides of the same coin, Lang is suggesting that linkages between practice and research are furthered by adoption of the same assumptions regarding human nature, namely, the goal orientation of human nature. Both Lawrence's and Lang's essays are projective, laying out a course in regard to theory development, research and practice, but their evocative suggestions need to be examined within the considerations offered by Altman and his valid concerns regarding the difficulties associated with such extensive connections proposed by both of the other authors.

Architectural Education

Chapters 6 through 9 all address the profession of architecture, either its practice or its educational system. Bob Beckley's "Amos Rapoport: Modernism's Apologist?" addresses Rapoport's (1984a; 1995) call for a radical reconceptualization of the architect as scientist. At it's heart, Beckley's essay questions the utility of the scientist metaphor arguing that the architectural problem is fundamentally different in nature than is the scientific problem. Groat's chapter expounds upon Beckley's by promoting a different metaphor — that of architect-as-cultivator. Groat begins by critically examining Rapoport's critique of architectural education, with which for the most part she agrees, but develops a very different systemic response to those issues than the one advanced by Rapoport. Her architect-as-cultivator model embodies the sense of connection underlying the Altman, Lang and Lawrence chapters, shaping its implications for architectural curricula.

Wes Janz's "Studious Questions, Studio Responses" takes Rapoport's thoughts on architectural education into the trenches of the architectural design studio class setting. In an inventive interpretive journal, Janz illustrates the challenges of reconceptualizing the role of the architect within the stringent constraints of most architectural curricula. There is a transformational aspect to all three essays that stems from the clear articulation of a problem; deliberate, conscious reflection directed towards reconciling the problem; and examination of relevant information from multiple perspectives and formation of a reasonable conclusion. In so doing, all of these essays emphasize the necessity of practicing critical inquiry in addressing issues of culture and the environment.

Architectural Anthropology

The last four essays address what may presumptuously called architectural anthropology. Chapter 11 by Yasser Elsheshtawy examines how Rapoport's approach to culture-environment studies shaped his own inquiry into urban public spaces and the relevance of such an approach in traditional cultures facing environmental conflict. His articulated multi-method approach provides a natural segue into Setha Low's essay "Culture, Politics and the Plaza: An Ethnographic Approach to the Study of Urban Public Spaces in Latin America." Low outlines an ethnographic approach to Environment-Behavior research (EBR) that emphasizes sociocultural processes. Her methodology is multi-method, producing both verbal and non-verbal data which through analysis she suggests can produce understanding that can lead to more culturally-appropriate design. Low brings front and center the concept of meaning as central to the linkage between culture and architecture.

Chapter 13 by Charles Goodsell examines a discrete aspect of meaning, the mnemonic function of the built environment. In this essay Goodsell illustrates the utility of dismantling the broad concept of meaning into three sub-divisions: one that guides behavior; one that conveys social expectations; and one that produces an emotional response to a deep symbolism. Goodsell then examines American state capitol buildings for their mnemonic meanings arguing that they do indeed possess symbolic meaning, contrary to the hypothesis forwarded by Rapoport. Finally, Sue Kent's essay "The Cultural Revolution in Architecture" states that the impact of Rapoport's work was to reinvent anthropology by positing that culture was a socially-constructed abstraction that is expressed in the concrete realm of architecture and behavior. Therefore, the interpretation and meaning of the built environment differs for each culture (Kent, this volume, 1). It is in the social construction of meaning that the heart of inquiry into the relationship between the theoretical construct of culture and the concrete expression of the built environment lay.

All of these essays reflect the vibrancy and richness of inquiry into the nexus of culture and architecture. It is astonishing how much work is currently being conducted in other fields that do not find currency in architectural discourse but are so relevant. These all reflect the importance of the conduct of research and the development of a knowledge base, as well as for the need of an integrative framework by which to structure understanding.

Attributes and Themes of the Volume

The importance of linear and lateral connections, the importance of critical thinking and the development of a cumulative knowledge base, are what perhaps can be called three attributes that characterize inquiry into the relationship between the built environment and culture. While each attribute was referred to most succinctly in regard to a specific substantive area, it is arguable that all three of the attributes in some form or fashion are evident in each area. While such attributes are interesting and begin to offer descriptors for the inquiry found in the domain addressing culture and built form, they do not offer much critical insight into the domain. If we take a sectional view, cross-cutting all of the independent essays which form this volume as a collective, there are three themes that emerge as predominant: the recognition of the systemic nature of culture as a construct; the multiplicity of human environments; and meaning as a primary integrator linking culture and the built environment.

The Systemic and Dynamic Nature of Culture

As Rapoport (1984b, p.9) rightly points out, culture is a theoretical construct, providing a conceptual shorthand for understanding "a group of people who have a set of values and beliefs which embody ideals, and are transmitted to members of the group through enculturation." This notion of ideals embodying values and beliefs can be related to held world views.[1] The concept of world views and their impact on the understanding of the person-environment nexus is a predominant theme that runs through this collection.

Beginning with Altman, who raises the issue with the most vigor, world views are seen as a significant challenge facing the development of Environment-Behavior studies (EBS). Within the domain of people-environment relations, Altman identifies four different world views at work which he terms Trait, Interactional, Organismic and Transactional. The difficulty Altman suggests is that such underlying world views informs the data we collect, the methodologies we adopt and the form of our theories and conceptualizations. Because the domain of person-environment relations has scholars from different disciplines, very likely operating with different philosophical assumptions, it has proved difficult to link their separate knowledge and theory; a condition Altman characterizes as a "Tower of Babel." "The ultimate results of our failure to state clearly, or to even know, our own and others assumptions are: isolated islands of knowledge and understanding; mutual ignorance or neglect; and a pattern of fragmented scholarship" (Altman, this volume, p. 50-1).

Kent's essay also addresses world view in two important ways: one, in suggesting that the world view held by a culture fundamentally structures a society's built environment (which she illustrates with empirical examples); and second, that the world view of archaeology was significantly transformed upon the introduction of the revolutionary work of Amos Rapoport (e.g. 1969; 1990b) regarding the influence of culture upon built form. She writes,

> it was generally thought that climate, available building materials, and local topography were the most influential factors shaping architecture. Instrumental in challenging this deterministic and non-cultural view of the built environment, Rapoport demonstrated that people were not passive slaves to their environment. Instead, they used culture and architecture to modify their physical environment, rather than the other way around.

Thus the assumption of the "given" nature of architecture held within anthropology was overturned, upsetting the definition of the domain and opening new areas of inquiry for anthropologists.

Linda Groat picks up on the importance of philosophical assumptions in her chapter, "The Architect as Artist? or Scientist?: A modest proposal for the architect-as-cultivator." She asserts that particularly in the case of architecture, there has been a failure in sustaining a viable conceptualization of culture, resulting "in a contemporary culture that is 'hostile to itself' in that it denies the intrinsic value of artifacts, including architecture" (Groat, this volume, p.138). There is a "subjectivism" to both the architect-as-scientist (technician) and architect-as-artist models in the dichotomy presented by Beckley. Groat asserts a model of an architect that should be "more fully engaged in relations with and among people, and benefit by the cumulative and diverse inheritance of the culture" (ibid.). In so stating, Groat raises the dialogic endeavor that architecture engenders, negotiating between myriad sociocultural factors.

Elsheshtawy personalizes this debate regarding world view in suggesting how at variance his own ideals regarding the role of the architect are with that of his mentor, Amos Rapoport. Rapoport, he suggests (this volume), "refrains from viewing the architect as an agent of change," a position from which Elsheshtawy radically departs. Elsheshtawy's research in the Middle East reflects the necessity for culture-environment studies to not only concern itself with the traditional, but accept the transitory nature of this nexus and the significant impact that economics and politics play in this transience.

The importance of the political and economic in addressing built form and culture is apparent in several other essays. Goodsell's piece on American capitols specifically addresses the relationship between politics and the environment linked through the meaning of these environments. Lawrence and Lang both mention the impact of the economic and political on the built environment and refer to its necessary inclusion in any framework of culture-built form relations. Both also extend the multi-dimensionality of culture in other ways: Lang discussing social expressions of culture such as gender differences, stage in lifecycle and social status; Lawrence in regard to historical and ecological considerations. For many of these factors, Rapoport (1994) suggests that their relevancy is tied to the degree of impact they have on a definable lifestyle. Lifestyles are seen "as the choices people make about how to allocate resources" (Rapoport, 1994, p.16), which reflect the values the members associated with that lifestyle hold dear, and values are shaped by one's world view.

The most manifest and visible expression of lifestyle is human activity and thus it should not be surprising that in articulating a methodological approach that addresses the multivariate construct of "culture," Low stresses the importance of ethnography. For Low this entails a multiplicity of methods centered on participant observation, and behavioral mapping — the documentation of human activity. Integrating methods of interviews, surveys and questionnaires, Low argues that the ethnographic study of human activity implies "that meanings and interpretations that emerge are those of the cultural group(s)." She raises the important concept of perspective that cultural research brings to the fore, evidenced by her discussion of "etic/emic" considerations. Low also argues for inclusion of ethnohistorical, semantic and proxemic methodologies in any culture-environment research design. Together, all of the methodologies Setha Low argues for present the researcher with a convolution of data, each rendering insight into the meaning that particular place holds for its participants.

Multiple methods, multiple perspectives, multiple dimensions of culture bring with them a need for triangulation between all of these various data types and sources. Thus a search for one commonly held understanding seems fool-hearty within cultural-environment research. Any such finding would need to be of such abstraction and generality that it is difficult to imagine the enlightenment it would render.

Rather, acceptance of the notion of the social construction of understanding seems mandated; recognizing the plurality of groups and sub-groups. Each culture that shares a common set of values and beliefs will develop their own meanings and expectations in regard to particular environments. When thrust together — either in terms of being a sub-group nested within a larger culture or two equivalent scales of human groupings sharing a common setting or a combination of the two — these various cultures, the activities they engage in, and the meanings and expectations they possess regarding the fixed, semi-fixed and non-fixed components of the setting, will come into negotiation with one another. This dynamic interplay is what forms the central role meaning plays at the nexus of culture and the built environment.

The Multiplicity inEenvironmental Definitions

Part of the complexity surrounding culture-environment relations is how one defines the environment.[2] In the articles which form this compilation, there is a multiplicity of definitions for the environment. The range of environment types range from Goodsell's analysis of American capitols as monuments to vernacular housing (Lawrence and Kent), to urban plazas and streets (Elsheshtawy and Low). Hence even in this small sampling, the environment can be thought of as having scalar variability, from particular rooms or spaces, to buildings, to neighborhoods, to the cultural landscape, but at each level the environment can be considered the organization of physical space.

Lang's essay (this volume, p.88) suggests this is the definition of environment most often applied by architectural theoreticians who "have generally thought of the built environment as consisting of spaces which are enclosed to a greater or lesser extent. Their attention has largely focused on the geometries of these spaces and the sequence between them." This argument suggests that architects typically think of the environment in terms of built form. Lang goes on to suggest that for architects, their built form can be conceptualized as creating physical settings that consist of "fixed and semi-fixed features defined by surfaces, textures, and objects which afford specific sets of activities and do not afford others." Not only can environment be conceptualized at multiple scales, but also in terms of fixed and semi-fixed features. Low adds the importance of non-fixed elements, most importantly people, that are defining elements in the environment that one experiences. This reflects what may be a significant shortcoming in terms of the traditional architectural definition of the environment, although an understandable one. If environmental designers limit their conceptualizations of the environment solely to those elements under their "control," they are addressing but part of the problem.

As Beckley points out, the architectural problem is the *relation of form and function*. This comment raises two points. First, is the addition of the concept of function to the consideration of environments. Both Beckley and Lang relate the concept of functionality to that of human purpose. Lang suggests that environments have three purposes: affording activities; providing shelter; and acting "as displays that contain information," adding that this third purpose is often considered an add-on. Beckley, Lang and Goodsell illuminate the limited approach to functionality Lang implies is prevalent, all suggesting that aesthetics, instead of being an additional virtue, is rather a fundamental aspect of environmental purpose. One of the conundrums this point raises is how one can possibly "model the physical surroundings in ways that will capture the qualities of pleasure and delight as well as issues of function and comfort" (Canter, in press, p.8).

The second point Beckley's comment raises is the importance of the relationship itself between form and function. Perhaps this point is best addressed by Lang's third purpose of environments, which he identifies as containing information. In theory, a building's form, broadly conceived, would provide information to users about its function, again broadly conceived. In a restaurant one could imagine this information as being of the sort that cues where one may sit, the conversation level that is expected, which could be cued by arrangement of chairs and tables, light levels, and the actions of others. Thus this information is not best conceptualized as contained in the environment but rather interpreted reflexively by those experiencing that environment. Lawrence's essay (this volume, p.66) suggests that environments have instrumental functions and roles attributed to it that are developed and maintained through "the interrelations between people and their surroundings (which) are characterized by discursive and reflexive knowledge."

It should be of little wonder why Lawrence stresses the importance of the societal context in understanding housing environments, or why Kent simply refers to "architecture as socio-physical in nature." If indeed environments have instrumental functions and roles, they either need to be intrinsic to the environments or are understandings which have been experienced time and time again and have become enculturated. While certainly the former posits an interesting question (that being the possibility of pan-cultural, or archetypal environments that will embody all of Lang's three purposes of environments, do so universally, and result in universally-common human experiences), the latter suggests that our environments are integrally related to cultural phenomena. It is because of this inseparable, intangible, integral relationship between culture and the environment that there is the vast variability in environments found across the earth.

One of the manifestations of this inseparability of culture and the environment has been the usage of terms such as context and milieu in lieu of environment. Each of these suggest that the word environment all too often limits consideration solely to the physical, and that one's experience needs to be understood as being shaped and influenced not only by the physical system of settings which they actively experience, but also by the whole range of cultural phenomena with which the person transacts. Conversely, in this light, while both Janz and Groat address the culture of architectural education in their essays, surprisingly missing is any consideration of the physical setting and hence the complete milieu in which architectural education takes place.[3] In any case, what becomes clear is that it is the context, or milieu created by the interrelations of culture and the environment that is of significance to human experience and that any milieu "is a function both of variations between people and of variations in the settings and how they interact" (Canter, in press, p.8). Because of this complexity, it should be of little surprise that there has been and will continue to be a multiplicity of definitions for the environment.

How one defines and operationalizes culture and environment in a particular study will depend upon the question(s) posed.[4] As Rapoport (1994,p.6) suggests, "Different types of definitions and conceptualizations are useful for particular types of questions and problems, of different degrees of generality, at different scales, and consequently for different disciplines and fields.[4] This makes the parceling of culture and environment more a function of adequate conceptual clarity than of basic principles. Rather the anchor around which culture-environment studies revolve are the processes by which culture and the environment interrelate. This manifests itself in discussions of such issues as the use of mnemonics (Goodsell, Kent and Low), the production of identity (Beckley, Elsheshtawy, Groat) and symbolism (Lawrence). All of these are subordinate to the primary connection of meaning that all of the authors, in some fashion, address.

The Negotiation of Meaning

In discussing culture it became evident that culture is ideational in nature, whose attributes are both systemic and dynamic. Regarding the definition of environment, the essays reflect a diversity of opinion; one that reflects the current state of plurality in the study of person-environment relations. This diversity stems from the level of abstraction at which environment, and most certainly, culture exist.[5] Because of the myriad fashions in which both may be dismantled, there becomes a plurality an almost endless list of conceptualizations that rightly may be part of the culture-environment relations domain. How to structure relationships in an insightful fashion when there is such diversity is a difficult question but of extreme criticality if these studies are to constitute a building of understanding that may inform more insightful place-making. In each of the essays the concept of meaning is addressed, if not finding itself central in each case. Here it is suggested that a potential means for organizing culture-environment relation studies would be around the core concept of meaning. There emerge from the articles three themes that would appear to be important in addressing meaning: first is the importance of perspective; the second is the intentionality of human activity; and the third is the negotiable nature of meaning.

The Importance of Perspective. This point is addressed in several of the essays. Beginning with Altman who suggests that one's view of the world impacts how problems are defined and how phenomena are understood, the role of the researcher in the development of a knowledge base becomes critical. Low develops this further in raising the classic "etic versus emic" debate in her essay on positing an ethnographic methodology to culture-environment studies. She rhetorically asks if it is ever possible for a researcher to understand another culture, given the "gulf between our existential realities." Her methodological approach of mixing multiple methods is designed to triangulate upon an understanding. Low also posits that any description or finding a researcher makes is "only one interpretation of many." Kent's essay dramatically reflects the importance of perspective by illuminating the inaccuracy in understanding that was developed by applying Western civilization norms and assumptions to non-Western cultures.

Perspective is also important in the world of practice as reflected in several of the chapters. Lang (this volume, p.99) makes the important point that "simply, the attitudes towards what is important and what is not shapes designs." Shaping those attitudes are people's view of the world, their ideals, their knowledge and their values, and in turn, those attitudes inform the choices they make as designers. Janz (this volume, p.165) asserts a negative vision of the attitudes of the architectural profession when he writes, "until the profession values asking critical questions of itself and others, setting intentions clearly, and designing quality environments, well-prepared graduates will encounter working environments marked by avoidance, quick compromise, mediocrity, and little passion." Both suggest that one's perspective will influence the intentions one has and the choices that person will make to achieve those intentions.

The Intentionality of Human Activity. Intentionality is core to all of human activity. Lang (this volume, p.90) simply states "the meaning of an activity lies in the purposes it fulfils -- activities are means to achieving ends." These purposes may take myriad forms from supporting a particular behavior, to conveying cosmological and/or political overtones (see Goodsell and Kent). Beckley goes as far as to suggest a legitimate purpose of designed built environments is the architect's "urge to self-display." These range of purposes are certainly individual in nature, but they are also consensual. This consensual aspect of human purpose is often overlooked, but if environments provide cues for socially-expected behavior, as discussed above, then individuals act in a manner that takes into account their own agenda but within the context of what is socially-expected within the given setting. Socially-expected behavior, in this way, can only be defined through a process of negotiation between the participants in a place and the intentions they seek to achieve.

In other words the social understanding of particular settings is perpetually reconstituted by individuals through their collective actions, obeying the socially-held expectations or rules regarding that setting and the activity occur therein. This allows for the evaluation of an act being rebellious by definition, in violation of the expectations of the collective. If enough participants rebel, the expectations of the setting are altered and the intentions underlying the rebellious act come to the fore. Thus settings, the activities they afford, their meanings, and the socially-shared goals they are to achieve are dynamic in nature. Canter (in press, 10-11) nicely summarizes the assumption of purposiveness in environment-behavior relations by stating,

> I take it as axiomatic that the purposes and repertoires are defined through contacts with other people. Social processes are thus not superficial additions to fundamental human processes...but rather they are the fundamental constituents of our world that underlay all purpose and meaning.

The Negotiable Nature of Meaning. Elsheshtawy presents the dynamic nature of vernacular housing to his students by having them search for what he calls the "cultural core" — those aspects that did not change over time. This of course suggests that many of the aspects of place-types have indeed evolved. As Lawrence indicates such cultural cores are of decreasing relevance in a contemporary world that expresses "an increasing level of pluralism in contrast to consensus." This pluralistic and diverse nature asserted by Lawrence reflects one of the three characteristics of culture of Cahoone as summarized in Groat's article. The other two are: "that individuals derive their essential characters from relations with and among people;" and "that cultural artifacts (including architecture) would not be what they are without their meanings (Cahoone, 1988: 247)" (Groat: 12).

From these three characteristics it is evident that culture and identity are directly related to the production of meaning. It is also clear that meaning is created amongst the environments people occupy, the activities in which people are engaged, the purposes they seek to achieve, and the resulting interpretation of this entire milieu. Hence meaning is fundamentally socially-constructed: negotiated dialogically between all of the participants active in the setting and all of the social worlds they represent.[6] If culture-environment studies have informed us of anything, they have revealed that meaning is integrally related to a given setting. Culture-environment relations can be viewed as producing meaning; meaning resulting from the negotiation amongst the multiple dimensions of the culture-environment nexus.

If placing meaning front and center makes sense, then the dynamic process of negotiation by which meaning is produced may serve Altman's call for the human phenomenon environment-behavior studies needs in order to mature into a field with a coherent body of knowledge. Negotiation is a human process that has been studied in organizational analysis, political science and sociology to name but a few domains. Negotiation theory begins with the assumption that the various participants in a setting or situation possess a variety of perspectives from which they interpret the ongoing situation (e.g. Goffman, 1974). It is between these various interpretations that a negotiated commonality needs to emerge in order for co-action to be possible. These negotiated commonalities become habitualized (c.f. Berger & Luckmann, 1966) and typified (Schutz, 1967), forming patterns of experience upon which individuals may call upon in order to either reproduce it or challenge it (depending upon their purpose). The meanings of these patterns and how various alternative activities would be assessed if enacted would vary between the various social expressions of culture (e.g. social worlds). In regard to individuals, these patterns can be related to the constructs of schema or scripts (e.g. Abelson, 1981) in cognitive psychology, but they may also be related to the concept of program associated with behavior settings (e.g. Barker, 1968). Barker suggests that to utilize a setting effectively implies an understanding of the commonly held set of expected roles people are to enact and the rules for enacting those roles. Wicker (1987: 623) extends behavior setting theory by suggesting that settings are themselves "social constructions that are continually being built and rebuilt through the deliberate actions of individuals." Thus there is this dynamic relationship between individuals, social expressions of culture, and the physical environment (and the cues it provides) which is in continuous negotiation constructing meaning. Meaning is thus not static and a given but rather is constructed and variable.

That being the case, with the centrality of meaning evident in these essays, lateral connections to the work of people such as Gerson (1976), Goffman (1974), and particularly Strauss (i.e. 1978; 1993) may enhance theory development in understanding how such meaning is negotiated and is negotiable. Concomitantly, it would appear that the domain of culture-environment relations would have equally as important concepts and understandings to illuminate and refine approaches to studies of negotiation found in the more traditional fields of sociology and organizational analysis, where the role of the physical environment is all too often overlooked.

Conclusion

Both the attributes and themes that have emerged in this volume are reflective of the work of Amos Rapoport, which served as the initial locus for this collection. In this light it is appropriate to reflect upon the work and influence of the work of Amos Rapoport. In the thirty years since Rapoport published the landmark *House Form and Culture*, essentially marking the birth of culture-environment relations and environment-behavior studies, much has been learned, conceptualized, theorized, developed and discarded regarding the linkage of culture and the environment. The development of gender studies, lifestyle studies, attempts at linkage with biological and ecological levels of inquiry, links with economical and political analysis, inquiry into hidden curricula, are no doubt directions in which the early participants of culture-environment relations would have not envisioned the domain branching into and perhaps are dismayed at seeing. Still much is left unknown and there is much fertile ground to be explored.

The key themes found in this collection broadly outline the armature Rapoport has developed for structuring culture-environment inquiry. In broad terms, culture and environment are conceptualized as two ideational constructs in whose nexus is formed meaning (See Figure 1). Rapoport's work (1990b) has dismantled these two constructs of environment and culture in ways which make them more manageable, more useable and hence more enlightening. This framework is reflected in Rapoport's three basic questions of environment-behavior relations:

> 1. What are the characteristics of people, as members of the species, as individuals and as members of various groups ranging from families to societies that shape the environment and, in design, should shape the environment so that it is congruent with these characteristics and supportive of them?
> 2. In what ways do which attributes of environments affect what groups of people in which ways, under what sets of circumstances, why and how?
> 3. Given this two-way interaction of people and environments they must be linked in some ways: What are the mechanisms that link them? (Rapoport, 1994, 3).

The first question addresses culture and gives a sketch as to how Rapoport dismantles that term. The second question addresses environment, while the third discusses the mechanism which links the previous two. Certainly his final question does not mention meaning, but it is clear that this is one aspect of that interrelationship that is central to culture-environment relations and is also central to Rapoport's own work (1982; 1990c).[7] Together, this framework is loose and encompassing enough to accommodate much if not all of the work referred to in these essays and do so in a comprehensible fashion. Beckley cites Rapoport (1969, p.135) himself as recognizing "the value of constraints to establish generalized, loose frameworks where the interplay of the constant and the changeable aspects of man (sic) can find expression." The framework Rapoport has developed meets this goal he set thirty years ago.

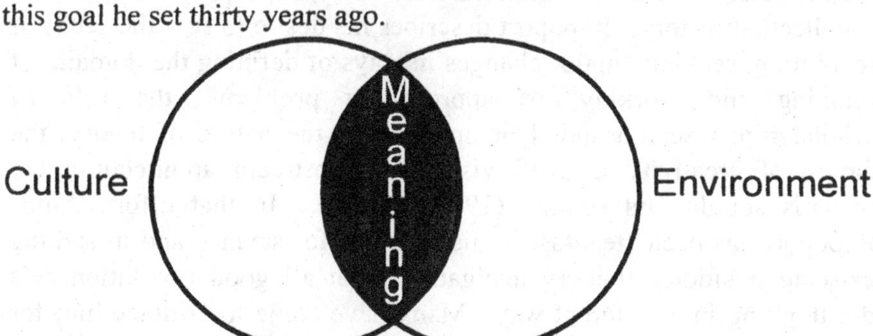

Figure 1.1 Framework of Place

Thought of in terms of the armature diagrammed in Figure 1.1, Rapoport's work can be seen to have much in common with the research on place. Groat's (1995) excellent introduction to *Giving Places Meaning* reveals a similar tripartition to person-environment relations in the work of the environmental psychologist David Canter, and the phenomenological geographer Ted Relph. Together these approaches to EBS may begin to articulate the domain most clearly and also shed light on each others' perspectives.

Because of the pluralism of cultures and sub-cultures and the systems of settings which exist, meaning has come to be viewed as dialogical in nature and human understanding as being socially-constructed. Goodsell's interpretive approach to research, Low's methodological triangulation, Lawrence's pluralism, Groat's "negotiated hypotheses," and Kent's "architecture as socio-physical in nature," all derive from the acceptance of the social construction of reality (e.g. Berger & Luckmann, 1966). By making us aware of the multiplicity of cultures and perspectives necessarily considered to understand an environment, Rapoport's work naturally leads to this assumption.

Both of the preceding paragraphs I am sure bother Rapoport to no end. I have no doubt he vehemently disagrees with my assessment on both counts. However I suggest both are important to his work's overall legacy.[8] They suggest a completely different way of thinking than existed prior to *House Form and Culture* and the rest of Rapoport's work. Not only does Rapoport's extensive body of work and the concepts held therein possess a lasting influence, so too does the zeitgeist associated with culture-environment inquiry. In his 1990 'intellectual history,' Rapoport describes his desire to sow the seeds of revolution, seeking "major changes in ways of defining the domain, of thinking and working, of approaching problems, the role of scholarship, research and their application, the nature of theory, the nature of creativity in EBS vis-a-vis mainstream architecture, the rewards sought and so on" (1990a, p. 81). In that effort, Amos Rapoport has been steadfast in his idealism for science and in staking extreme positions, thereby instigating what all good revolutionary's do: thinking in a different way. Many have come to criticize him for being overly critical, obstinate, a 'curmudgeon.' But in all his writings and lectures Rapoport has always made us think. This is evidenced in the essays which form this book.

In that same intellectual history, Rapoport (1990a, p.108) wrote, "Thus I will continue to cultivate my own garden, doing what I do, pursuing ideas wherever they lead, and above all, enjoying myself...it has all been great fun." Amos, if you are reading this, rest assured that not only was it fun, your cultivation was fruitful; your seed has fallen on fertile ground as these essays make clear. In fields from architecture to social psychology, anthropology to landscape design, there are students who when exposed to your work and the cultural issues of the built environment perk up and, in the words of your beloved Monod quote, say, "I want to know..."

Notes

1 Rapoport argues for this linkage as well (see Rapoport, 1990b; 1994).

2 This is true in regard to environment-behavior studies in general (see Wohlwill, 1976; Groat, 1983).

3 For instance, what are the implications of the physical design where design studios form the perimeter of a building and overlook a central atrium while all support courses are taught in the basement as was true of my graduate school? A former student of Rapoport's, Henry Sanoff, is currently exploring this issue (Sanoff, 1999).

4 For instance, if researchers are examining schoolyard bullies, as a given level of human aggregation, those bullies would operate within a physical environment but also within a context that includes their classmates, the entirety of the school's student body, the teachers and administration, the school board, the neighborhood, the community, the nation and so on.

5 Rapoport (1994), in fact, suggests that built form may be considered a subset of culture; the former embedded in the latter.

6 This is all too often an overlooked point in that people can associate themselves with myriad social worlds simultaneously and relate to them in varying degrees of entrenchment. Thus people bring a wide range of expectations to any given setting which shapes their interpretations and hence experience of that setting.

7 Rapoport (1994) actually argues that meaning is central to all three questions -- a point with which I do not disagree but with which I have always struggled in terms of conceptual clarity.

8 If I am wrong, I take solace in knowing I have provided more fertilization for the continuance of brilliant scholarship which will come from Amos in the upcoming years.

References

Abelson, R.P. (1981). Psychological status of the script concept. *American Psychologist, 36*, pp. 715-729.

Barker, R. (1968). *Ecological psychology: Concepts and methods for studying the environment for human behavior.* Stanford, CA: Stanford University.

Berger, P. & Luckmann, T. (1966). *The social construction of reality.* New York: Anchor Books.

Cahoone, L. (1988). *The dilemma of modernity: Philosophy, culture, and anti-culture.* Albany, NY: SUNY Press.

Canter, D. (in press). Seven assumptions for an investigative environmental psychology. In S. Wapner, J. Derrick, T. Yamamoto & H. Minami (Eds.), *Theoretical perspectives in environment-behavior research: Underlying assumptions, research problems and methodologies.* New York: Plenum Press.

Dutton, T. & Mann, L.H., Eds. (1996). *Reconstructing architecture: Critical discourses and social practice.* Minneapolis, MN: University of Minnesota Press.

Gerson, E. (1976). On quality of life. *American Sociological Review, 41*, 793-806.

Goffman, E. (1961). *Asylums.* Garden City, NY: Anchor Press.

Goffman, E. (1974). *Frame analysis: An essay on the organization of experience.* New York: Harper and Row.

Groat, L. (1983). The past and future of research on meaning in architecture. In D. Amadeo, J. Griffin & J. Potter (Eds.). *Proceedings of the Environmental Design Research Association.* Washington, DC: EDRA.

Groat, L. (1995). *Readings in environmental psychology: Giving places meaning.* London: Academic Press.

Groat, L. & Despres, C. (1991). The significance of architectural theory for environmental design research. In E. Zube & G.T. Moore (Eds.), *Advances in environment, behavior and design. Volume 3.* New York: Plenum Press.

Jackson, J.B. (1953a). Pueblo architecture and our own. *Landscape, 3*(2), pp. 20-25.

Jackson, J.B. (1953b). The westward moving house. *Landscape, 2*(1), pp. 8-21.

Jencks, C. (1997). *The architecture of the jumping universe.* London: Academy Editions.

Jencks, C. & Baird, C. (Eds.) (1970). *Meaning in architecture.* New York: Braziller.

Kent, S. (1982). Hogans, sacred circles, and symbols -- The Navajo use of space. In D. Brugge and C. Frisbie (Eds)., *Navajo Religion and Culture: Selected Views*, pp. 128-137. Santa Fe: Museum of New Mexico Press.

Oppenheimer Dean, A. (1999). Listening to critics: The stage is set. *Architectural Record,* (1), pp. 68-73.

Rapoport, A. (1969). *House form and culture.* Englewood Cliffs, NJ: Prentice-Hill.

Rapoport, A. (1982). *Meaning of the built environment: A nonverbal communication approach.* Beverly Hills, CA: Sage.

Rapoport, A. (1984a). There is an urgent need to reduce or eliminate the dominance of the studio. *Architectural Record.* October 1984. New York, NY: McGraw Hill.

Rapoport, A. (1984b). Cross-cultural aspects of environmental design. I. Altman, A. Rapoport & J. Wohlwill (Eds.), *Environment and culture. Human behavior and environment: Advances in theory and research, Volume 4.* New York: Plenum Press.

Rapoport, A. (1990a). Science and the failure of architecture. I. Altman & K. Christensen (Eds.), *Environment and behavior studies: Emergence of intellectual traditions. Human behavior and environment: Advances in theory and research, Volume 11.* New York: Plenum Press.

Rapoport, A. (1990b). Systems of activities and systems of settings. In S. Kent (ed.), *Domestic architecture and the use of space.* Cambridge: Cambridge University Press.

Rapoport, A. (1990c). *Meaning of the built environment: A nonverbal communication approach.* Second Edition. University of Arizona Press.

Rapoport, A. (1994). On the relation between culture and environment. *Aris, 1994.* Pittsburgh, PA: Carnegie-Mellon.

Rapoport, A. (1995). On the nature of design. *Practices (3/4)*, 32-43.

Rossi, A. (1966). *The architecture of the city.* Cambridge, MA: MIT Press.

Rykwert, J. & Tavernor, R. (1988). *On the art of building in ten books.* Cambridge, MA: MIT Press.

Sanoff, H. (1999). *Student responses to architecture schools.* Paper presented at the thirtieth annual Environmental Design Research Association Meeting; Orlando, Florida.

Schutz, A. (1967). *The phenomenology of the social world.* Evanston, IL: Northwestern University Press.

Strauss, A. (1978). *Negotiations: Varieties, contexts, processes and social order.* San Francisco: Jossey-Bass.

Strauss, A. (1993). *Continual permutations of action.* New York: Aldine de Gruyter.

Venturi, R. (1966). *Complexity and contradiction in architecture.* New York: Museum of Modern Art.

Wicker, A. (1987). Behavior settings reconsidered: Temporal stages, resources, internal dynamics, context. I. Altman & D. Stokols (Eds.), *Handbook of Environment Psychology.* New York: Plenum Press.

Wohlwill, J. (1976). Environmental aesthetics: The environment as a source of affect. I. Altman & J. Wohlwill (Eds.), *Human behavior and environment: Advances in theory and research, Volume 1.* New York: Plenum Press.

PART I: THEORETICAL INQUIRY

2 On the Importance of Theory

Amos Rapoport

Prelude

I am grateful to all who took it upon themselves to organize, edit and contribute to this book. It is certainly gratifying to have been deemed worthy by one's colleagues and students of what is a great honor. At the same time there is a feeling of sadness because, in effect, it signifies and marks the end (or approaching end) of one's active career, even if one intends to continue working — as I certainly do.

The division of this book into three sections (theoretical inquiry, architectural education and architectural anthropology) does not necessarily correspond to the way I think of my work. Having recently had occasion to review it for the bibliography, other patterns seem more consistent: Identifying reasons for the great variety of built environments, the nature of environmental quality, the need to agree about, dismantle and operationalize concepts, defining "environment," "activity systems" and other such terms, the use of systems of settings and cultural landscapes and so on.

One of the three topics used, however, is indeed central and the key to everything else — the need for an explanatory theory of Environment-Behavior Relations (EBR). The more specific themes all derive from a perceived critical need for such theory. Also, all this work (starting as an undergraduate) is, in essence, a research program, so that it is possible to find almost all later work latent in my theses and first published work and single sentences in *House Form and Culture*. These have become papers and parts of books and are being developed further (cf. Rapoport 1990a).

The Domain of Environment-Behavior Studies

The need for explanatory theory, in turn, leads to the need to define the domain, which I do in terms of what I have called the three basic questions of Environment-Behavior Studies (EBS) (Rapoport 1997a, in press a). These, in turn, derive from an even more basic commitment—that science provides the only reliable way of acquiring knowledge. This raises a series of questions about the nature of science, the nature of theory, the meaning of explanation and many others on which I have been concentrating since 1982 (Rapoport 1990a, 1997a, in press a).[1]

In order to be able to develop theory (and even valid generalizations) the largest and most diverse body of evidence is needed. This has led to what I call the four-fold expansion of that evidence, and which is another way to organize the bibliography. This involved including (i) all types of environments (including vernacular, popular, spontaneous settlements, etc.), (ii) the whole environment (cultural landscape, system of settings and also semi-fixed and non-fixed features), (iii) all of history (possibly via hominids to animals origins of both built environments and culture) and (iv) all cultures.

Also, underlying all this work is an effort at maximum possible objectivity and detachment from the specific topics. I am rather proud of the fact that, as far as I am aware, nowhere in my work is there a statement about my own likes and dislikes, evaluations of environments and the like. There are two reasons for this. The first is that one's own preferences are irrelevant (except to one's own environment); the second is that one thereby avoids so-called architectural 'theory' which is, in essence, a normative position about how buildings should be.

Clearly these characteristics also follow from the meta-value (which I *do* hold very strongly)—a commitment to science and, therefore, the view that if one is trying to achieve 'good' or 'better' environments, one needs to ask (and should be able to answer) what is 'good?' Better for whom?' Why is it good? How do we know it is better? etc. (Rapoport 1983a).

A commitment to science also involves making minimal (especially metaphysical) assumptions. Among these, that there exists a real, mind-independent world which is simple in principle, logical, self-consistent and causal, and hence can be understood and explained. Further, that science provides the only way to achieve this goal and that objectivity and detachment are not only necessary, but possible. I would also argue that, contrary to dogma, our domain is *simpler* than that of many other sciences. It is at the mesoscale (avoiding the very large, the very fast and the very small) and, moreover, we evolved in it.

The supposed 'difficulty' of understanding EBR is due largely to a desire to obfuscate (as in the recent anti-science literature [see references in Rapoport in press a]) and also to disguise the fact that the (architectural) emperor has no clothes.

This striving for objectivity and detachment from one's objects of study also follows from my motives for becoming involved with EBS which seem very different to others' (as becomes clear from Altman and Christensen 1990). Put most briefly and simply, my goal was always to *understand* the world (or a particular part of it) which is what explanatory theory is about, rather than to *change* it. This clearly bears on ones evaluation of the field, which always depends on what one takes it to be and, hence, what one expects it to have achieved. Also, the distinction between *obtaining* knowledge (a cognitive, objective, detached process) and *using* knowledge (a much more subjective, conotative process involving many more values, ethical judgements, etc.) seems important. In addition, once a discipline exists, i.e. explanatory theory derived from *basic research*, one cannot avoid changing the world. For one thing, in the present case, the nature of 'design' will change; it will be seen as involving problem identification and solving, i.e. *research application*, relying also on *applied research*. This three-fold distinction is most important and, unfortunately has been confounded in EBS, the categories used in conferences and calls for papers, etc. The lack of this distinction has also meant that the products of some good applied work in some specific sub-domains (e.g. design guides, participation, programming, POE, regarding dementia, children's environments, offices, etc.) has not been useful in developing a science of EBR.

Culture in EBS

A good example of detachment is provided by the last of the three sections of this book. I am often (usually?) identified with "culture."[2] In fact, however, I do not take a 'normative position' about it. My apparent emphasis on culture was due to the fact that it seemed (and seems) to be an inescapable component of any understanding of how people interact with built environments. It seems significant that 'culture' is increasingly playing a role in psychology, psychiatry, medicine, sport, business and other fields. I do not, however, feel that I have any 'vested interest' in it, or even necessarily believe that it is the most important aspect in our understanding of EBR. It is a strictly empirical question how important culture is vis-à-vis other human characteristics. If its importance is shown to be less — so be it. I am not an upholder of 'cultural theories' as some have suggested (I do not even believe such things exist). One needs to go wherever the evidence leads, accepting it about how things are.

I drew attention to the role of culture in *House Form and Culture* (Rapoport, 1969), and since in many publications, not necessarily because it had been neglected (which is in order if it is, in fact, unimportant). Rather, it came up in trying to answer a very important question—why there are so many dwelling and settlement types when human activities seem so much fewer in number.[3] This led to the idea of the importance of latent aspects of activities (and also to their dismantling), the importance of meaning (and its dismantling), etc. 'Culture' also seemed to be an inevitable aspect in trying to deal with the three basic questions of EBS, i.e. it played some role in the domain. However, how important a role is an empirical question, as are the relative impacts of variability vs. constancy? The latter has been, and is, changing as a result of ongoing research in evolutionary science, behavioral genetics, molecular biology, sociobiology, evolutionary psychology and the like; the answer is not self-evident (Rapoport in press a). It is also the case that some variability may be due to *constraints*, which are sometimes difficult to distinguish from wants.[4]

As reliable answers begin to emerge, and as the evidence changes, so will my views about culture, any biological or genetic constraints on it (i.e. human nature), how it evolved, variability vs. constancy and so on. In effect, I am neutral about the role of culture and some of my views are in somewhat of a state of flux due to a constant stream of sometimes contradictory recent work (e.g. Rapoport in press a, in press c).

The Importance of Conceptual Clarity

Since I regard non-scientific 'holism' to be an impossibility (Rapoport in press a), 'culture' like many (if not most) concepts (e.g. meaning, 'vernacular,' tradition, environmental quality) needs to be dismantled in order to become usable. Without dismantling, I increasingly find that it cannot be used. In fact, already in my 1969 work, one can detect beginnings of dismantling which has since gone much further and can be traced in the bibliography (e.g. Rapoport 1977, 1986, 1993a, in press b). I am currently (June 1999) writing a paper for a new Swedish journal (*Housing, Theory and Society*) taking this even further. In effect, therefore, one no longer needs to argue that culture should be considered; by making it more *specific*, more *concrete* and hence operational, one can begin to use its components. Yet, because of the general problems due to the prevalent anti-scientific attitude, less operational terms (like 'home' and 'place') are replacing clear, simple, well-defined, and hence, more operational terms like 'dwelling' and 'setting' (Rapoport 1993b, 1994, 1995b).

There is another equally (if not more) important aspect of concepts — this is to reach agreement about their meaning and their use. I tried several times to have special meetings to deal with this issue, but unsuccessfully. Thus, at the very least it is essential to make *explicit* how any given concept is being used. The common, *implicit* and variable usage leads to chaos and confusion. A related problem is an increasing lack of awareness of what has already been done, what is known and where there are disagreements. Instead of starting at the 'state of the art,' the wheel seems continually to be reinvented. This is due partly to a seeming reluctance to get to know and use the literature (or rather *literatures* of the many relevant fields). It is also due partly to a tendency to see topics as independent, rather than as specific expressions of more general patterns. This ignores the internal logic of the field, and how different parts 'hang together.' One needs to operate at a sufficiently high, abstract conceptual level in order to identify such linkages. That also allows new material to fit into the growing conceptual framework. I find constantly, including in almost every class session, that new material, and not only from the research literature but from newspapers and other media, fits in (Rapoport in press a). Furthermore, one can often relate material at different scales, from the region to the room, both because they form a single system and because the *same principles* often apply (although scale invariance or variability are empirical questions).

Architectural Education

All these matters are important in my teaching. On the one hand all my courses are about one thing—the science of EBR—although using different vehicles. These (housing, urban design, vernacular design and developing countries) can then be treated as *model systems*, similar to those used in the bio-medical (and other) sciences.[5] Similarly dissertation, thesis and paper topics can also play this role.

Not working at the 'state of the art' involves not only the neglect of new work in fields which happen to have been part of EBS from the beginning, but also the failure to use new fields, some of which can be seen as *model disciplines* (e.g. my discussion of archaeology in Rapoport 1990b; c.f. Rapoport (in press a). Model disciplines can be such either because of their attempts to become more rigorous and scientific, or because of the speed with which they develop. For example, molecular biology is not that much older than EBS, yet its achievements and rate of development have been breathtaking. At best, EBS has been on a plateau for quite some time; more realistically it has deteriorated as the social so-called 'sciences' have adopted the worst excesses of the anti-science movement (cf. references in Rapoport in press a), and have become what the Australian philosopher David Stove refers to as 'festering intellectual slums.'

The notion of seeking patterns and making what I call lateral linkages or connections is another way to structure my work. Such connections can be both within the domain and with other fields and theories—looking for inter-field and inter-theory support. The development of such conceptual frameworks also involves seeking the mechanisms that link people and environments. These seem to be limited in number; a current list (in Rapoport in press a) identifies eight plus an uncertain number derived from dismantling 'culture.'

The development of such frameworks also involves using the largest and most diverse body of evidence (as discussed earlier). Such data can come from a variety of fields. Using large amounts of data and synthesizing/integrating them helps to turn a disparate collection of studies, an accumulation or pile (which can become counterproductive) into a unified, cumulative body of knowledge, a process brought to completion by the development of explanatory theory. An important aspect of the latter is that it makes teaching a great deal easier and more productive. This is due to what is called 'compressibility,' the fact that science is cumulative and that theory can reduce masses of information to relatively short, easy to communicate and remember, yet powerful frameworks (Rapoport 1990a). This also has implications for what is taught as well as how it is taught.[6]

Using my own ongoing synthesis I increasingly feel able in my courses to give an overview (or sketch) of EBS (as the science of EBR) in one or two sessions (cf. Rapoport in press a, part 2). As in the case of any science, specifics can then be introduced to deal with particular problems. What is being taught is a way of thinking, a way of approaching problems by *identifying* them rather than inventing them. Only then does one look for specific data that are needed in order to solve the problem (which can be conceptual). Also important is the logic of the argument, how the various sections (of a paper or dissertation) work together and are linked. Data are, of course, needed (one cannot even begin to construct theory without some minimal amount) but in classroom situations it is even possible to use 'hypothetical' data, i.e. "if I had X, I would use it at this point in such-and-such a way." This makes the problem presented by the difficulty of finding information easier. That problem is due not only to the lack of theory, but also to the scattered nature of the material, lack of standard sources, small circulations, going out of print and the like (which I discuss in the introduction to my *Thirty-Three Papers in Environment–Behavior Research* [Rapoport, 1995a]). Thus, in addition to the development of explanatory theory we badly need a unified, global, transdisciplinary database.

Another consequence of my approach is that I tend not to teach specifics. Not only do they change, but they are provided by the students' paper topics—and in all my courses papers have always been required, never examinations. This not only helps develop logical thinking skills and fosters the ability to be critical, to analyze and synthesize, but it also emphasizes the importance of communication. I would argue that clear writing means clear and critical thinking, logic, a sustained argument and the ability to establish linkages. Clear diagrams are equally important, and I believe that not nearly enough diagramming is taught as a tool for thinking, analysis, synthesis and so on. Yet it seems to be much more important than perspective drawing, let alone drafting.

Given this view of EBS as the science of EBR, one thinks of 'design' as a *science-based profession*. An essential part of this is pure, basic research which can only take place in universities (Rapoport 1979); both applied research and research application (= design) can (and often do) take place elsewhere. Also, rather than preparing students for the profession as it now is, the role of universities is to try to change the profession.

It is also important to emphasize the close link between research and university level teaching: They mutually influence one another. It is useful to recall that a professor is *someone who professes*; three things are important, however; (i) To make *explicit* and use data to justify one's position, (ii) to encourage criticism and (iii) not to take a normative position about specifics, but only regarding the domain and epistemology. Thus, I teach using my research as the starting point while encouraging a critical approach to it. Students' questions, arguments and criticisms have considerably influenced my research and have led to a significant number of new publications and to major revisions of others.

Conclusion

Thus, clearly theoretical inquiry is the most important and central of the three sections of this book — the others follow. Explanatory theory is what best characterizes science, and I want to conclude by re-emphasizing that I see EBS as the science of EBR. Many things follow. One is my objection to studio and what happens in it. Names may seem trivial but are important; thus, even calling 'studios' laboratories would help—because names project images and set up expectations. In a laboratory one would expect the application of research (more like in engineering or medicine) in the same way that I see environmental design as closer to the design of materials, molecules and the like than to art (which the term 'studio' suggests). But, in any case, I agree with Horace Judson (in his *The Search for Solutions*) that science is the art of the 20th [and 21st] century. With this in mind, I still hope, actually, to write the book on theory—but time will tell.

Notes

1 My 1997b deals with many of these issues in much more detail. Referring to it, and also my in press a, would help clarify many points only briefly touch upon here.
2 This was even the case in the announcement in the recent EDRA 30 registration packet about the 'Reflections on Rapoport' session.
3 Skimming through the new *Encyclopedia of Vernacular Architecture of the World* (edited by Paul Oliver) is instructive in this connection.
4 Culture seems to play a more important role in wants than in needs, and also in satisfying both.
5 All of those are useful but the most useful are developing countries (e.g. Rapoport 1983b) followed by vernacular design.
6 It also bears on the distinction between what has been called private science (what individuals do) and public science—the discipline. In EBS there has undoubtedly been good work produced by individuals but, as yet, no development of a discipline.

References

Altman, I. and K. Christensen (Eds.) (1990). *Environment and Behavior Studies: Emergence of Intellectual Traditions.* (Vol.11 of Human Behavior and Environment). New York: Plenum.

Rapoport, A. (1969). *House, form and culture.* Englewood Cliffs, NJ: Prentice-Hall.

Rapoport, A. (1977). *Human Aspects of Urban Form.* Oxford: Pergamon Press.

Rapoport, A. (1979). Pure research in architecture and urban planning. *Wisconsin Architect*, September, pp.5.

Rapoport, A. (1983a). Debating architectural alternatives. *RIBA Transactions 3, 2*(1), 105-109.

Rapoport, A. (1983b). Development, culture change and supportive design. *Habitat International,* 7(5/6), pp.249-268.

Rapoport, A. (1986). Culture and built form – a reconsideration. In D. Saile (Ed.), *Architecture in cultural change: Essays in built form and culture research.* Lawrence, KS: University of Kansas.

Rapoport, A. (1990a). Science and the failure of architecture – An intellectual history. In I. Altman & K. Christensen (Eds.) *Environment and Behavior Studies: Emergence of Intellectual Traditions* (Vol.11 of Human Behavior and Environment) New York, Plenum.

Rapoport, A. (1990b). *History and precedent in Environmental design.* New York: Plenum.

Rapoport, A. (1993a). *Cross-Cultural Studies and Urban Form.* College Park, MD: University of Maryland.

Rapoport, A. (1993b). A critical look at the concept 'place.' In R.P.B. Singh (Ed.), *The power of place: Human environment and sacrality.* Varanasi, India: Banaras Hindu University Press.

Rapoport, A. (1994). A critical look at the concept 'place.' *National Geographical Journal of India, 40*(1-4), 31-45.

Rapoport, A. (1995a). *Thirty-three papers in Environment Behavior Research.* Newcastle (UK): Urban International Press.

Rapoport, A. (1995b). A critical look at the concept 'home.' In D. Benjamin & D. Stea (Eds.), *The home: Words, interpretations, meanings and environments.* Aldershot (UK): Avebury.

Rapoport, A. (1997a). Theory in environment-behavior studies: Transcending times, settings and groups. In S. Wapner, et.al. (Eds.), *Handbook of Japan-U.S. Environment-behavior research (Toward a transactional approach).* New York: Plenum.

Rapoport, A. (1997b). The nature and role of neighborhoods. *Urban Design Studies, Vol. 3*, pp.93-118.

Rapoport, A. (in press a). Science, explanatory theory and environment-behavior studies. In S. Wapner, et.al. (Eds), *Theoretical perspectives in Environment-behavior research: Underlying assumptions, research problems and methodologies.* New York: Plenum.

Rapoport, A. (in press b). Using culture in housing design. *Housing and Society, 25*(1).

Rapoport, A. (in press c). Architectural anthropology or environment-behavior studies? In M. J. Amerlinck & J.F. Bontempo (Eds.), *Architectural Anthropology.* Westport. CT: Bergen and Garvey.

Rapoport, A. (in press d). Archaeological inference and environment-behavior studies. *Habitat, Source d'interppretation de l'Organization et de la Complexite Sociales.* Antibes, France: Editions APDCA.

3 Amos Rapoport: Scholar, Conscience and Citizen of the Environment and Behavior Field

Irwin Altman

I cannot say exactly when and where I first met Amos Rapoport, but I think that it was at one of the early conferences of the Environmental Design Research Association, some three decades ago. Since then we have been friends and colleagues-- co-editing a book in the *Human Behavior and Environment* series published by Plenum Press (Altman, Rapoport & Wohlwill, 1980), participating in conferences and panels all over the world, reading and commenting on one another's writings, enjoying more informal discussions, debates, agreements and disagreements than I can remember, and sharing many meals, drinks and social occasions over the years. Amos and I hold many of the same views and values about environment and behavior studies, but we also differ on a number of issues. Anyone who has spent even a little time with Amos Rapoport surely knows that there are no slow moments in his presence; he is alive and enthusiastic about intellectual issues, revels in discussion and debate, and has a quick wit and ever-sparkling eyes. Given our lengthy collegial and personal association, I am pleased to comment on Amos Rapoport's contributions to our field and to my own work.

The Scholar

First, let me speak of his wide-ranging contributions to the study of environment-behavior relationships. As one of the longest-term and continuously active participants in the field, Amos Rapoport symbolizes the importance of understanding people-environment relationships as a key to human viability and to the design of effective environments. His contributions in the service of this principle are wide-ranging, penetrating, and unique in content, concepts, energy, commitment, and productivity.

What are those contributions? Their content is enormously broad, but they are undergirded by his long-standing interest in culture-environment relationships. Between his early landmark work on house form and culture and his more recent writings on history, archeology, and environment, Amos Rapoport has addressed a tremendous variety of topics—homes and housing, community design, environmental meaning, concepts of place, privacy, and others (Rapoport, 1969; 1977; 1990a; 1990b). I recall many occasions at conference presentations when Amos whispered to me how he had already written about aspects of the material being presented. Not infrequently I often later discovered that he had, indeed done so! But more than volume and content, it is what underlies Amos Rapoport's writings that have always intrigued me, influenced my thinking, and lie at the heart of his value to our field.

Amos Rapoport is as close to a renaissance man as the environment and behavior field will ever have. Almost every topic he studies is linked to some extent to the content, philosophy, and epistemology of other fields, e.g., physics, chemistry, biology, archeology, anthropology, geography, psychology, and to various environmental design fields. He courageously leaps into other disciplines, thoroughly reads, absorbs, and uses a greater range of knowledge than anyone I know. Building connections, relying on substantive, theoretical and philosophical ideas in other disciplines are hallmarks of his work, and are crucial to our understanding of human-environment processes.

He is a voracious reader, and I have the image of Amos sitting in his study surrounded by mountains of books, a dozen or so open all at once, and from which he is reading and scribbling notes in his own distinctive style. I suspect his scribbles and scrawls are voluminous, and whenever I have stolen a peek at them at meetings I am impressed by their array of colored lines, arrows, boxes and circles—and their complete unintelligibility to anyone looking over his shoulder. And the intensity with which he makes notes at meetings matches his overall energy and enthusiasm. How often I have half-jokingly said to myself: "Wow, Amos knows everything! How does he do it?" I am ever astounded at his limitless energy and ability to draw on so many different fields and subject matters. Although I too rely heavily on writings from many social sciences and other fields, I am an amateur in comparison to Amos. He is a scholar with a capital S.

The Conscience of the Field

Amos Rapoport is the conscience and beacon of idealism in the environment and behavior field. It is often said that a best friend is one who is a constructive critic. Amos is such a friend to scholars, practitioners, and consumers of environment and behavior products. And he does the job at all levels--vigorously critiquing our use of terminology, theoretical concepts, methods and procedures, approaches to evidence, and the very state and direction of the field. He is a masterful critic of sloppy use of terms such as homes, place attachment, privacy, territory, and others (and these are some of my favorite terms and concepts!). He is enormously skillful in pointing out careless distinctions, imprecise analyses, and confounded meanings. His critiques of flawed methodologies are often penetrating and well justified. And, at another level, his recent comments on how the field as a whole has a knowledge base that is too atheoretical, redundant, ignores past work, and is not cumulative, are right on target.

It is easy to be defensive about his critiques and commentaries, or to write off Amos Rapoport as a "curmudgeon" who is ever critical of others' work. Personally, I am indebted to him for his critiques of my work, because they help me see my way to being clearer and more precise about the concepts and phenomena in which I am interested. He is my "high-priced, unpaid consultant," and an invaluable advisor--even if I don't always agree with him.

I view Amos Rapoport's critiques as constructive in two important ways. First, his personal and professional goal for the environment and behavior field is to be rigorous and systematic, in order to enhance our understanding and design of productive human environments. Second, Amos often does more than criticize; he usually proposes a positive alternative to better deal with the issue under consideration. Would that we all follow the practice of constructive criticism coupled with proposals for future directions. Taken together, Amos Rapoport serves us well as a first rate constructive critic.

The Theoretician

Amos Rapoport seeks to systematically theorize about environment and behavior phenomena in a way that is firmly anchored in a "scientific" philosophy and epistemology. He has repeatedly and vigorously called for the development of integrative theories of environment-behavior phenomena that will set the stage for progress in scholarly understanding and practical design. Although he acknowledges the difficulty of developing a "grand" and wholly unifying theory, he urges us to search for as comprehensive theory as is possible, in order to synthesize a broad array of environment and behavior knowledge.

I also heartily endorse theory development, and acknowledge efforts by some environment-behavior scholars to apply theoretical ideas from other fields (e.g., psychological concepts of overload, stress, and control perspectives in respect to crowding, developmental psychological theories regarding cognition and perception, psychological and sociological theory on interpersonal relationships, social support, role theory, social participation, and community organization, to name a few). At the same time, one might hope for more effort directed at theoretical application and development of concepts unique to environment and behavior phenomena, more integration of existing conceptual frameworks, and more systematic testing and evaluation of existing theories as they apply to people-environment relationships.

The development of theory is not easy because, among other things, it depends on a cumulative body of knowledge, reliable information and findings, and an appreciation of the contexts within which information was obtained. These requirements are not readily met in the environment and behavior field, given its diverse and ever-changing membership, the varying interests of participants from different disciplines, and the early stages of our knowledge. Complicating the situation is the fact that practicing environmental designers—a large and important constituency—are not always well-versed or able to spend time and energy in the development and assessment of theoretical constructs. Many practitioners are trained to focus on specific design problems, and must pragmatically move from project to project. Although they often creatively apply theoretical notions to design problems, they do not always have the opportunity to evaluate, expand, or reflect in depth on theoretical approaches.

Although theory development is crucial, we must also be realistic about the scope of theorizing that is possible in the environment and behavior field. I seriously question, for example, the feasibility of developing "grand" or broad-scale theories at the present time—or perhaps ever—regarding environment-behavior phenomena. At best, I believe that we will find it most useful to apply and extend existing theories or concepts, or develop new but limited approaches.

Grand Theory vs. Theories of the "Middle Range"

Why do I take this stance? From time to time scholars in many disciplines have proposed broad-ranging or "grand" theories of human functioning. Yet, the history of the social sciences, including my parent field of psychology, is replete with the failures of scholars who sought to develop "magic bullet" concepts designed to explain many domains of human functioning. The instinct theories of the late 19th and early 20th century didn't do the job. The behaviorist movement, culminating in radical operant "Skinnerian" theories of the mid-20th century positing the universal role of "reinforcement" as the motor driving all of human behavior, fell by the wayside. Nowadays, the so-called "cognitive revolution" and its many sub-variations, promulgated as a panacea for understanding all of human behavior, are also likely to fall short of the mark. And on the horizon is the rising popularity of "evolutionary psychology," which proposes a biological and evolutionary explanation of a vast array of human functioning, including social and interpersonal behaviors. Isn't it also the case that the "genetics revolution" is promising, explicitly or implicitly, to uncover the genetic explanations of disease? Yet, we already know that, except for rare diseases, the genetic underpinnings of health are complex, involve combinations of genes and a variety of environmental circumstances. Given the early and almost primitive state of knowledge in the environment and behavior field, I believe that searching for "grand," or large scale unifying theories, is not likely to be fruitful. Rather, as is the case in many disciplines, theories of the "middle range"—limited in scope and application—are likely to be the most productive approaches to understanding environment and behavior processes (c.f. Moore, 1997).

Perhaps my long term experience as a quantitatively trained researcher makes me appreciate first-hand the fragility, instability, weak replicability, and crude knowledge we have about social phenomena in relationship to the physical environment, and the low likelihood that we can presently progress toward broad- ranging theoretical statements. Frankly, I am not convinced that we will ever find an all-encompassing theory to account for social phenomena. I believe that there are multiple truths, multiple types and rules of evidence, and multiple twists of the kaleidoscope of human behavior, many of which have legitimacy and meaning, but none of which is "the answer."

A "Field" of Environment-Behavior Studies?

At the risk of sounding pessimistic—which I am not—I recently raised the rhetorical possibility that there may well not presently be, nor may there be in the future, a unified and coherent field or discipline of environment-behavior studies (Altman, 1997).

It is true that we have many of the institutional trappings of a field, in the form of at least two national or international organizations, regular conferences, journals, awards, books and book series, and educational programs. Yet, there are other institutional features that suggest a rather fragile structure to the field: variable numbers of participants in conferences, a modest number of journal subscribers, high turnover of membership in organizations with only a small core of continuing participants, modest growth of academic programs and courses in colleges and universities, relatively little recognition of the role of environment and behavior studies in design fields or design education.

Perhaps more important, I raised questions about whether or not it is possible to have a coherent and unified body of knowledge or theory associated with environment and behavior phenomena. I stated (Altman, 1997, p. 427):

> Although I am an agnostic on the question, I will argue for the moment that there can be no discipline of environment and behavior studies.

> Why not? Because new fields or disciplines, like traditional ones, must be organized around selective human processes, with the physical environment only one of several factors linked to those human processes. Thus I can conceive of new disciplines of family and interpersonal studies, life cycle processes, health, quality of life in communities and cities, cognitive science, and others, each focusing on different clusters of human processes. But it is inconceivable to me that there can be a discipline focused around the physical environment and all human processes. And that is what I think we have tried to do in environment and behavior studies—create a field that deals with all human activities in respect to the environment.

This somewhat disconcerting possibility, therefore, is that there may not now be, and may never be, a *single* field of environment and behavior studies. Rather, there are traditional and emerging disciplines, all defined by particular human processes, and each dealing with environmental contexts within which those human processes are embedded. It is the human processes that define these fields, not their interest in environmental issues.

Theoretical Development and Human Processes

If this line of reasoning is plausible, how can we speak of developing theory in environment-behavior studies? To my way of thinking, so doing requires one or both of two paths. First, one must begin with some human functional, social, or psychological process. Given the fact that extant theories in traditional disciplines address a given human process, e.g., privacy, stress, performance, emotional state, interpersonal relationships, or others, one may then pose conceptual and empirical questions about how the process and existing theories about it relate to environmental factors. In so doing one might extend, revamp, or scrap existing theories based on research and analysis. But note that the focus is on the human phenomenon as the anchor, with the physical environment only playing a role as an influence, effect, or milieu in relation to the human phenomenon. The physical environment is not what a theory is about; a theory is primarily associated with a human process.

A second approach is to draw on concepts and theoretical ideas from other disciplines, bring them to bear on a human process, and simultaneously weave in the role of the physical environment. However, most scholars trained and working in a discipline tend to rely primarily on the concepts, theories and methods of their parent field. It is certainly important to work within the framework of a traditional discipline. But it is also crucial to stretch our perspective beyond the philosophy, theory and epistemology of our parent field, to see how the human phenomena of interest to us can be understood through the lenses of other disciplines. So doing opens up the possibility of a more comprehensive and varied appreciation of the human processes we aspire to understand. However, note again that the human social process—not the physical environment—is the starting point.

Amos Rapoport is a premier example of one who has aggressively and successfully drawn on the ideas, concepts, and theories of a variety of disciplines in the social sciences, and even in the physical and natural sciences. He casts a wide conceptual net, and will surely continue doing so as he pursues theoretical ideas. I am also not quite sure about the scope of human processes he intends to capture in his future theorizing. Nevertheless, we can be certain that Amos Rapoport will bring to bear an array of ideas from different disciplines to whatever he addresses.

Some Philosophical Issues

Amos Rapoport and I agree about the importance of continuity, accumulation, rigor, and need for syntheses of knowledge and development of theory that can guide research and practice in the environment and behavior field. At the same time, I am not sure that we share a common vision of what some of these ideals mean, especially in terms of epistemology, the nature of theory and, most important, the alternative philosophical assumptions that can legitimately underlie our work and thinking.

I grew up professionally in the field of psychology during an era when it sought to be a "true science" along the lines of chemistry and physics. I was socialized in a value system that revered and promulgated the laboratory experiment (and its key features of random assignment of people to experimental conditions, and experimental and control groups) as the essence of science. In addition, this value system advocated the concept of rigorous operational definition of variables, the idea of antecedent-consequent causation as the premier indicator of cause effect relationships (i.e., if A is followed closely in time by B, then A is a "cause" of B), replicability of findings and data as a requirement for generalization, the search for broadly based "universal" laws of relationships between variables, a molecular and analytic approach involving precise statements of variables in their most fundamental form, parsimony in theoretical statements, the importance of "objectivity" and multiple observers separate from the phenomenon who ideally view it in a consistent way.

These and related philosophical guidelines have dominated psychological research for most of this century, and have resulted in a voluminous and valuable array of knowledge and theory about human psychological processes. And it is this confluence of values and approaches to knowledge that I believe Amos Rapoport subscribes to and vigorously encourages others to apply to environment and behavior phenomenon. I do not disagree; so doing will be invaluable. At the same time, I believe that there are alternative "ways of knowing," alternative forms of scholarship that can be informative, and alternative philosophical assumptions that enable us to achieve legitimate knowledge and theory about human -environment relationships. Simply put, I do not subscribe to the thesis that all of our research and scholarship on human-environment processes must be cast within the dicta of the philosophy of science that has prevailed historically in psychology and other fields.

Growing up professionally in the tradition just described—having done quantitative empirical work, hypothesis formulation and testing, and laboratory experiments and field research according to that tradition—left me both satisfied and dissatisfied. Yes, useful research and theory resulted. Yet, over the years I came to see how restrictive and limited were the results and concepts, especially in respect to the complexities of everyday interpersonal relationships, and the role of the physical environment in relationships. Simple A-leads-to-B causal analyses were insufficient; replicating findings in different environmental settings was almost impossible in the face of complex contextual factors; the idea of control groups often made no sense or added little meaningful comparisons; I questioned whether there could be truly "objective" observers of complex social relationships in different environmental contexts, and accepted the possibility that there might be useful multiple observers--participants, scientists, visitors, etc. Furthermore, I wondered about how to deal with changing relationships and changing environmental confluences in a controlled, replicable, or generalizable way in a naturalistic setting? And, I speculated about what was the ideal unit of analysis to study? It may not *invariably* be the molecular or isolated behavior that is usually sought in the ideal laboratory setting and that follows strict principles of precise operational definition.

World Views in Person-Environment Relations

These perplexities led to my attempt to understand underlying philosophical "world views" or alternative approaches and assumptions to the study of psychological processes, including people-environment relations (Altman & Rogoff, 1987). Based on the writings of philosophers John Dewey, Arthur Bentley, and Stephen Pepper, Barbara Rogoff and I described four world views that differ in their assumptions regarding:

1) unit of analysis of psychological processes to be studied;
2) time, change and temporal aspects of psychological processes; and
3) philosophy of science or rules for assessing the legitimacy of knowledge and information (Altman and Rogoff, 1987).

With respect to units of analysis, the *trait* world view emphasizes internal qualities of individuals, e.g., instincts, personality qualities, etc., as the main drivers of individual behavior, with environments and contexts playing a qualifying role. Trait approaches are infrequent in contemporary psychology, whereas a second world view, the *interactional*, is prevalent nowadays. The interactional world view treats psychological qualities and environmental features as independently defined entities which may interact to affect human functioning. The third world view, the *organismic*, emphasizes holistic units of study, with complex sets of relationships existing between individual qualities and environments. Trait, interactional, and organismic world views all assume that psychological processes (and sometimes environmental features) are the fundamental units of analysis to be studied, with these elements independently defined and separate from one another. The preferred strategy of study in these approaches is to isolate psychological phenomena and environmental features into their parts or dimensions, study relationships between elements or clusters of elements, and systematically define and control dimensions and properties of variables.

The fourth world view, the *transactional* perspective, treats phenomena as composed of inseparable psychological and environmental aspects that jointly define the whole and one another. The transactional world view does not focus on relationships *between* separate elements, but assumes that the person and context jointly define one another, and mutually contribute to a holistic unity. Thus the transactional approach treats phenomena as an *inseparable* unity of psychological processes and physical and social features of settings.

World views also differ in their approach to time and change. The *trait* world view usually assumes stability of psychological processes; the *interactional* world view treats change as deriving from the interaction of separate person and environmental events, possibly also linked to underlying regulatory mechanisms. In the *organismic* world view change is associated with predetermined teleological processes. In contrast, the *transactional* perspective assumes that change and stability are inseparable aspects of psychological phenomena. Furthermore, this approach does not assume that change proceeds in a particular direction or is under the control of guiding mechanisms. Stability and change are emergent in their occurrence, direction, and other qualities.

The four world views also differ in their approach to science, modes of inquiry, or rules of evidence. *Trait* world views highlight Aristotelian "material" cause, or the idea that causation is associated with the "essence" and intrinsic properties of a phenomenon, e.g., instincts, personality traits. *Interactional* world views focus on "efficient" causation or antecedent/consequent relationships between variables. *Organismic* approaches highlight "final" causation or the teleological qualities that pull social and psychological processes toward some end state. In contrast, *transactional* world views emphasize "formal" cause, or identifying patterns and organization of events that include inseparable configurations of people, space, and time.

World views also differ in other aspects of philosophy of science. For example, *trait*, *interactional* and *organismic* perspectives seek observers of situations who are separate, objective, and detached from phenomena. *Transactional* world views rely on a variety of observers to an event--investigators, participants, and others — each in different "psychological locations," and each of whom may provide different but potentially valuable information about a phenomena.

Furthermore, the *transactional* world view, although interested in general principles, focuses on understanding particular events in terms of whatever theoretical principles may apply, acknowledging that different concepts may be necessary to understand particular events. In contrast to this pragmatic and relativistic approach, the other world views seek to discover universal explanatory principles and, ideally, an ultimate synthesis and unity of knowledge based on limited theoretical principles.

Our analysis states that *none* of these world views provides the "correct" or "best" way to understand phenomena. Each offers a distinctive form of inquiry, understanding, and theory development, and all are ideally necessary to comprehend a phenomenon. At the same time, our assessment is that the transactional perspective is underutilized in research and theory, and the time is at hand to give more attention to this philosophical perspective — without rejecting the value of the other world views.

I am reluctant to stereotypically categorize Amos Rapoport's approach to scholarship, but I believe that he adheres in many ways to an *interactional* world view. Although I recognize the value of the *interactional* paradigm, and understand its central role in the development of the social sciences, our analysis of world views encouraged me to explore other ways of "knowing," especially the transactional approach (or what some call a *contextualist* perspective, e.g. Stokols, 1987). In so doing I have come to believe that there are no true and perfect ways of knowing and understanding, and I feel compelled to adopt any strategy that seems to facilitate my understanding of a phenomenon. For some purposes an *interactional* or another perspective may be most useful. Given the issues I wish to explore regarding interpersonal relationships — their dynamic, environmental, and cross-cultural features — I consider it most productive, at least for the time being, to work from a *transactional* world view, rather than from the traditionally most favored *interactional* perspective.

Those who question this strategy may argue that this is a "nonscientific" approach, claiming that it fails to identify efficient causes, does not isolate variables precisely, has limited predictability, testability, replicability, generalizability, and does not satisfy many of the traditional hallmarks of 20th century interactional "science." To this I say that social sciences in this century have arbitrarily selected the *interactional* world view as the only meaning of "good science." In contrast, one may argue that application of *all* world views is necessary to fully comprehend a phenomenon. Any world view, taken alone, provides only a fragmentary, albeit useful and legitimate, perspective on a phenomenon. Labeling one or the other strategy as "science," "history," or "story-telling" ignores the utility of different world views and severely limits our ability to broadly comprehend phenomena. Whether inquiry is labeled as "science" or not because it uses an alternative to the presently normative *interactional* world view is less important than the utility of the products of our scholarship.

There are many examples of empirical and conceptual work that my colleagues and I have done within a *transactional* world view: quantitative and empirical analyses of neighborhood social networks and their links to environmental design (e.g. Oxley, Haggard, Werner & Altman, 1986); archival analyses of ethnographic material on courtships, weddings and placemaking (e.g. Altman, Brown, Staples & Werner, 1992); qualitative, empirical analyses of husband- wife and wife-wife relationships in modern polygamous families (e.g. Altman & Ginat, 1996); studies of the temporal qualities of homes based on ethnographic material and direct observations of house blessing ceremonies (e.g. Werner, Altman & Oxley, 1985; Werner, Haggard, Altman & Oxley, 1988); conceptual analyses of fundamental dialectic processes in close relationships (e.g. Altman, Vinsel & Brown, 1981; Brown, Werner & Altman, 1998), theoretical statements regarding privacy and territoriality (e.g. Altman, 1975), historical analyses of homes and interpersonal relationships (Isaac & Altman, 1998) to name a few. Our blend of quantitative and qualitative analyses, archival and direct ethnographic research, and conceptualizations and syntheses of knowledge in a variety of disciplines, are all cast within a transactional world view.

Are the products of our research and theorizing useful, scholarly and systematic? My colleagues and I believe that the transactional perspective has enriched our understanding of close interpersonal relationships . Yet, we fully acknowledge that this philosophical approach is only one strategy, albeit one that is widely neglected in modern social science. And we certainly encourage the application of other world views. Indeed, the complexity of environment-behavior phenomena cries for alternative paths of investigation.

This is *not* to say that "anything goes." Sloppy scholarship, inconsistent conceptualization, unclear or inappropriate methodology, neglect of earlier work, and other flaws are unacceptable, regardless of mode of scholarship. Although serious, these are phenotypic or superficial errors. For me, the most egregious error in our scholarship is the failure to know and state our underlying philosophical assumptions. It is essential that we always attempt to explicate our assumptions about the social, psychological, social and environmental units of analysis we believe to be worthy of study, the ways in which we deal with time, stability and change, and the rules of evidence or philosophy of science to which we subscribe. The data we collect, the methodologies we adopt, and the form of our theories and conceptualizations are inextricably linked to our underlying world views and their associated philosophical assumptions. Too often we do our scholarly work without explicating our assumptions, and the consequences are significant. Thus we risk unknowingly casting every phenomenon we study in the mold of a particular world view, thereby theorizing and researching in a mechanical and constricted fashion. Furthermore, scholars from different disciplines, who may operate according to different philosophical assumptions, will find it difficult to link their separate knowledge and theory if their underlying assumptions are unstated--yielding a modern Tower of Babel not infrequent in the behavior and environment field! In addition, being ignorant of alternative assumption frameworks makes it easy to reject out of hand findings and theories of others, and seduces us into thinking that our own approach is the only "correct" one. The ultimate results of our failure to state clearly, or to even know, our own and others' assumptions are: isolated "islands" of knowledge and understanding; mutual ignorance or neglect; and a pattern of fragmented scholarship.

Although I strongly encourage alternative approaches to knowledge in the environment and behavior field, I also call for rigorous scholarship in any world view perspective, and especially urge that we be fully aware of, and explicitly state, the underlying assumptions that guide our work. So doing is the only way to connect islands of knowledge and theory, and to build a more comprehensive network of understanding.

Postscript

Amos Rapoport's contributions to the environment and behavior field are notable and wide-ranging. He is a premier scholar who has unflinchingly set and maintained standards of quality in research on environment and behavior phenomena from the very beginnings of the field thirty years ago. Rigor of analysis, breadth of interdisciplinary perspective, concepts and theories buttressed by solid evidence, and a steady stream of high quality work all reflect Amos Rapoport's stamp that will last well into the future. Whether or not one shares exactly the strategy and direction of his scholarship, there can be no disagreement about the importance of his sustained and high quality work. He is a paragon and standard of what we should all strive to achieve. His physical and intellectual energy, courage in the face of personal crises, continuing presence in conferences, lectures and informal conversations, coupled with his talent at speaking out, listening, and debating, make Amos Rapoport a fine scholar, noteworthy citizen, and good conscience of the environment and behavior field. Your many friends and colleagues, thank you, Amos, for all you have done for the field.

References

Altman, I. (1975). *Environment and social behavior: Privacy, personal space, territory, and crowding.* Monterrey, CA: Brooks/Cole (reprinted by Irvington Press, New York, 1981).

Altman, I. and Rogoff, B. (1987). World views in psychology: Trait, interactional, organismic, and transactional perspectives. In D. Stokols & I. Altman (Eds.) *Handbook of Environmental Psychology. Volume 1.* (pp. 1- 40). New York: Wiley.

Altman, I. (1997). Environment and behavior studies. A discipline? Not a discipline? Becoming a discipline? In S. Wapner, T. Yamomoto, T. Takahashi

& J. Demick (Eds.). *Handbook of Japan-United States environment-behavior research: Towards a transactional approach.* (pp. 423- 434) New York: Plenum.

Altman, I. & Ginat, J. (1996). *Polygamous families in contemporary society.* New York: Cambridge University Press.

Altman, I., Rapoport, A., & Wohlwill, J. (Eds.). (1980). *Environment and culture. Volume 4: Human Behavior and Environment.* New York: Plenum.

Altman, I., Vinsel, A., & Brown, B. B. (1981). Dialectic conceptions in social psychology: An application to social penetration and privacy regulation. In L. Berkowitz (Ed.) *Advances in Experimental Social Psychology. Volume 14.* (pp. 107-160). New York: Academic Press.

Altman, I., Brown, B. B., Staples, B., and Werner, C. M. (1992). A transactional approach to close relationships: Courtship, weddings, and placemaking. In B. Walsh, K. Craik and R. Price (Eds.) *Person-environment psychology: Contemporary models and perspectives* (pp. 193-241). Hillsdale, NJ: Erlbaum.

Brown, B. B., Werner, C. M. & Altman, I. (1998). Choicepoints for dialecticians: A dialectical/transactional perspective on close relationships. In L. Baxter and B. Montgomery (Eds.) *Dialectical approaches to studying personal relationships.* (pp. 137-152). Hillsdale, NJ: Erlbaum.

Isaac, J. & Altman, I. (1998). Interpersonal processes in nineteenth century utopian communities: Shakers and Oneida Perfectionists. *Utopia*, 9 (1), pp. 26-49.

Moore, G. T. (1997). Toward environment-behavior and design theories of the middle range: Their structure and relation to normative design theories. In G. T. Moore & R. W. Marans (Eds.) *Advances in environment, behavior, and design. Volume 4. Toward the integration of theory, methods, research, and utilization.* (pp. 1-40). New York: Plenum Press.

Oxley, D., Haggard, L. M., Werner, C. M., and Altman, I. (1986). Transactional qualities of neighborhood social networks: A case study of "Christmas Street". *Environment and Behavior.* 18, pp. 640-677.

Rapoport, A. (1969). *House form and Culture.* Englewood Cliffs, NJ: Prentice Hall.

Rapoport, A. (1977). *Human aspects of urban form.* Oxford: Pergamon Press.

Rapoport, A. (1990a). *History and precedent in environmental design.* New York: Plenum Press.

Rapoport, A. (1990b). *The Meaning of the Built Environment. A Non-verbal communication Approach.* Tucson: The University of Arizona Press.

Stokols, D. (1987). Conceptual strategies of environmental psychology. In D. Stokols & I. Altman (Eds.) *Handbook of Environmental Psychology. Volume 1.* (pp. 41-70). New York: Wiley.

Werner, C. M., Altman, I. & Oxley, D. (1985). Temporal aspects of homes: A transactional perspective. In I. Altman & C. M. Werner (Eds.) *Home environments. Volume 8: Human behavior and environment.* (pp. 1-32). New York: Plenum.

Werner, C. M., Haggard, L. M., Altman, I. & Oxley, D. (1988). Temporal qualities of rituals and celebrations: A comparison of Christmas Street and Zuni Shalako. In J. E. McGrath (Ed.) *The social psychology of time: New perspectives.* (pp. 203-232). Beverly Hills, CA: Sage.

4 House Form and Culture: What have we Learnt in Thirty Years?

Roderick J. Lawrence

The design and use of houses reflect certain cultural and social beliefs, ideas, meanings and values. This principle was made explicit for architects when *House Form and Culture* was published by Amos Rapoport in 1969. In that book Rapoport challenged common interpretations of the layout, design and use of vernacular houses. The book is an explicit critique of geographical, physical and technical determinism that has been (and still is) used to explain vernacular and other kinds of houses. Although there is no consensus about the meaning of the term vernacular architecture, it usually refers to folk, indigenous, tribal, peasant and traditional buildings. The term is also used with reference to a wide range of building forms, traditions, types and uses around the World (Oliver, 1997). The majority of vernacular buildings are built to accommodate domestic ways of life. They are usually related to the local environmental conditions and available resources and often they are constructed by those who occupy them using traditional construction materials and methods.

In contrast, formal architecture usually refers to public buildings and monuments designed by architects and constructed by master builders and specialists using aesthetic styles, building layouts and construction materials and methods transposed from other localities. These distinctions between vernacular and non-vernacular buildings were made by Alexander (1964) when he contrasted those processes of unselfconscious housing construction (including iterative responses to local conditions and incremental adaptation over time) to self-conscious processes in which the rate of change is greater and varied owing to the diverse interests of all those involved in the design and construction of modern buildings. In sum, the implication of administrative, economic, political, symbolic and other kinds of societal and cultural factors in the layout, construction and use of these two classes of buildings is quite different and ought to be recognized by housing researchers.

In Rapoport's own words, *House Form and Culture* was meant to be "an exploratory study" of the ways in which people construct and use domestic space. The main thesis is that "house form is not simply the result of physical forces or any single causal factor, but is the consequence of a whole range of socio-cultural factors seen in their broadest terms" (Rapoport, 1969: 47). In addition, house form "is modified by climatic conditions (the physical environment which makes some things impossible and encourages others) and by methods of construction, materials available, and technology (the tools for achieving the desired environment). Rapoport wrote that "the socio-cultural factors (are) primary, and the others secondary or modifying" (ibid.). The main reasons he used to support this thesis stem from the degree of choice people have when they construct and use domestic space: Choices reflect the degree of constraint which is explained in relation to the concept of criticality: the forms of houses are not determined by physical forces and hence can show great variety because of the relatively low criticality of buildings....because physical criticality is low, socio-cultural factors can operate; because they can operate, purely physical forces cannot determine form." (Rapoport, 1969: 59)

Thirty years after the first publication of *House Form and Culture* it is now clear that many contemporary scholars have apparently ignored, or rejected, Rapoport's overriding note of caution that this book was "an exploratory study". Given the fact that this book has been widely quoted to uphold the view that cultural factors have a primary influence upon the design of houses, it is not only appropriate but important to acknowledge, as Rapoport did, the strengths and the limitations of this book. These have been discussed in detail elsewhere and will not be repeated (Lawrence, 1987). This essay will examine how cultural dimensions are attributed to and expressed in the design, meaning and use of houses in contemporary societies. Then a discussion of methodological issues related to cultural studies of the residential environment includes some recommendations for future housing studies.

Housing: a Complex Subject

This essay argues that housing cannot be studied adequately by applying traditional academic theories or methods that rarely transcend disciplinary boundaries or sectoral approaches. Today we live at a time in the history of human civilization when the design, layout, meaning and use of housing warrants a reappraisal. Unfortunately, despite the rapid growth of housing studies during the last two decades, academics and professionals have rarely developed and applied innovative theories and methods (Aries, 1993; Low and Chambers, 1989; Tognoli, 1987; van Vliet, 1998). However, owing to the complex nature of housing, an integrative historical perspective ought to be formulated in order to identify and study the multidimensional characteristics as well as the interrelations between them. This kind of approach can generate a contextual understanding of housing, either at a specific point in time or over an extended period.

In order to redirect contemporary interpretations of housing it is fruitful to ask and answer the following questions:

1. What meanings do researchers attribute to housing in a precise locality at specific points in time?
2. What philosophical and ideological frameworks are commonly underlying these meanings and other interpretations of housing?
3. How can current knowledge of these frameworks and meanings be developed and applied?

These are not simple questions that can be easily answered as *House Form and Culture* indicated in relation to vernacular houses. Moreover, in contemporary societies, there is a lack of consensus about uses of terminology including "housing," "dwelling" and "home" (Altman and Werner 1985; Benjamin 1995; Saegert, 1985). There have been a number of ironical reversals of the meaning and uses of terms in recent centuries; for example, the common use of "home" as an euphemism for "house" when the real estate sector refers to "homes for sale." In principle, however, a person can purchase a house but one cannot buy a home! Similarly, architects can design houses but not homes. A house may be uninhabited temporarily, or abandoned, but a home has a experiential dimension at one or more geographical scales — generally, from a dwelling unit to a country —

as well as over time.

Housing can be interpreted with respect to sets of human relationships between individuals and society which are contextually located in time and place. These relationships are meaningful not simply functional. They are created and maintained over time by the experience of daily life (Somerville, 1997). These relationships are mediated by at least seven sets of affiliations including the family, community, government, education, employment, religion, and recreation. Collectively these affiliations define and are mutually defined by the duties and claims, the rights and obligations, and the social status and role of a person. They also underlie self-, social- and place- identities (Duncan, 1981). These are associated with how housing is interpreted in precise situations by individuals and groups. All these dimensions are complex and the interrelations between them can change in specific localities over time. During the last thirty years there have been a large contribution of theoretical and applied housing research that has tried to advance knowledge and understanding. The next section of this essay will present an overview and critique of these contributions. Then an integrated conceptual framework will be presented as a reference model. This model is currently being applied to study the qualitative characteristics of habitat in the Canton of Geneva, Switzerland (Lawrence, 1996).

Overview of Housing Studies

In 1969, as Rapoport underlined, housing was not a priority subject of study for researchers in the social sciences, or for professional planners and architects. Since then many theoretical perspectives, concepts and research methods have been used by authors from a wide range of academic disciplines and professions. Both housing studies and research on the meaning and use of domestic space have grown rapidly in scope and volume (Aries, 1993; Low and Chambers, 1989; Tognoli, 1987; van Vliet, 1998). Although this section is not meant to provide an exhaustive account of all these theoretical and methodological contributions, it is suggested that an overview of recent publications enables the formulation of two broad classes of studies:
first, historical, sociological and policy studies concerned with urban and housing policies, institutions, markets and especially those factors

related to the construction ("supply") and requirements ("demand") of housing; and

second, a wide range of architectural psychological and sociological approaches of people and their surroundings at the geographical scales of housing units, residential buildings and neighborhoods.

This essay briefly outlines and comments on the underlying theoretical and methodological frameworks that have guided research in both these classes of studies (see Table 4.1). Like Després (1991) and Somerville (1997) it suggests that owing to selective and interpretative biases it has been extremely difficult to develop and apply a comparative perspective. In addition the interrelations between the vast number of dimensions that define and are mutually defined by the design, meaning and use of housing have not been studied in detail.

Urban and Housing Politics and Sociology

During recent decades, a large volume of housing studies has examined the interrelations between broad societal dimensions and the provision, regulation and use of residential neighborhoods and housing units (see Lawrence 1985 for an overview). Subjects of study in this class of contributions include housing economics, national and local housing policies and legislation, housing construction methods and domestic technology. In general, these contributions have examined societal dimensions related to mechanisms of the "supply and demand" for housing and/or the living conditions of specific categories of people in precise cities and towns (e.g. the size of households and housing units, landlord-tenant relations, and official housing and land-use policies and practices). Many authors have adopted an economic interpretation that considers housing primarily as a form of financial investment. As Daunton (1983) noted, this interpretation suggests that supply and demand are related to 'macro'-economic parameters, whereas little concern is given to household income and how residents use their resources. One exception to this approach is a contribution by Englander (1983). A different interpretation examines housing standards and legislation, especially about construction materials and methods, the number and size of rooms, and the provision of gas, water and sanitary facilities (Burnett, 1978). There are very few studies that

Table 4.1 Comparison of Frameworks to Classes of Housing Studies

THE DESIGN, MEANING AND USE OF HOUSING

	Themes	Subjects	Examples
URBAN AND HOUSING HISTORY AND SOCIOLOGY OF INSTITUTIONS	HOUSING POLICY & HISTORY		
		Housing politics and policies	Burnett, 1978
	(Diachronic approach)	Socioeconomic account of "supply and demand"	Dunleavy, 1981
		Households and housing conditions	OECD, 1996
		Tenure, subsidies and allowances	
		Developments in public services and domestic technology	
			Michelson, 1977; 1980
	HOUSING SOCIOLOGY & INSTITUTIONS		Ravetz, 1974
	(Synchronic usually)		van Vliet et al. 1985
	MORPHOLOGICAL STUDIES	Morphology of residential quarters	Daunton, 1983
	(Synchronic & diachronic)	Layout and size of dwelling units (sometimes with households)	Lawrence, 1986
		Architecture of housing types (sometimes in larger context)	Vernez Moudon, 1986
PEOPLE AND SURROUNDINGS STUDIES	PHYSCHOLOGICAL & SOCIOLOGICAL STUDIES		
	(Synchronic approach)	Cultural, societal and individual factors	Cooper Marcus, 1995
		How residents perceive, value and assess residential environments	Dovey, 1985
			Duncan, 1981
	STUDIES OF DOMESTIC LIFE		
	(Synchronic approach)	Architectural studies	Allen & Crow, 1989
		Ergonomic studies	Franck et al. 1989
		Socioeconomic class, age, professional status	van Vliet et al. 1985
		Household demographics: Structure and composition of households	

explicitly include a study of morphological or spatial dimensions, but Daunton (1983) and Lawrence (1986) are two exceptions. Swenarton (1983) maintains that housing historians have dealt with the economics, politics and society while ignoring housing design, whereas architectural historians have discarded everything except the built form of housing. This leads Swenarton (1983, p.3) to argue that "both these approaches imply that design and society are not involved in a single process but are separate and distinct." This means that it is impossible to identify changes in the design and use of housing units over time, and relate these changes to broad trends in the societal context including evolving life styles, social values and government housing policy.

There has been a limited amount of demographic research concerning the structure and composition of households and families, which have undergone significant changes in many industrialized and developing countries during this century. For example there has been a significant increase in the share of one-person households, in the decline in household size and in the increase in one-parent families (van Vliet, Huttman and Fava, 1985). In general, many studies in this category of housing research give scant attention to the changing nature of the design and composition of the housing stock, or the values of residents concerning the meaning and use of domestic space and facilities. Two exceptions to this custom are Ravetz (1974) and Wright (1981). This oversight illustrates a more general shortcoming of this category of research: in general, the interrelations between the societal context and its embedded processes have rarely been associated or examined in conjunction with personal ideas and values, as well as household customs, either at one point in time, or over an extended period.

Studies of People and their Surroundings

This class of housing research includes contributions from ergonomics, environmental psychology, architecture, geography and housing sociology. These have commonly examined the point-of-view of the individual, usually the tenants, owner-occupiers or the property managers using either:

1. Psychological and socio-psychological concepts such as identity, place-identity, appropriation, self and social-self in order to interpret how people perceive, use and value residential environments. Many of these interpretations interpret housing in terms of individual needs for identity, control, privacy, security, intimacy and social status (cf. Després, 1991, for an overview). Some contributions have explicitly used social surveys about housing design to formulate guidelines for professionals from the geographical scale of specific rooms in housing units to urban neighborhoods (Altman and Werner, 1985; Duncan, 1981). Another set of contributions apply phenomenological approaches and symbolism to interpret how mental representations, rituals and values are implicated in the personal attachment to and the appropriation of houses and domestic objects (Cooper Marcus, 1995; Dovey 1985).

2. Architectural and sociological interpretations stemming from either large-scale (at the national or regional level) or small-scale (at the neighborhood level) household surveys, including interpretations of housing aspirations and "needs" and lifestyles (see Tognoli, 1987, for an overview). Some surveys identify how the age, gender, education, household composition, socio-economic class and residential mobility of the studied population can be interpreted (Michelson, 1977; 1980). There are also architectural surveys of the composition of the housing stock at one point in time and other contributions that analyze how the design and use of houses change in specific localities over time (Vernez Moudon, 1986). These contributions have enabled differences between residents in the same and different localities to be identified and interpreted in terms of cultural, demographic and socio-economic variables (Allan and Crow, 1989).

The majority of these studies in this category have examined biological and psychological dimensions without explicitly accounting for the broader societal context in which the studied population resided. This means that ideologies concerning housing, in general, and housing policies, economics, and domestic life, in particular, are not integrated into these studies. (It is noteworthy that Ravetz, 1974, and Dunleavy, 1981, do not follow this custom because they explicitly address this context). Moreover, research of this kind has frequently adopted a selective bias by focusing on the so-called "typical" or "average" house type or household, while rarely examining representative samples of resident populations (e.g. single-parent households or the unemployed), as well as representative samples of the housing stock (e.g. studying single-family houses or recurrent apartment buildings at the expense of other types of residential accommodation). Indeed there has been very little concern for identifying and studying differences in housing conditions or households in western societies (Franck and Ahrentzen, 1989). However there has been an increase in studies of vernacular houses, including informal settlements (Hamdi, 1991). Last, but not least, and in contrast to the first category of studies, this kind of research has rarely adopted a temporal perspective or accounted for changes to the societal context.

What is Societal Context ?

The term context was first used in linguistics to analyze literary works in relation to their cultural and historical circumstances. In the discipline of philosophy, contextualism is defined as any doctrine that establishes the meaning of terms or emphasizes the importance of the circumstance of enquiry in order to solve problems. These definitions can be applied to study the design, meaning and use of housing. In this essay it implies that not only the intrinsic characteristics of houses and household behavior warrant analysis, but also the sets of ecological, societal and individual human factors that are directly or indirectly involved. This interpretation of "societal context" can be contrasted with its common interpretation in contemporary housing studies, in general, and particularly in the fields of architecture and urban sociology. For example, in contrast to definitions that explicitly mention cultural dimensions and underline the relativity of meaning, "contextualism" "contextual compatibility" and "contextual fit" are increasingly used in contemporary architectural publications to refer only to the massing, formal composition and aesthetic treatment of buildings, and their façades in particular. Architects have been provided with guidelines and pattern books that are meant to serve as "contextual design strategies" (Forty and Moss, 1980). Nonetheless, these documents are only based on the external appearance of buildings, sometimes in relation to the formal composition of the elevations of neighboring buildings. This essay argues that because this architectural orthodoxy only considers buildings in terms of their appearance, it is a restrictive interpretation of context and contextualism that ignores cultural, societal and historical dimensions. This architectural orthodoxy has a long history as some authors including Collins (1965) and Macleod (1971) have shown.

Since the 1970s, this approach has not been limited to the treatment of new buildings, but also increasingly applied to the conservation and restoration of old structures that may present inaccurate interpretations of particular architectural styles. These kinds of arguments illustrate the preoccupation of the architectural profession with style. However, the restrictive interpretation of contemporary architects ought to be contrasted with those earlier in this century. Although leaders of the Modern Movement in architecture debated the aesthetic and formal composition of new buildings in detail, concurrently, they also challenged static formalism and they sought to formulate and apply new principles of spatial organization, as well as the innovative use of materials and technology for 20th century architecture and urban design. The contemporary architectural debate about the styling of buildings considers aesthetics at the expense of other principles or parameters, and it does not examine precedent in a critical manner. Rather, it reduces precedent in architecture and urban design to a warehouse of aesthetic and formal traits, from which a designer can freely select and duplicate according to past or current fashions, or personal preference. Furthermore, the aesthetic preferences of the users of buildings are not considered (Harries, Lipman and Purden, 1988). According to current architectural discourse, the appearance of buildings is *decontextualized* to become both acultural and ahistorical as well as devoid of any economic, political or other societal dimensions. Unfortunately, this interpretation of architecture has been supported by recent studies of the design and meaning of housing (Forty and Moss, 1980; Richardson, 1981). In contrast, the interpretation of societal context in this essay implies that the distinctly different classes of approaches used in housing studies today ought to be applied simultaneously and in a complimentary way in order to implement an integrated perspective.

Principles for a Reorientation of Housing Studies

The preceding sections of this essay have classified and given a broad assessment of studies of housing. Some limitations of the two categories of studies have been briefly presented here and other assessments can be found elsewhere (e.g. Després, 1991; Lawrence, 1987; and Somerville, 1997). Given these criticisms, the task of some researchers, during the last decade, has been the redefinition and the reinterpretation of housing and home. Some of these researchers including Lawrence (1993) and Somerville (1997) argue that an integrative perspective is necessary. This kind of perspective ought to overcome the either/or approach shared by the two classes of studies presented above. This goal can be achieved if (and only if) the dimensions of study in any particular research project are explicitly related to the contextual conditions in which they occur. These contextual conditions define and are mutually defined by a range of cultural, societal and individual human dimensions that are interrelated, that occur at diverse scales, and that are susceptible to change over time.

If an integrated perspective is to be applied, it is necessary to reject any hierarchical model which is commonly used to order "variables" in terms of their relative importance. In this respect, and to cite but one example, it is noteworthy that Rapoport's (1969) thesis in *House Form and Culture* that cultural variables have primacy over all others in the determination of house form is still frequently accepted *a priori* by scholars who study vernacular and other types of housing in contemporary societies. This hierarchical interpretation is partial, as Lawrence (1987) has shown. In order to understand how cultural dimensions function in the design and use of houses in specific localities it is necessary to limit and specify the reciprocal relations between buildings and people by "cutting the culture concept down to size" as Geertz (1973) advocated. This can be achieved by replacing extremely broad conceptual tools that obscure rather than reveal the essence of social processes and cultural ideals, by intensive analyses which define not only those parameters operative in specific localities but also the reciprocal relations between them.

It is also necessary to reject any atomistic-mechanistic model, used in some housing studies. This model underlies those interpretations that identify cause-effect interactions between two "variables" isolated from the context in which they occur. One example of this kind of interpretations is the study of residential mobility and housing choice in terms of "pushes and pulls". This kind of interpretation has been challenged by Michelson (1977; 1980). Another example is those studies that try to correlate residential satisfaction with the floor level of housing units above the ground without considering all the other factors that are implicated in the experience and evaluation of housing. A critique of these approaches is included in Lawrence (1987).

In contrast to the two models just mentioned it is necessary to develop and apply a holistic, conceptual framework which not only reconciles the divergence between the two classes of housing studies presented earlier, but also accounts for the environmental and societal dimensions of housing as well as the reciprocal relations between them over time. This approach implies the application of an ecological perspective which is systemic rather than atomistic or hierarchical. This kind of approach has been used by Netting (1981) in his analysis of Törbel, a Swiss alpine village in the valley of the River Visp at an altitude of 1500 meters. Another example is the study by Boyden (1981) and his colleagues of the development of Hong Kong and its hinterlands from the period before British colonial settlement until the 1970s.

An Ecological Perspective

Although the term "ecology" has been used by natural sciences since the late 19th century, it has acquired a political connotation in recent decades. General ecology refers to the study of the interrelations between animals, plants and their immediate surroundings. Human ecology explicitly deals with people-environment relations. It provides a conceptual framework for academics and practitioners from both the natural sciences (e.g. biology, chemistry and geology) and the human sciences (e.g. anthropology, sociology and psychology) to accept divergent disciplinary concepts and methods and develop an integrated approach. From this perspective, the residential environment is multi-dimensional and complex and it should not be interpreted as a neutral background. Human ecology is an holistic interpretation of those processes, products, orders and mediating factors that regulate natural and human ecosystems at all scales of the earth's surface and its atmosphere. It implies a systemic framework for the analysis and the comprehension of three logics and the interrelations between their constituents using a historical perspective. These logics are a *bio-logic*, or the orders of biological organisms including animals and plants; an *eco-logic*, or the orders of all inorganic constituents such as air, water, soil and the sun; and an *anthropo-logic*, or the ordering of cultural, societal and individual human factors including myths, rituals and symbolism. This interpretation is not new. Although it should not be equated with environmental sociology or ecological psychology (Barker, 1968), it does have common ground with some basic principles of ecological anthropology, which explicitly includes economic and political dimensions (Hardesty, 1977). It implies that the following set of principles should be applied.

First, the interrelations between humans and their surroundings are manifested through a wide range of physiological and psychological processes. These not only include sensations and perceptions (which animals also share) but also beliefs, doctrines, ideas and representations, which are unique characteristics of the human intellect.

Second, unlike other biological organisms, the interrelations between people and their surroundings are characterized by discursive and reflexive knowledge including symbols. This characteristic differentiates anthropoid and human behavior (Lévi-Strauss, 1979).

Third, the "human environment" can be contrasted with the environment of other biological organisms by the instrumental functions and roles attributed to it. Human processes and products transform the constituents of the environment in order to meet prescribed aspirations, goals and needs. In addition, human activities can provoke unintended consequences on environmental constituents and, in return, impact on human health and well-being. This is one reason why studies of the *interrelations* between the characteristics of the residential environment are crucial if an integrated perspective is to be applied effectively.

Issues of an Evolving Societal Context

Professional practitioners, researchers and teachers in the field of people-environment relations need to address those changes in our societies that have consequences on the design and use of housing, and the meanings and functions of home. Some of these will now be summarized.

Societal Developments, Trends and Transformations

During this century, and especially since *House Form and Culture* was published in 1969, many industrialized and undeveloped societies around the World have undergone important developments that have had direct consequences on the meaning and use of housing and home. For example, there have been significant demographic changes in many countries. Much attention has focused on the consequences of an aging population, of the effects of a steady decline in household size, as well as changes to household composition and structure (Allan and Crow, 1989; van Vliet, Huttman and Fava, 1985). Today most societies around the World have reached a level of complexity previously unknown, and often unpredictable. With respect to demographic trends, for example, the complete reversal of the "baby boom" after the Second World War was not forecast. Today it is difficult to predict whether the current decline in the birth rate, or the aging of the population in many European countries, will continue well beyond the year 2000. It is noteworthy that these demographic trends have been more significant than changes to the provision of kinds of housing units in most industrialized countries. Hence, the disparity between the housing stock and households has increased during the last three decades in many countries as shown by the Organization for Economic Co-operation and Development (OECD, 1996).

Evolving Household Structures and the Meaning and Use of Housing

In Europe, there has been much media coverage about aging populations and the significant increase in households of one or two elderly persons. In addition, today marriage and the family have been discarded by a large portion of society, so that nuclear families (e.g. a married couple with children) are now a minority in some countries whereas post-war housing research and policy considered them as the norm. In addition to one parent households, there has been a rapid increase in recomposed households. Therefore it is appropriate to identify what home means for the growing number of children who have *two* places of residence that they use on an alternating basis, then to underline any implications on the design/use and management of the housing stock. The same kind of study could examine the homeless person (including an increasing number of youth and young adults) and the itinerant business man who often sleeps in hotel rooms.

These examples illustrate that today societies in Europe (and other parts of the World) have reached a level of diversity and complexity that ought to be studied by researchers and also understood by policy decision-makers. This means that:

1. Traditions are no longer a core influence in all sectors of daily life like they were during the lives of our forefathers. Today, marriage and the family have not only been challenged but also discarded by a large portion of the population of industrialized countries. Consequently, although housing administrations still often refer to a household as a married couple with two children, such households are a minority in many countries (OECD, 1996). Consequently, it is necessary to identify what home means to an elderly person who is confined to live in an institution; likewise to the hostage, or the prisoner; or the person who is obliged to sleep on the pavement. The meaning of housing and home will be different for each of these citizens (Cooper Marcus, 1995).
2. Societal values reflect and express an increasing level of pluralism in contrast to consensus. It is precisely for this reason that there is no shared definition of housing and home. From this perspective it is necessary to identify what home means for the immigrant, the foreign worker, the refugee, or the local citizen who has been obliged to move from his or her place of residence owing to a projected highway and redevelopment project (Porteous, 1989). The meaning and experience of housing will be different for each of these citizens.
3. Technological innovations are transforming the use of space and time at a faster rate than at any other period since Antiquity. Following the agricultural and the industrial revolutions, and more recently the impact of mass transportation, the radio, telegraph and television, today micro-technology is effacing some of the traditional spatial and temporal demarcations in the World (Mitchell, 1995).

It is necessary to identify the consequences of all these transformations on the design and use of housing. First, face to face contacts associated with many traditional forms of exchange - banking and shopping for example - have declined or become redundant, owing to innovations in communication technology, economic exchange and transportation (Castells, 1989). This means that social exchanges (indeed society itself) are maintained by less tangible ties between people, whereas in the past people were obliged to meet face to face to enact exchanges. This trend reflects and expresses the growing individualization of societies. Second, the corollary of the decline of face to face contact is that social relations have been stretched over space and time (Mitchell, 1995). Consequently, peoples' daily lives may no longer be directly related to their place of domicile, or their place of birth. The consequences of a much greater mobility in our society have not been well understood. The implications on the design and use of housing may be significant. There may be direct implications on the use of domestic space, such as when one's place of domicile serves only the function of a dormitory, as shown by a recent study in Geneva (Lawrence, 1996). Last, but not least, the effects of all these trends may be compounded so that individuals have difficulty in locating a place of belonging (Dovey, 1985). When such consequences are reality, the human costs and benefits can be grave, resulting in anxiety, stress and anomie. These are important subjects of study for researchers as well as for policy decision makers.

Reinterpretations of Culture

In view of the preceding developments during the last three decades, it is not wholly surprising that this essay argues that it is not only important to accept diverse interpretations of housing but also reconsider our interpretation of culture. In general, culture is a complex concept that often refers to an integrated pattern of human beliefs, customs, norms, knowledge, morals, values, behaviors and institutions shared by a group, the inhabitants of a region or a nation. In the past, culture was commonly considered to be a monolithic and static concept that could inhibit change. Today, culture refers to a relativistic and a multidimensional concept with its components evolving over time (Tuan, 1982). The consequences of this more complex and dynamic interpretation of culture ought to be recognized in our research, teaching and practice about housing. In an innovative agenda for housing research and policy new dimensions of people - residential environment interrelationships need to be addressed by:

1. Identifying and understanding differences in a broader sense than age, gender and the requirements of other specific groups without ignoring the importance of personal experience and individual differences.
2. Developing a broader concern with environmental values (including the use of resources of all kinds) and how these can influence the design, meaning and use of housing in specific localities.
3. Studying the growing diversity and complexity of spatial and temporal scales of daily experiences in and outside housing using new technologies.

Recommendations for Future Housing Studies

There are diverse approaches to understanding the interrelationship between cultural variables and residential environments. To appreciate the contribution of these diverse approaches it is useful to consider a framework and definitions pertinent to comparative cross-cultural studies of the built environment and human behavior over time.

Domestic architecture and human behavior can be interpreted on four interrelated levels. First, there are spatial and activity patterns which are universal to a culture, including behavior protocols and building regulations. Second, there are spatial and activity patterns which are consistently shared by members of a group or a community during a specific period of time, such as prescriptions for the preparation of food according to religious beliefs and practices (Goody, 1982). Third, other spatial and behavioral patterns are shared by an individual with a number of people who form a group - a household, and extended family or a club - including customary ways of preparing, serving and eating meals at home (Lawrence, 1982). Finally, the individual has certain ways of behaving and of evaluating which are unique to her/him, such as the preparation of a particular recipe. Such idiosyncratic behavior may not be social if it is not handed down to other persons.

The manner in which cultural, social and psychological

dimensions are interrelated is interesting, yet there are few studies of buildings or urban spaces in terms of the interrelations between these variables. Yet the understanding of such interrelationships is essential as is illustrated by the difficulty discussed earlier of undertaking a study of the interrelationships between architectural and behavioral variables without producing ambiguous results. Three methodological issues especially acute in research of this kind are the units of analysis, sampling problems and interpretation of data.

Units of Analysis

Many contemporary scholars have not identified a unit of analysis in order to conduct comparative research of buildings in different cultures or societies. As Rapoport (1990) has noted in several of his publications since 1969, it is important for architects and social scientists to analyze comparable residential settings rather than those which, only at first sight, appear to be the same. In this respect it is quite misleading to compare a room labeled "the kitchen" in Australian and English houses. Instead, Lawrence (1982) has shown that it is appropriate to consider a range of extant facilities for the preparation and eating of food — including several rooms inside the house, outdoor private spaces and public food facilities — rather than ascribing arbitrary boundaries to delimit a unit of analysis. Facilities for cooking and eating food were chosen for some very important reasons discussed by Goody (1982) and Lévi-Strauss (1979). First, the fact that the preparation and eating of food in spaces associated with the house is common to all cultures and societies and provides the necessary ingredients for comparisons between different cultures and within national boundaries. Second, activities involved in the preparation and eating of food reveal the socially and culturally defined demarcations (if they exist) between male and female and between parent and child roles which are not evident in the use of other spaces and facilities inside the house. Finally, the development of facilities for the preparation and eating of food is largely related to the history of ideas and values upheld by people in specific contexts at specific points in time.

Research by Khare (1976), for example, studies the implicit conceptual orders and explicit rules and conventions that Hindus in the city of Lucknow, India, employ to transform substances into food that is morally edible. According to Khare, the preparation, cooking and eating of food reflects the logic of Hindu cosmology. He shows that Hindu concepts of the natural, the social and the divine — including castes — are expressed by the structure and content of ceremonial, festive and secular events. There are prescriptions that define who can eat and drink what edible matter that have been prepared by a specific class of person according to precise recipes and customs using particular utensils. Hence food is a means of expressing self and group identities. Moreover, it is also a vehicle for the expression and transmission of religious and secular meanings. Khare explicitly shows how these meanings are transcribed on to the layout of facilities for preparing and cooking food, as well as the conditions for their use.

Khare identifies the spatial, social and ritual categories and practices that order what he terms "food areas". These areas include all those spaces, utensils and produce in a homestead that are related to the storage, the preparation and the eating of food. He illustrates the pertinence of the inclusive concept of "food area", which he contrasts to that of "the kitchen" and "the dining area", because they are too restrictive to include all localities related to the preparation and eating of food. This inclusive concept has been reapplied in other research, including comparative study of the houses and domestic life of settlers in the Province of South Australia during the mid-19th century (Lawrence, 1988). This study found that Cornish, German and other groups of pioneers transposed village layouts and house designs from their homelands. In the case of the German settlers at Bethanien, for example, houses with passage-kitchens and black-kitchens were rebuilt and used according to known designs and methods. Hence, this study shows the high value attributed to customary ways for preparing food and how these customs were maintained despite the heat from the hearth during the long, hot summer months in South Australia. In essence, it reminds us that the preparation and eating of food not only meets a vital need but it is a means of producing and reproducing human culture.

Limits of Case Studies

Several authors in diverse disciplines have commented on the limitations of the conventional case study approach for social research. Dunleavy (1981, p.198) for example, states that:

> One must confront the problems of inductive reasoning when (case studies) are used in certain ways; generalizations from one or a few cases can only be made in terms of their typicality and ultimately differing results across cases must be interpreted either as indicative of incorrect methodology in one set of studies, or an indicative of the extent of variation across different areas.

Dunleavy stresses that these problems are not inherent to the case study method "but are indicative of the limitations on the use of this method." The interpretation of case studies can consider them as a description of extant objects or events in a specific context. Traditionally, these objects and events have been studied in terms of one of the following intentions: to relate an abstract event to a concrete setting without any development over time; to analyze a series of events of short duration in order to uncover their theoretical implications; and to observe events over an extended period of time in order to establish necessary dependencies amongst variables in a specific context.

Unlike the first and second alternatives, and in contrast to social surveys which generally consider surface or explicit correlation amongst dimensions, case studies of the third kind can explore the logical relations between variables. As Dunleavy notes, it follows that the basis for generalization from a real case study is not the typicality of the units of analysis, but how that study illustrates the operation of general principles in a precise situation. Thus, "problems of choosing a typical case in this approach disappear, and the uniqueness and particularity of each study is explicitly recognized" (Dunleavy, 1981, p.199). The key element in this interpretation of case studies is the level of "theoretical interpretation" which is intended. One becomes concerned with the "use of case material to penetrate beyond a surface correlation to detect the more fundamental and general processes involved" (ibid.). Moreover, the problem of typicality is dissolved and those structural relations which operate in areas with the same form can be studied: "There is no guarantee involved that a plausible account in terms of structural relations will be forthcoming. But the attempt to establish such an account places our use of case material on a radically different plane from that of previous research" (Dunleavy, 1981, p.199).

Interpretation of Data

There are three essential components of cultural research which ought to be borne in mind when examining how cultural and social dimensions are implicated in the design and use of houses.

First, this research cannot be restricted to quantifiable dimensions as Rapoport has repeatedly argued since *House Form and Culture* was published.

Second, it encompasses social processes including activities and behavior or what Rapoport terms "systems of activities and systems of settings" (Rapoport, 1990).

Third it is grounded in a specific social, political, cultural and historical context.

From these perspectives, cultural dimensions are no longer defined in terms of innate capacities, nor simply by observing human behavior. Rather, both implicit and explicit social dimensions impinge upon the design and use of buildings in precise ways (Lawrence, 1993). In essence, cultural dimensions are ordered set of normative and value-laden concepts and meanings: they include moral and aesthetic principles which form an idealized framework or model of "how the world ought to be." In contrast, social dimensions include patterned processes of everyday life: they encompass the existential being of people, the actuality of their daily life and its surroundings, and the interpretation of idealized concepts. Hence, on one level there is a framework of expressive and normative concepts which enable each individual to comprehend what Langer (1953) called the "ethnic domain." On another level there are activity processes related to the goal-oriented behavior of individuals and groups which interpret this framework of meaning. Although these two kinds of dimensions are interrelated there is no automatic fit or congruence between them. With respect to the design and use of domestic buildings, congruence is more likely to be achieved in preliterate societies than industrialized societies, owing to the impact of a wide range of intermediary or regulatory factors in the latter as Alexander (1964) underlined. It is noteworthy that researchers and practitioners have commonly transposed research findings and housing policy instruments from one society to another without accounting for these different social and political dimensions.

Conclusion

House Form and Culture was meant to illustrate the implication of tacit and manifest "socio-cultural" factors in the design and use of vernacular houses. It was, however, in Rapoport's own words, an "exploratory study" of the ways in which people organize and use domestic space in primitive and vernacular buildings and settlements. The conceptual framework found in *House Form and Culture* for studying the variety of house designs and the number of factors that influence them has been widely cited by researchers who have misinterpreted it as a definitive contribution that is applicable to non-vernacular housing in countries around the world. The concept of societal context is still largely overlooked while the growing pace of change in household life has not been well understood. To conclude, therefore, this essay suggests that in order to conduct housing research that is relevant to people from all walks of life in our pluralistic world there is a need for:

1. Integrative approaches rather than exclusive ones;
2. More collaboration rather than disciplinary confinement;
3. Conceptual innovation rather than theoretical conservatism; and
4. Multiple methods and measures.

These directives can be applied using an ecological perspective in which all the dimensions implicated in the design, meaning and use of housing, as well as the interrelations between them, are explicitly borne in mind.

References

Alexander, C. (1964). *Notes on the Synthesis of Form*. Cambridge MA: Harvard University Press.

Allan, G and Crow, G. (Eds.) (1989). *Home and Family: Creating the domestic sphere*. Basingstoke UK: Macmillan.

Altman, I. and Werner, C. (Eds.) (1985). *Home Environments: Human Behavior and Environment. Advances in Theory and Research, vol. 8.* New York: Plenum Press.

Aries, E. (Ed.) (1993). *The Meaning and Use of Housing: International Perspectives, Approaches and their Applications.* Aldershot UK: Avebury.

Barker, R. (1968). *Ecological Psychology: concepts and methods for studying the environment of human behavior.* Stanford: Stanford University Press.

Benjamin, D. (Ed) (1995). *The Home: Interpretations, Meanings and Environments.* Aldershot UK: Avebury.

Boyden, S., et.al. (1981). *The ecology of a city and its people: The case of Hong Kong*. Canberra: Australian National University Press.
Burnett, J. (1978). *A Social History of Housing 1815-1970*. Newton Abbot UK: David and Charles.
Castells, M. (1989). *The Informational City: Information, technology, economic restructuring and the urban regional process*. Oxford: Basil Blackwell.
Collins, P. (1965). *Changing Ideals in Modern Architecture 1750-1950*. London: Faber and Faber.
Cooper Marcus, C. (1995). *House as a Mirror of Self: Exploring the deeper meaning of home*. Berkeley CA: Conari Press.
Daunton, M. (1983). *House and Home in the Victorian City: Working-Class Housing 1850-1914*. London: Edward Arnold.
Després, C. (1991). "The meaning of home: literature review and directions for future research and theoretical development" *The Journal of Architectural and Planning Research*, vol.8, no.2: pp. 96-115.
Dovey, K. (1985). "Home and Homelessness" pp. 33-64 in I. Altman and C. Werner (Eds) *Home Environments: Human Behavior and Environment. Advances in Theory and Research, Vol. 8* New York: Plenum Press.
Duncan, J. (Ed.) (1981). *Housing and Identity: cross-cultural perspectives*. London: Croom Helm.
Dunleavy, P. (1981). *The Politics of Mass Housing in Britain, 1945-1975*. Oxford : Clarendon Press.
Englander, D. (1983). *Landlord and Tenant in Urban Britain, 1838-1918*. Oxford: Clarendon Press.
Forty, A. & Moss, H. (1980). "A housing style for troubled consumers: the success of pseudo-vernacular" *Architectural Review* no. 996 (February) 1980: pp. 73-78.
Franck, K. and Ahrentzen, S. (Eds.) (1989). *New Households, New Housing*. New York: Van Nostrand Reinhold.
Goody, J. (1982). *Cooking, Cuisine and Class: a study in comparative sociology*. Cambridge: Cambridge University Press.
Hamdi, N. (1991). *Housing Without Houses: Participation, Flexibility, Enablement*. New York: Van Nostrand Reinhold.
Hardesty, D. (1977). *Ecological Anthropology*. New York: Alfred A. Knopf.
Harries, P., A. Lipman and S. Purden (1988). "Meaning in Architecture : Post Modernism, Hustling and the Big Sell" pp. 188-199 in D. Canter, M., Krampen and D. Stea (Eds). *Environmental Perspectives*. Aldershot, UK: Avebury.
Kent, S. (Ed) 1990. *Domestic Architecture and the Use of Space*. Cambridge: Cambridge University Press.
Khare, R. (1976). *The Hindu Hearth and Home*. New Delhi: Vikas Publishing House.
Langer, S. (1953). *Feeling and Form: A theory of art*. New York: Routledge and Kegan Paul.
Lawrence, R. (1982). "Domestic space and society: A cross-cultural study" *Comparative Studies in Society and History*, vol.24, no.1: pp. 104-130.
Lawrence, R. (1985). "Urban history, housing, and politics in Britain" *Environment and Planning D: Society and Space* vol.3, no. 4: pp. 323-336.
Lawrence, R. (1986). *Le Seuil franchi: logement populaire et vie quotidienne en Suisse romande, 1860-1960*. Geneva: Georg Editeur.
Lawrence, R. (1987). *Housing, Dwellings and Homes: Design Theory, Research and Practice*. Chichester UK: John Wiley.
Lawrence, R. (1988). "Learning from colonial houses and lifestyles" pp.219-257 in M. Turan (Ed) *Vernacular Architecture: Paradigms of environmental response*. Aldershot UK: Avebury.
Lawrence, R. (1993). "Reinterpretation of cognitive institutional and material structure in an integrated historical perspective" *The Quarterly Newsletter of the Laboratory of Comparative Human Cognition* vol.15, no. 1: pp. 16-23.

Lawrence, R. (1996). “Building bridges for studies of housing quality” *Nordic Journal of Architectural Research*. vol.9, no.3: pp. 41-52.

Lévi-Strauss, C. (1979). *The Origin of Table Manners*. New York: Harper Row. (English translation by John and Doreen Weightman of L’Origine des mannières de table. Paris,: Librarie Plon, 1968).

Low, S. and Chambers, E. (Eds.) (1989) *Housing, Culture and Design*. Philadelphia: University of Pennsylvania Press.

Michelson, W. (1977). *Environmental Choice, Human Behavior and Residential Satisfaction*. New York: Oxford University Press.

Michelson, W. (1980). “Long and short range criteria for housing choice and environmental behavior” *Journal of Social Issues*, vol.36, no. 3: pp.135-149.

Mitchell, W. (1995). City of Bits : Space, Place and the Infobahn. Cambridge MA: MIT Press.

Macleod, R. (1971). *Style and Society: Architectural Ideology in Britain, 1835-1914*. London: Royal Institute of British Architects Publications.

Netting, R. (1981). *Balancing on an Alp: Ecological change and continuity in a Swiss mountain community*. New York: Cambridge University Press.

Oliver, P. (Ed) (1997). *The Encyclopedia of Vernacular Architecture of the World*. Cambridge: Cambridge University Press.

Organization for Economic Co-operation and Development (OECD), (1996). *Strategies for Housing and Social Integration in Cities*. Paris: OECD.

Porteous, D. (1989). *Planned to Death: The annihilation of a place called Howdendyke*. Toronto: University of Toronto Press.

Rapoport, A. (1969). *House Form and Culture*. Englewood Cliffs NJ: Prentice Hall.

Rapoport, A. (1990). “Activity areas and architecture: an interdisciplinary view of the relationship between use of space and domestic built environments” pp. 1-20 in S. Kent (Ed.) *Domestic Architecture and the Use of Space*. Cambridge: Cambridge University Press.

Ravetz, A. (1974). *Model Estate: Planned Housing at Quarry Hill, Leeds*. London : Croom Helm.

Richardson, M. (1981). Pattern book design: English housing and the vernacular. *International Architect, 1* (6): 27-34.

Saegert, S. (1985). “The role of housing in the experience of dwelling” pp.287-309 in I. Altman and C. Werner (Eds.) *Home Environments: Human Behavior and Environment. Advances in Theory and Research, vol. 8*, , New York: Plenum Press.

Sommerville, P. (1997). “The Social Construction of home” *Journal of Architectural and Planning Research*, vol.14, no.3: pp.226-239.

Swenarton, M. (1983). *Homes Fit for Heroes: the politics and architecture of early State housing*. London: Heinemann Educational Books.

Tognoli, J. (1987). “Residential Environments” pp. 655-690 in D. Stokols and I. Altman (Eds.) *Handbook of Environmental Psychology, Vol. 1*: New York: Plenum Press.

Tuan, Yi-Fu (1982). *Segmented Worlds and Self : A study of group life and individual consciousness*. Minneapolis: University of Minnesota Press.

van Vliet, W., Huttman, E. and Fava, S. (Eds) (1985). *Housing Needs and Policy Approaches: Trends in thirteen countries*. Durham NC: Duke University Press.

van Vliet, W. (ed) (1998). *The Encyclopedia of Housing*. Newbury CA: Sage Publications.

Vernez Moudon, A. (1986). *Built for Change: Neighborhood Architecture in San Francisco*. Cambridge MA: MIT Press.

Wright, G. (1981). *Building the Dream: A social history of housing in America*. New York: Pantheon Books.

5 The 'New' Functionalism and Architectural Theory

Jon Lang

Amos Rapoport has made a number of pleas for the integration of Environment-Behavior studies within a theoretical construct. He seeks an explanatory framework for the field in which the environment is conceptualized as "the organization of space, time, meaning and communication which leads to systems of settings/cultural landscapes made up of fixed, semi-fixed and non-fixed features, linked to behavior via systems of activities (including latent aspects) and communicated by cues" (Rapoport, 1997). He is striving for a cognitive map of the field. This effort is crucial for Environment-Behavior studies. Such a body of theoretical knowledge could provide the basis for the development of architectural ideologies (generally known as architectural theory). It must be recognized, however, that the design fields generally show great reluctance to draw on such bodies of knowledge. Their knowledge tends to be organized in a different manner – in generic solutions, or design paradigms — not abstract models.

It now seems possible to meet designer's attitudes halfway — to present a relatively simple framework for the synthesis of the disparate findings of Environment-Behavior research that relates to the concept of *function*. This paper suggests a type of integration, but it is not the one that Rapoport advocates. It is one based on the needs of an applied professional field — architecture — rather than the requirements of Environment-Behavior studies as an academic discipline. The thesis of this synthesis is that the design of architecture should be based on a consideration of the functions they are supposed to serve — not only for the people that inhabit them but also for society as a whole and, inevitably, to fulfill their designers' own needs.

The focus of this paper is, however, narrower than on the full consideration of functionalism in architecture. It is on the intellectual area in which Amos Rapoport has made his major substantive contribution — Environment-Behavior studies — and its contribution to understanding the nature of architectural functionalism. The synthesis involves imposing a model of the purposes served by built form — a model of functionalism based on a model of human motivations — on the vast array of empirical findings yielded by the environment and behavior research of the last three decades. This model is shown in graphic form in Figure 1 later in this paper.

The model draws on the conceptual insights of a remarkably small band of researchers in the field given the total number of people active within it. The members of the group (people such as Irwin Altman, Roger Baker, Kevin Lynch and Amos Rapoport) have focused their endeavors on more than establishing empirical findings; they have developed theoretical underpinnings to the research and/or conceptual models which make useful generalizations about their findings. Of them, Rapoport's remarkable efforts at synthesis provide the basis for much further exploration by people, academics and practitioners alike, in the design fields.

The model to be presented in this paper draws on three distinct branches of ecological research: 1) ecological psychology (Barker 1968) and ecological optics (Gibson 1977), 2) on the humanist psychology of Abraham Maslow (1987), and 3) on the work on environmental meanings of Amos Rapoport (1982). It provides one synthetic framework for ordering our knowledge of the built environment and human behavior within a cultural framework of which the social order is an important component. The goal is to enhance the quality of architectural theory and practice at a time when multinational architectural firms are carrying out a considerable body of work around the world and are in a position to incorporate culture-based thinking into their current professional endeavors.

The Context Of Architectural Theory

As generally understood, architectural theory consists of the explanation by architects (or schools of architectural thought) for why a building's design is the way it is. It also embraces the interpretations of architectural critics about the design goals and mechanisms used for achieving them of an architect or a set of architects. It consists of 'architalk' (Johnson 1994). Often a set of architects is given a label because of the similarity of the values and design orientations of its members: Modernists, Post-Modernists, Metabolists, Neo-traditionalists, etc.. Architectural theory, in this sense, focuses largely, although by no means entirely, on the design ideologies of architects. Often it is solely the aesthetic ideology that attracts attention. Much architectural theory focuses on the repetitive visual patterns in architects' vocabularies, thus allying itself with art criticism. The current debate amongst architectural theoreticians is far removed from the norms of most current practice. It focuses on a narrow band of practitioners, the architectural elite who see building as works of self-expression, rather than a product of the building industry in service of a broad spectrum of people. The aesthetics of an architect's ideas tend to overwhelm the aesthetics of built form.

The focus of concern is on what the normative positions, or manifestoes, of architects are and how they have shifted and shift over time (see Conrad 1970, Jencks & Kropf 1997). This orientation has been recognized in the field nowadays calling itself 'History and Theory'. Much less concern is placed within it on understanding the functioning of the designed product, a building, landscape or urban design, in terms of the multiplicity of the purposes that they actually do or do not serve. The focus is on the current interpretation by historians of the geometries used by architects in the formation of internal 'spaces' and in the formation of outward appearances. These aspects of design are important. They do, however, portray a limited, indeed naïve model of the functions of architecture, one frequently narrower than that of the Modernist of the 1930s that is so criticized today. This situation is unfortunate because the concept of functionalism is really central to architectural programming and design. All buildings serve some human purposes, otherwise they would not be built.

Functionalism

It is difficult now to reconstruct how different architects have thought at different periods of architectural history of the *functions* served by buildings. Until recently the words 'function' and/or 'functional' were seldom used in architectural discourse. The concept has, however, always been implicit in it and has had to do with various interpretations of the fitness of built form to accommodate, in comfort, activities, physical or mental. Although often associated with Gottfried Semper in the late nineteenth century, the concern about the functions a building serves has a long history traceable back to, at least, the writings of Vitruvius especially as propagated by Henry Wotton (see Lang 1987). Shifts in its definition have throughout history been correlated with contemporary concerns. In the eighteenth century, for instance, the concern was with the purposes to which materials and structural systems could be put in enclosing space. At mid-nineteenth century, the concerns were with the operation of manufacturing equipment as well as such things as modes of transportation. Muthesius (1902) at the turn of the century was worried about the over-reliance in the nineteenth century of the application of reason, science and technology in intellectual thought and thus on contemporary conceptions of function implied in the buildings that architects and engineers created. Thus the types of constructions to celebrate turned out to be bridges and railway stations despite the concern for meanings associated with different architectural styles such as the Gothic and the Classical.

A number of architects, such as Tony Garnier (1917), at the turn of the century, were very much concerned with the nature of good behavioral systems and their relationship to the physical environment. So the concern was very much with specifying the nature of a well-functioning social order and the physical environment that provided for it and the privacy for life within pleasant surroundings (De Zurko 1957). The social order in their thinking dealt with both the formal and informal interactions and the behavioral controls on them that *should* take place within an idealized cultural framework. Neither were fully defined so the contextual applicability of the architectural and urban paradigms they created is implicit not explicit in the physical design frameworks they created. Within these models, the functions to be designed for were themselves designed and signified the thought that considerable social engineering was possible through changing the nature of the built forms of human settlements. This attitude permeated Modern architectural thought. It is a worthwhile ideology as long as the functions so identified or designed as the appropriate ones have some external validity – some validity for the people who might later live in the environment designed to that model of the functions to be served.

As the twentieth century progressed so the model of functionalism shifted. The term was reduced to a focus on efficiency in activity systems and problems of efficiency in constructional, constructional and technological integrity. The aesthetic purposes became regarded as something different, as the designer's prerogative and thus not a function to be filled by a building on behalf of anybody else. This division, with the hindsight of six decades of experience, is now illogical.

In 1928, CIAM (Congrès Internationaux d'Architecture Moderne) was concerned with economic efficiency, rationalization and standardization that would 'require a reduction in certain individual needs. . [that are] . . devoid of real justification" (see the statement in Conrad 1970). Emotional needs were seen as irrational. During the 1930s, building function thus became thought of in narrow terms. The concern was with ergonomics and with the minimum sizes of spaces. The resulting architecture (and, even more so, urban design and planning ideas) was thus based on a limited model of the human being and a limited model of the functions of architecture. The rise of Post-modern architecture was a response to this line of Modernist thought and the perceived failures of the products that resulted from it (Brolin 1976). Paralleling the stylistic change in architecture during the 1960s was a more deep-seated questioning of the purpose served by built forms and how the fulfilment of these purposes and the built form consequences varied from culture to culture (e.g., Rapoport 1969).

The field of Environment–Behavior Studies grew, at least partially, out of the necessity of developing a stronger intellectual base for architectural design than that which existed. Much of the attention was focused on the mass housing built since World War II according to the tenets of Modern architectural thought and to the discrepancy between its universalist assumptions and the experiences of the housing's residents. The discrepancy between predicted and actual behavior within the built forms (indoors and outdoors) created by architects to better serve people came as a shock. It was shocking because architects were well intentioned and really thought they were serving the best interests of people: adults and children, sponsors and administrators alike. At the same time, books such as *House Form and*

Culture (Rapoport 1969) brought attention to the cultural relativity of design. It became clear that the models of the human being and human behaviors (physical, intellectual and emotional) and the design paradigms architects were wont to use needed considerable rethinking.

'Form follows function' is a slogan closely associated with the Rationalist school of Modern architecture. It could equally be associated with the Empiricist. The so-called failure of Modern architecture (Brolin 1976) led to the abandonment of this slogan because it was perceived as being a limiting definition of the goal of design. It has now become clear that the slogan is still a useful one provided the understanding of the range purposes that buildings serve is clearly understood. It also depends on architects being willing to recognize the functions that buildings serve as 'functions'! From a designer's viewpoint, the whole field of Environment-Behavior Studies has piece by piece, concept by concept, made the understanding of the functions of built form clearer, even though much remains vaguely understood.

Toward A 'New' Functionalism

Rapport argues that 'if Environment-Behavior Studies are to be more than an *ad hoc* attempt to improve design' it must be considered as a discipline (Rapoport, 1997). It must, nevertheless, be recognized that the field also serves as what I have called, correctly but short-sightedly (because of the confusion with positivism) the positive theoretical basis for design (Lang 1987) -- what others more sensibly call the empirical theoretical basis. It might also be called functional theory (e.g., Lynch 1984).

At a generic level, the functions that the built environment serves have not changed since time immemorial. At a specific level debates arise. The operational definitions of function that we have been using for the last hundred odd years include only a limited proportion of the whole set of functions. In architectural criticism this set has not only been limited but has shifted from time to time (Belgasem 1987). If the functions that built forms serve have not changed over time what we pay attention to has. As James Marston Fitch (1965) suggested over thirty years ago, the definition of function that we use in designing needs to be broadened. In particular, he argues that the aesthetic purposes that patterns of built form serve are as much functional concerns as the housing of activity patterns and the structural purposes of building techniques. A closer examination of building suggests that the concept of function needs to be even broader than Fitch suggested. The New Functionalism in architectural thinking represents an ideological position, that attempts to broaden the definition of function by stating that all the purposes (tangible and intangible, measurable or otherwise) that a building serves should be regarded as functions. It is an attempt to refocus architects' concerns.

The same patterns of built form, either as an environment or as an object, may serve different functions for different people. For the architect it may serve as a vehicle for carrying a message about society. In this sense it can serve as a means of self-expression, as a work of art. It can also be a display of an architect's technological knowledge and skills in the application of that knowledge. Indeed, there are a number of much admired buildings which represent an 'architecture of structural dexterity' in which the focus of attention is on new ways of enclosing space and/or new ways of putting the fabric of a building together. Observers and users can respond to the work based on their own experiences with the world or by interpreting the work based on the construct the architect has developed for designing and/or explaining it. Only a small group of cognoscenti are likely to be aware of the architect's intentions. Most, but not all, of this group will be other architects. For architects, their work also represents an attempt to corner a segment of the market for services. Architects are, after all, generally small business people although some are members of large multinational corporations. Indeed the history of architecture could be as much a history of clients as a history of buildings.

For the sponsors of buildings, such as banks and other lending institutions, and for building owners, buildings represent a substantial investment on which they hope to make a profit in the long, if not short, term. Buildings thus function as a financial investment. The majority of city buildings, including apartment buildings, is speculative and is designed by *developers' architects* for profit but few *architects' architects* think of buildings in this way. Most, however, are conscious of this investment aspect of design when it comes to their own homes. There is often a trade-off between the expectations of financial return based directly on a capital gain in property and the utility of the house as an advertisement of their tastes and skills that will yield indirect profits through the obtaining of additional work. If urban design is concerned with enhancing the quality of the public realm of human settlements, the financial function of built form is clearly different.

Environment-Behavior Studies do not deal with all these issues, nor does this paper. If, however, the design professions wish to better understand their own work and its relationship to human activities and aspirations, the Environment-Behavior research of the past four decades offers much. It presents an increasingly important source of understanding of the richness of functions served by buildings. In particular, those aspects of the field which have yielded concepts which describe and explain the ecological experiencing of buildings, landscapes and urban settings provide the basis for enriching our understanding of the functions of built form. This observation only holds if one takes the ideological position that how the environment is experienced by those who inhabit or use a building is important. Not all architects do (see the statements in Conrad (1970) and Ellis and Cuff (1989)). If one does, the Modernist distinction between the *functional* and *aesthetic* purposes of architecture becomes largely irrelevant.

Experiencing the Environment: Perceptions and Settings

The manner in which we perceive and cognize the world around us is the basis of environmental experience. It is the basis for the decisions we make about how to act in the settings we encounter and the way we respond to them emotionally. A number of mutually exclusive theories of perception coexist. There are, nevertheless, a number of matters on which they all agree. Perception is multi-modal and the role of movement is fundamental to the experiencing of the world around us. This movement may be as small as the slight movement of the head or it may involve moving through the world at a high speed. A distinction is also made between environmental perception – seeing the world as the surroundings of everyday life — and object perception — seeing the world from the outside. Certainly, buildings can be and are perceived in both ways. Their interiors are, however, difficult to see as objects although they may be full of them.

What does one pay attention to in the environment? Architectural theoreticians have generally thought of the built environment as consisting of spaces which are enclosed to a greater or lesser extent. Their attention has largely focused on the geometries of these spaces and the sequence between them. The concern has been largely with the visual world. Increasingly, it has become important to think of the environment as consisting of settings for behavior.

The concept that has attracted many architects and those in the field of Environment-Behavior studies is that of *behavior setting* developed by Roger Barker (Barker 1968; see also Lang 1987, 1994). To Barker, a behavior setting consists of a standing pattern of behavior that occurs in a physical environment — the milieu — for a particular time period. Thus the same physical setting can afford many behavior settings. The world of every day experience — the ecological world — is seen as a system of settings. For architects, however, it is probably more important to think of the physical environment as consisting of physical settings consisting of fixed and semi-fixed features defined by surfaces, textures, and objects which afford specific set of activities and do not afford others (see also Rapoport 1990c, 1997).

The 'failure' of Modern architecture is as much a failure in programming as in design. The fundamental questions that have arisen about Modernist work have to do with the decisions on the systems and sub-systems of settings and their characteristics that should exist. Implicit in the questions is those about what behavioral systems and aesthetic values should be afforded and for what purpose. Understanding the potential array of functions that can be served by the built environment is fundamental to creating good building programs and thus good designs.

Functions, Purposes, Needs and Motivations

If one considers the built environment as a system of interrelated settings formed by illuminated (and thus pigmented) surfaces and textures that enclose (to a greater or lesser degree) behavior – i.e., they surround -- but also as objects which can be examined, then there are three basic purposes that settings serve: they afford activities; provide shelter; and act as displays that contain information available to be discerned. Modernism considered the first two as the functional goal and the third as the aesthetic goal. Thus architects have often thought of the first two as the most basic and the third as an add-on. All three are, however, really of the same nature.

Although the aesthetic (really symbolic) purposes often overwhelm the other two, the basic concern in practice, if not in architectural rhetoric, is usually that for supporting and sheltering activities. For a long time the concept of 'activity' has been loosely defined. Recently, Amos Rapoport has noted that the concerns ". . . range from (1) instrumental aspects which are the most manifest . . . through (2) how activities are carried out, (3) how they are associated into systems, to (4) their meaning, their most latent aspect" (Rapoport 1996). What is important in programming in architecture and urban design is to think of activities as systems and to consider who is involved and who is excluded from specific activities. The meaning of an activity lies in the purposes, the needs, it fulfils — activities are means to achieving ends. They have functions themselves.

Beyond activities *per se*, Environment-Behavior Studies have yielded a host of purposes that activities and specific patterns of the milieu serve: territorial control, privacy, identity, a sense of self-worth, an aid to orientation, etc. What designers need to have at their disposal is some model that structures these purposes, or functions, in some form that informs the whole process of designing. It must inform the processes of programming (i.e., asking the question "what is the problem to be solved?"), designing ("what are the possible ways of solving it?"), predicting ("how will each possible way function) and making a choice (selecting the best way). There are many empirical findings and concepts that should be of use in this process but they are unordered and designers are overwhelmed by piecemeal and fragmentary research results.

Relating Human Needs to Building Purpose

One way of moving ahead is to develop a model of functionalism in architecture that relates built form to the fulfilling of human needs through its affordances for activities and symbolic interpretations. There is nothing new in this approach. It was essential to the Bauhaus

(Wingler 1969). What limited the Bauhaus approach is that it had no clearly articulated model of human needs from which to work. Instead the Bauhaus masters listed activity patterns that buildings had to allow. These activities were identified based on a Rational analysis of what a good (often highly austere) life is, not on empirical evidence of how people wished to live nor the constraints imposed on them in meeting their ends. The Bauhaus masters had the right idea but not the models on which to draw. We do.

There are indeed a number of models of human needs and each has attracted the attention of one architect or other. The clearest model, and the most widely used in the professional fields such as business and education, appears to be that of Abraham Maslow. First formulated in the 1950s, it has been much criticized but not replaced. It is a comprehensive ecological model onto which all others can be mapped. His model, in its most recent form, was developed by his intellectual colleagues (Maslow 1987). The model suggests that there is a hierarchy of human needs from the most basic (survival) to the most abstract (aesthetic). These needs trigger motivations to behave in one way or another and to aspire to own objects or be in settings that display specific characteristics. These motivations may result from inner drives but they are also culturally shaped by a number of agents: family, peers, educators, advertisers, etc. — indeed by the whole socialization process. The fundamental motivations as identified by Maslow are universal, as may be the psychological mechanisms to achieve them. The actual manifestations of these mechanisms in overt actions and in aesthetic choices will differ from culture to culture and will change within a society as the culture evolves.

An effort to use Maslow's model to synthesize the concepts yielded by Environment-Behavior research into a unifying model for design purposes is shown in Figure 1. The model draws on the professional architectural and urban design programming work of the Environmental Research Group [ERG] under the direction of Walter Moleski in Philadelphia. It is an adaptation of an earlier effort at the same synthesis (see Lang 1994). With the exception of that noting the importance of the biological environment, all the bubbles refer to Maslow's concepts. Terms outside the bubbles refer to some aspect of Environment-Behavior research that informs us about the socio-physical mechanism for attaining those ends. At the apex of the

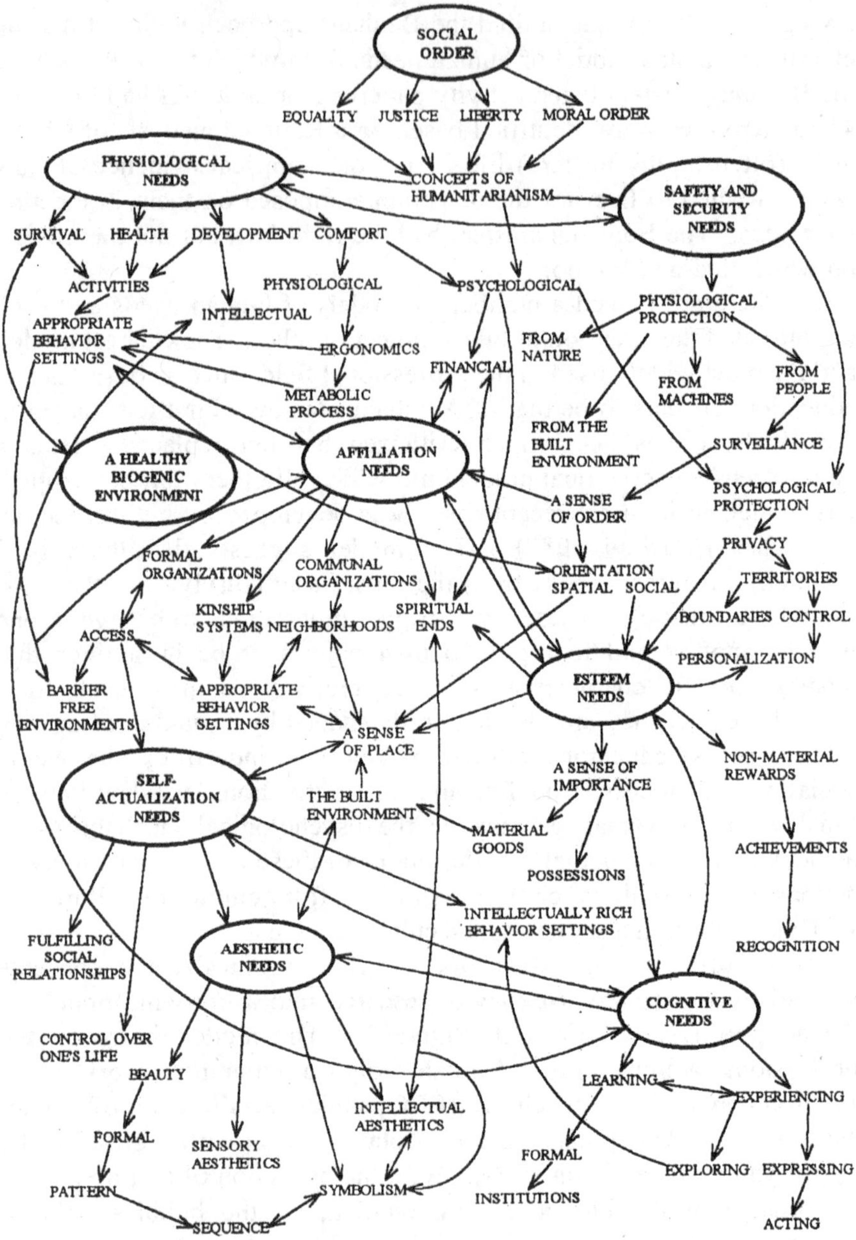

Figure 5.1 A Human Needs Based Model of Functionalism in Architecture

diagram is the specification that the manifestation of human motivations, its outcomes, must be seen within a social order. The cultural environment is what defines the social order of a society — its concepts of equality, justice, liberty and moral order. These in turn define its concepts of humanitarianism.

The thesis is that physical design patterns, existing or proposed, need to be seen with a particular social order. This social order is shaped by and shapes the broader cultural framework of which it is a part. Human motivations and their behavioral consequences are made manifest by how people shape, consciously or subconsciously, their non-material culture — their social order — and their material culture — their artifacts including the built environment. Thus the physical form within which a society exists can be analyzed in terms of the efforts of it members to fulfil their needs within a specific cultural umbrella. Changes in built form occur when people perceive a misfit between their needs and that form and they have the resources to do something about it. Major changes in built form paradigms (either those created by designers or those that evolve from the operation of the market place as developers seek to meet their own needs) result when there are major changes in the social order. These changes may occur as the result of the affordances of new technologies being recognized and exploited or as the result of a redesign of the social order *per se*.

The most basic needs, according to Maslow, are physiological and the most basic of these is for survival although many people have given up this need to meet some higher motivation. Martyrs have given their lives for their beliefs and, more curious to us today, European explorers, in order to maintain their own identities and feelings of self-worth, have died of starvation when surrounded by indigenous populations living comfortably off the land. In terms of design the concerns are with the provision of shelter and, at a higher level, comfort and access to the activities that allow us to maintain our lives and to develop them. There are major cultural differences in levels of acceptance of discomfort and we often trade-off comfort levels to obtain environments that enhance our feelings of identity and self-worth.

Once those primary needs are at least partially fulfilled we are then motivated to achieve a sense of safety and security. Our needs at this level are both physiological and psychological. In building design, architects have, until recently when the work of Oscar Newman (1974) seeped into architect's consciousness, paid more explicit attention to the former than the latter. Providing for people's psychological, and aspects of physiological security, involves them having the appropriate levels of privacy in and control over their environments. What behaviors are regarded as private and what gradations of privacy people require vary from culture to culture. Behaviors expected of each gender and of people at different stages in life cycle vary considerably across the world. They have major implications for design, both interior and outdoors. Providing for people's privacy needs is one of the fundamental functions of the built environment.

It is clear from the diagram that the socio-physical mechanisms used by people to achieve safety and security needs also play a substantial role in meeting affiliation and esteem needs. People are motivated to engage in certain activities to maintain and develop relationships with other people for survival and to further themselves. The milieu, whether it is chosen or imposed, is also a fundamental communicator of people's identity and status to themselves and to others (Rapoport 1990b). For many people, these needs are also met through spiritual beliefs about the ordering of the world and their perceptions of a place within it. Here too cultural differences have a major effect on what we are motivated to have around us.

The highest level of Maslow's hierarchy of basic needs is the need for self-actualization. The design implications at this level are hard to discern. Perhaps having access to opportunities for nurturing others has design implications. Cognitive and aesthetic needs, however, have clearer implications for what we design. They are manifest throughout our lives. There is a need for learning for survival but learning also serves essentially aesthetic functions, to learn for its own sake. Aesthetic needs vary from having the built form signify status to an understanding of an architect's aesthetic logic in appreciating the built, or natural, environment for the sheer joy of appreciating it. At this level there is no instrumental purpose involved.

In looking at the functions served by the built environment in this way, a number of factors become clear. It is both a richer and a more abstract way than most designers consider the functions of architecture. It also becomes clear that many if not most of the ways of fulfilling human needs are social and psychological and have little to do with the built environment. It is clear that the functions of built form are clearly intertwined and cannot be reduced to simplistic formulae. There is tremendous human variability in what is important and what is not. The same behavioral mechanisms (e.g., privacy) serve many purposes. Many seemingly irrational needs are important and thinking of them as unnecessary and "devoid of justification" is shortsighted. For many people the fulfillment of spiritual ends, that to others are irrational, is of high importance.

The model is not all-inclusive. It needs to be taken to another level in which the patterns of the environment that fulfil the behavioral mechanisms need to be described. Similarly, the functions of the built environment included in the model have to compete with all the other functions that the built environment serves: as a capital investment for public and private organization and individuals, as a self-aggrandizement mechanism for the designer, etc.. The technological mechanisms that a building houses also have their own needs as do many other machines, such as those for transportation. Often their needs are more important than human ones. Many office workers only received air-conditioned comfort when computers required it to function properly. The biological environment in which buildings function also has its own requirement to survive well. We are only just becoming conscious of those needs and only beginning to have the political will to address them. Kyoto Izumi drew a diagram (Figure 5.2) some time ago now, which distinguishes among those types of environments where questions of fulfilling human motivations are paramount and those in which the needs of machines are (see Lang 1987).

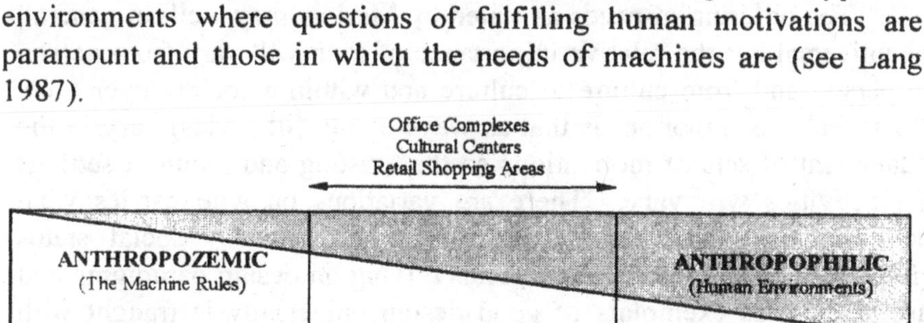

Figure 5.2 Range of Environments from those Primarily for Humans to those Serving Machines

The biological environment in which buildings function also has its own requirement to survive well. We are only just becoming conscious of those needs and only beginning to have the political will to address them. Buildings work as heat islands and as channelers of winds. A building fabric affects the energy consumption within and the materials of which a building is constructed all have embodied energy within them. Our attitudes to these matters will no doubt shift over time and these shifts will indicate shifts within our culture. So too will the patterns of the environment and the utility of their perceived functions shift.

The Cultural Dimension

One of the major criticisms of the Modern architectural ideologies was their assumption of the universality of the manifestation of human needs. They, to the best of our knowledge, quite rightly assumed the view that "all people have the same needs". Assuming, however, that the built forms needed by people to meet their ends could be reduced to a number of universal paradigms has proven to be a costly error financially and/or psychologically. This outcome was clear twenty years ago (see Brolin 1976, for example) with the result that much attention is now being paid to the cultural dimension of design types. The anthropological perspective on environmental design has been most clearly articulated by Amos Rapoport (1969, 1977, 1990c).

The ordering of needs as stated by Maslow may well, in general, be universal but the relative importance of each will vary from person to person and from culture to culture and within a society over time. What really is important is that as ways of life (lifestyles) vary in the attainment of sets of motivations so the existing and required settings for activities will vary. There are variations on who carries what activities by gender, by stage in life cycle and by social status (Rapoport 1969, 1977, 1990c). Thus relying on design paradigms that are held up as exemplars of good design universally is fraught with problems (Rapoport 1977). When working within culturally homogenous countries (although even here there are often major socio-economic differences amongst components of the population) the basic behavior patterns can be identified in designing the program for a building or an urban design. In multi-cultural countries, it is possible to tailor-make buildings for specific sub-populations. What one should do, however, is an ideological question.

It is not simply the activity patterns that vary cross-culturally, but also concepts of privacy, and territoriality, and the need for psychological security generally. So do aesthetic tastes. Patterns of the environment, the materials of which it is made, its color and whole manner in which it is illuminated carry meaning based on learnt associations. These associations may have been learnt as part and parcel of everyday experience or may result from a formal education. In some societies, the coding of status through design is readily observable by all that understand the code; in others the lines are blurred because there is no generally recognized social convention. Thus the plethora of interlocking identity and esteem motivations, shown in Figure 1, which lead us to seek specific patterns of the environment as statements of who we are shows the complexity and multi-dimensionality of the functions served by the built environment.

The New Functionalism

The model described above can be applied to the analysis and design for individuals, organizations (formal and communal) and to larger societies. The larger the system the more complex the issues. For whatever level one is designing, in thinking about the functions to be served by the built environment in the manner described here, two questions immediately arise. To what extent does the built form dictate human behavior? How good a fit between built forms and present behaviors should architects seek in their designs? The answer to the first question is conceptual if not mathematically clear; the answer to the second depends on a multiplicity of factors, many ideological but others have to do with our level of understanding of the issues.

It is probably wisest to think of patterns of built form within a possibilistic framework — as afforders of behavior, physical, metabolic and mental. Any pattern of the built environment affords some activities and aesthetic interpretations and not others. Yet based on empirical observations of how people use present patterns of cities, buildings and landscapes, and their behavioral tendencies one can make probabilistic statements of how people will respond to the opportunities for activities and aesthetic interpretations a pattern will provide them. The relationship between built patterns and behavioral patterns is not a simple stimulus-response relationship that is implicit in much architectural theory and criticism. Rather it is some complex function of the strength of a person's motivations, their ability to perceive the opportunities provided by a pattern of built form (i.e., their experience) and other opportunities for them to have their needs fulfilled.

The manifestations of needs change; the systems of activities required by a society, and organizations (formal or communal) or households within it change over time. The present can be observed but the future cannot. Certainly, future behaviors and aesthetic values can be predicted based on current trends, but still the future is unknown. How tightly should the built environment be designed to fulfil the functions we specify that it should fulfil it at the present? If one recognizes that such questions are wicked ones, the answers will depend on the confidence that one has in looking ahead. Designing buildings for the ease of later adaptations seems sensible unless an extremely tight fit is crucial for the behavior to take place; for instance, possibly, in a operating theatre. The underlying question of how far one can take this line of thought remains. One observation is simply to design buildings to be well fitting for the functions at the present and to allow future changes to be taken care of by others when necessary. Such a statement is not an empirical one; it is ideological. The built environment is constantly being altered. Only abandoned buildings are static and even they deteriorate over time.

What is emerging from this line of thought is a new concept of functionalism. The model presented here serves two very different purposes. It provides an umbrella for locating the theoretical findings of empirical research within the field of Environment-Behavior studies and it provides the basis for architects to ask questions about what it is that they are paying attention to and to what they should be paying attention during the design process.

What the model does show is that we need to think of the functions of built form much more broadly than we have done heretofore. Form follows function remains a good slogan for design provided function is considered comprehensively. It is also clear that the needs that a particular built environment is required to fulfil shift over time. Accommodating such shifts well is often a major consideration in design and so is one of the functions that a building has to fulfil. Thus one of the ideological questions in design is always: "To what extent does the form have to deal with future needs?" Sometimes the future for at least one step ahead is known (e.g., when it is known that housing for Olympic athletes is to be changed to family accommodation after a games is over). At other times, it is largely unknown, as the recent spate of conversion of office buildings to residential housing attests.

The New Functionalism and Architectural Theory

To understand an architectural theory – the set of propositions used by an architect or a school of architectural thought to generate designs — requires an understanding of the assumptions about the relationship of people and built form on which it is based. Implicit in any building, landscape architecture or urban design is a set of attitudes — beliefs and values — on which the work is based. These attitudes may not be the same as the professed attitudes of its designer or designers, clients, and the public interest (as defined by the law). They, nevertheless, are the behavioral correlate, or evidence, of the position actually held by the architect.

Some time ago, I attempted to identify a series of attitudes that guide an architect's work (see Lang 1987). The list is incomplete, but acts as a starting point: attitudes towards an existing societal culture and the settings that describe it; attitudes towards people, the young, the elderly, the powerful and the weak; attitudes towards nature and the role of flora and fauna in everyday life; attitudes towards how the design process should be carried out; attitudes towards the built environment; and, attitudes towards harnessing technology. More simply, the attitudes towards what is important and what is not shapes designs. Implicit in this statement is a statement of the attitudes towards the various functions of the built environment.

Any pattern of the environment serves a multiplicity of functions. In many cases the patterns that fulfil identity needs also fulfil esteem needs. During the 1990s there has been a worry that the globalization of the world's economy has resulted in a uniformity of corporate architectural expressions across the world and the concomitant loss of a sense of place. A clash in architectural ideologies exists between those who favor a local expression and those who aspire to an international expression in order to satisfy their self-esteem. In achieving the latter, they very often use design patterns that function poorly in meeting basic comfort needs. The trade-off, as with the ones made by many consumers of the high-fashion products of the garment and shoe industries, is seen as worthwhile.

All designs involve a trade-off between achieving some goals and other goals. All designs are created under some constraints; apart from space stations, they all exist in some terrestrial context. For all intents and purposes, all designs are created within financial limitations. Except when designing for themselves, and seldom even then, do architects have freedom of action. Architects are constrained by the task environment in which they work. In terms of both understanding the architect's work and for building the knowledge base that will inform the profession, it is important for the performance of designed products to be understood. The performance can be analyzed at two levels: in relationship to what the architects say about the design and in relation to how it is experienced by critics (presumably experts) and the people who inhabit the building or place.

The model of functionalism presented here is only partial and focuses on how the environment is experienced. It fails to deal with the economic functioning of buildings and how buildings shape the biogenic environment. Both are fundamental concerns, the latter especially so if one takes the energy crisis and global warming predictions seriously. The model is human-centric and pays little attention to the quality of cities for songbirds, butterflies and other fauna that enrich the lives of urban dwellers. All these limitations need to be recognized.

Conclusion

One of the disappointments of a sub-set of Environment-Behavior researchers is that their findings have been slow to seep into architectural thinking. The model of functionalism presented here may be indicative of how, if at all, those researchers' work does or should inform practice and, secondly, of the direction in which they can shape their research if they are interested in its applicability. An observation which can be made about the model is that it assumes that architectural practice takes place within a problem solving mode of thought in which architects work from the abstract to the particular. It has been observed that the work of most architects involves the adaptation of a standard set of design solutions — a set of paradigms that signal good practice — to the problem at hand. If this is so, then the model of functionalism presented here has a different utility.

The existing set of paradigms that are used by architects can be examined in terms of what functions they afford and what they do not. This analysis can be done within a terrestrial and cultural context for people at different stages in life cycle and of different socio-economic groupings. Using the same logic the model can also be the basis for the designing of new paradigms based on the accumulated wisdom of both the design fields and of Environment-Behavior researchers.

Applicability to design is neither a necessary or even desirable goal for Environment-Behavior researchers — theory building is. There are, however, ways in which those concerned with the design applicability of their work can shape their endeavors. One way is to use the framework provided here for examining the urban forms and architecture of specific cultures or, alternatively specific motivations cross-culturally. Another is to specify their research findings in the form of deontological design principles as Christopher Alexander and his colleagues (1977) have done but within the more abstract framework provide here rather than in terms of towns, buildings, and construction. A third way would be to take sets of such design principles and cast them in the form of new design paradigms or model solutions. Following the first of these suggestions means that Environment-Behavior researchers would have to be careful to place their work within the type of framework that Rapoport advocates. Following the second and third would involve them changing intellectual hats and becoming, if not designers, the shapers of design policies by shaping design theory. If they can add to the explanations of why built forms are the way they are and, as importantly, how well those forms serve society, they will have contributed much.

There is, in reality, little new in these statements. What is created is a niche for a behavioral science and design cooperation either in dealing with specific design situations or in terms of organizing behavioral science findings for design. Amos Rapoport has shown the way for Environment-Behavior Studies to advance in traditional scientific terms (e.g. Rapoport 1997). The way proposed here is one in which design theory can be advanced. In both cases it is for a new generation of researchers to move ahead.

References

Alexander, C., Ishakawa, S., & Silverstein, M. (1997). *A Pattern Language: Towns, Buildings, Construction.* New York: Oxford University Press.

Barker, R. (1968). *Ecological Psychology: Concepts and Methods for Studying Human Behavior.* Stanford: Stanford University Press.

Belgasem, R. (1987). *Human Needs and Building Criticism.* Unpublished doctoral dissertation, University of Pennsylvania.

Brolin, B. (1976). *The Failure of Modern Architecture.* New York: Van Nostrand Reinhold.

Conrad, U. (Ed.) (1970). *Programs and Manifestoes on Twentieth Century Architecture.* Cambridge, MA: MIT Press.

De Zurko, E. R. (1957). *Origins of Functionalist Theory.* New York: Columbia University Press.

Ellis and Cuff (Eds.). (1987). *Architects' People.* New York: Oxford University Press.

Fitch, J. M. (1965). Experiential Basis for Aesthetic Decision. In *Annals of the New York Academy of Science.* New York: The Academy: 706-714.

Garnier, T. (1917). *The Cité Industrielle.* Reprinted New York: Rizzoli 1990.

Gibson, J. J. (1977). *The Senses Considered as Perceptual Systems. Boston: Houghton Mifflin.*

Izumi, K. (1968). *Some psycho-social considerations of environmental design* (mimeographed).

Jencks, C. & Kropf, K. (Eds.). *Theories and Manifestoes of Contemporary Architecture.* Chichester: Academy Editions.

Johnson, P. A. (1994). *The Theory of Architecture, Concepts, Themes & Practices.* New York: Van Nostrand Reinhold.

Lang, J. (1985). Problems, Paradigms, Architecture, City Planning and Urban Design. *Journal of Planning Education* 5 (1): 26-27.

Lang, J. (1987), *Creating Architectural Theory.* New York: Van Nostrand Reinhold.

Lang, J. (1994). *Urban Design: The American Experience.* New York: Van Nostrand Reinhold.

Lynch, K. (1984). *Good City Form.* Cambridge, MA: MIT Press.

Maslow, A. (1987). *Motivation and Personality.* 3rd Edition. Revised by Robert Frager, James Fadiman, Cynthia McReynolds and Ruth Cox. New York: McGraw Hill.

Motalebi E. G. (1998). *A Theory of Meaning in Architecture and Urban Design: An Ecological Approach.* Unpublished doctoral dissertation, University of New South Wales, Sydney.

Muthesius, H. (1902). *Style-Architecture and Building Art: Transformations of Architecture in the Nineteenth Century and its Present Condition.* Republished in 1994. Introduction and Translation by Stanford Anderson. Santa Monica CA: The Getty Center for the History of Art and The Humanities, 1994.

Newman, O. (1974). *Defensible Space: Crime Prevention through Urban Design.* New York: MacMillan.

Rapoport, A. (1969). *House Form and Culture*. Englewood Cliffs, NJ: Prentice Hall

Rapoport, A. (1977). *Human Aspects of Urban Form.* New York: Pergamon.

Rapoport, A. (1982). *The Meaning of the Built Environment: A Non-Verbal Communications approach:* Beverly Hills, CA: Sage.

Rapoport, A. (1990a). *History and Precedent in Environmental Design.* New York: Plenum.

Rapoport, A. (1990b). *The Meaning of the Built Environment.* Tucson. AZ: University of Arizona Press.

Rapoport, A. (1990c). Systems of Activities and Systems of Settings. In S. Kent (Ed.), *Domestic Architecture and the Use of Space.* Cambridge: Cambridge University Press: 9-20.

Rapoport, A. (1997). Theory in Environment-Behavior Studies: Transcending Times, Settings and Groups. In S. Wapner et al. (Eds.) *Handbook of U.S.-Japan Environment-Behavior Research.* New York: Plenum Press.

Sadalla, E. J. (1987). Identity Symbolism in Housing. *Environment and Behavior* 19 (5): 569-87.

Wingler, Hans (1969). *The Bauhaus: Weimar, Dessau, Berlin,Chicago.* Translated by Wolfgang Jabs and Basil Gilbert, edited by Joseph Stein. Cambridge. MA: MIT Press.

PART II: ARCHITECTURAL EDUCATION

6 Studious Questions[1]

Amos Rapoport

This article first appeared in the October 16, 1983 issue of *The Architects' Journal*, The Architectural Press, Ltd., London. "Studious questions" (not my title) is the only thing I have ever written specifically about pedagogy. As I have indicated above, it seems clear that my most important work, that on theory, has major (and revolutionary) implications for architectural education (and the profession). There are however, three recent papers which deal with the nature of design and, as such, have a more direct relationship to pedagogy (Rapoport 1989, 1995a, b). – Amos Rapoport

The following remarks may be seen as heretical since they question the most central characteristic feature of architectural education – the design studio. In doing so, two distinct aspects need to be examined. First, what is taught – the rationale, theory and subject matter, and second, how is it taught – the manner of teaching.

Although my major objective is to examine critically how it is taught, it is essential that the other aspect be addressed briefly. In doing so an even more heretical position will need to be adopted: I will be asking highly critical questions about design and its central role in architectural education. In effect, questions are raised about what it is we do – and should do.

Design should be based on Theory, not Likes and Dislikes

The nature of design is something about which I have had various things to say over the years (Rapoport, 1983). The essence of my argument has been that the purpose of design is to provide settings appropriate to the bio-social, psychological, cultural and other characteristics and needs of the different people for whom design is done. This means that the most important decision is *what* to do and *why* to do it rather than *how* it is to be done (which comes later), with which design has traditionally been more concerned. (I neglect, for purposes of this discussion, issues such as how much design should be done – the minimum rather than the maximum—the degree and nature of open-endedness, and questions of participation).

Furthermore the decision about what to do and why must be based on the best available information, on a body of literature, on research on man-environment interaction, on "theory rather than the likes and dislikes of designers. In fact I have argued that in its strong form this position may involve designing something that the designer dislikes or even detests.

In setting explicit objectives for design, criteria are also set for evaluating how successfully goals have been met. When this process is repeated, there is hope of developing a cumulative body of knowledge and theory.

At the moment architectural design is the best example of what Sorokin called the New Columbus Syndrome: the tendency to rediscover America anew each time, or to reinvent the wheel.

It seems self-evident that both design goals and criteria of evaluation are always necessarily related to, and dependent on, a theory; one needs first to know what built environments can do before one can assess whether any given specimen does it well or badly.

Yet there is no valid theory of design involved in design teaching. In fact there is no theory of design worth that name. Without such a theory, design cannot be taught and is not really suitable as a university subject. Its approach is personal, subjective, illogical and not cumulative. One can also argue that it should not be taught since it perpetuates a highly undesirable state of affairs.

What to Do should be Stressed over How

As an illustration consider a recent study that seems to support my criticisms. This study deals with decision-making in architectural practice. It examines the relative allocation of time to the different stages of projects (Mackinder & Marvin, 1982). From this study it seems quite clear that the question of *what to do* receives least attention—the initial idea is developed rapidly using little information and research but it also rarely changes much. This fundamental decision is based on the designers' decision experience which, they believe, is best obtained by *doing* one's own design. Most time is devoted to refinement, minor matters of detail, small changes, choosing materials; in other words, the stress is on the *how*.

The teaching of design tends to perpetuate this manner of working. For example, a recent article comparing architectural design to music points out that the skills and knowledge assumed to be necessary for design are sketching, drawing, construction, planning, detailing and modelmaking (Zuk, 1982). None of these helps to deal with the question of what to do.

The result of this teaching approach was summarized well in a recent book review where an unnamed "leading publicist of postmodern architectural theory" is quoted as saying that "architecture is comprised of behavior, environment and form. Since I know nothing about environment or behavior I will restrict my discussion to form." The author comments that "such know-nothingism is inexcusable" (Watson, 1982). Yet, unfortunately, such "know-nothingism" is the norm in design as it is done, and is a result of design as it is taught; the two are intimately linked.

That design is the principal thing is not self-evident. Let us assume that not all design taught is as bad (in my terms) or that, by some miracle, it has changed overnight into a genuine body of theory and knowledge. The question would still remain: how is that new design to be taught? The studio basically sees design purely as a craft approached subjectively, stressing the personality of the designer rather than ideas (this is of course typical of architecture generally) (Kostoff, 1983).

In effect the studio presupposes that apprentices learn from a master—it perpetuates the archaic master-apprentice system no matter how disguised. This has several problems. Lacking clear evaluative criteria there is no way of defining who is a "master", what constitutes mastery, or what is one master of. This system also nullifies what I think design should be and the essence of university teaching — a stress on ideas, theory and knowledge rather than personality, for example.

It also perpetuates the emphasis on one's own experience and resources (as described in the BRE study cited above). But questions about the studio format go beyond even these questions, which I will now examine.

It is implied in the central position of "design" in architectural education—and reflected in the amount of time and resources devoted to it in studio teaching — that "design" (however conceived) is the principal thing architects do — and hence should know. This is far from self-evident and I suspect that a study of how architects spend their time would reveal otherwise. Certainly it seems evident from my own experience and observation that architects spend more time doing various sorts of analyses, in meetings and writing reports, so they need skills to help them do all this.

A Whole Range of New Disciplines is Needed

This conclusion was also reached recently for engineers. A survey of engineering graduates in major firms in Britain showed that their main weaknesses were in writing reports, in researching arguments, in a lack of language skills such as their reading ability, and in handling meetings. (It should be stressed that, unlike architectural design, engineering design has a greater body of theory, so engineers are likely to have an inadequate grasp of theory.) It was concluded that engineers needed skills in other disciplines (Wilby, 1983, Dixon, 1983).

Architects need corresponding skills and, if my view of design is correct, they also need knowledge of a whole range of new disciplines.

Too much Time is Wasted in Studio Teaching

Most of us who have gone through years of design studio, and who might even have taught it, know how much time is wasted in the studio, how much time is spent chatting and playing cards. Serious thought and research are needed to determine how much time is required to achieve certain objectives that are supposed to be achieved in the studio; even assuming that "design" and studio are important, we need to know how much time is needed and by how much it can be reduced without loss. I was involved several times in major reduction in the time devoted to studio work (once to half) without any apparent loss of quality (however that was judged by studio teachers).

If other skills are needed, as argued above, they will require time, most of which could be provided by using time hitherto spent in the design studio.

Another inefficiency that the design studio introduces is that it isolates students from the rest of the university, from the library and form reading and writing. In one Canadian faculty of environmental design, which brought together a number of disciplines so that they could learn from each other, the architects are conspicuously uninvolved. The reason I was given was that "studio takes all their time."

There are Many Ways of Teaching Architecture

It seems to have been forgotten that the studio is nothing but one method of teaching (and learning) among many others. There is no evidence to suggest that it is effective, although of course one cannot judge since it has never been clearly stated what is supposed to be taught here.

Let us assume that synthesis is one of the things to be taught in a studio. One could first ask: does it get taught? I rather doubt it. I would argue that most studios are not even aware of the range of variables and most of what is taught in other courses is forgotten upon passing the sacred portals of the studio. Most studios certainly do not deal formally with priorities, trade-offs, integration and synthesis among the full range of variables (including, for example, those related to man-environment interaction). As the evidence quoted in the previous comments on "Design" suggests, synthesis does not seem to be learned (even if it is right). This raises the question of whether there are other ways to teach synthesis which are more like those used to teach analysis.

One could also ask: how important is synthesis vis-à-vis analysis? The goals of teaching synthesis have never been articulated nor has its effectiveness been tested (as has the effectiveness of teaching clinical skills in medicine, for example, which most closely correspond to "design") (e.g., Elstein et al., 1978). Similarly unexamined has been the implicit emphasis on "creativity"—is it desirable or necessary? What does it mean? How is it best encouraged? At least one recent study of creativity in art argues that problem definition is much more important than problem solution, yet most studios stress the latter (Getzels & Csikszentmihalyi, 1976). Similarly unexamined, as far as I know, have been the many other objectives that no doubt are implicitly present in studio design teaching. In spite of this lack of analysis most resources in schools of architecture—material, human and temporal—are devoted to it.

Yet surely such an analysis, and a clear definition of goals and objectives, should precede such a major emphasis on a single method of teaching—and one as time-intensive as studio.

A Body of Knowledge and Theory must be Developed

It follows from my argument in the first part of this article that at the moment design teaching is really impossible since no evaluation of design (in or out of the studio) is possible, other than the subjective "I do/don't like it."

This is not good enough and a case could be made for it to cease. At some point the circle must be broken so that ways of setting objectives, evaluating their validity, testing whether objectives have been met, developing and refining theory and building a cumulative body of theory and knowledge can be begun. The obvious place to break that circle is the university and, more specifically, in the weakest link — the design studio.

Only thus can one begin to develop ways of knowing what design is, what it should do, what environmental quality is for various people, how design successes ca be judged, how one can decide how important design is, and so on. No longer can it be assumed that one can avoid defining and analyzing problems, nor can one assume any longer that the "solution" to any "problem" will be "building".

We Need a New View of what Architects Are and Do

It can also no longer be assumed that the goal of architectural education is a Renaissance man — a single architect/designer. It is more likely that we need a whole range of people with different skills — hyphenated architects, as it were: architect-programmers, architect-evaluators, architect-researchers, architect-theoreticians.

The studio may be the major mechanism for perpetuating an invalid view of what architects are and what they should do.

One of the things wrong with most schools of architecture and which affects the profession is the absence of scholarship, research and publication compared to other disciplines. Part of the reason for this is lack of time — what little is done is often in one's own time. One can only do scholarly work if there is uninterrupted time for it — and that can only happen if that most wasteful method of teaching, in terms of time — the studio — s reduced. One does not have time to sit around with students, do desk crits, repeat the same thing to each student, go through project after project in juries, again repeating the same thing, and deal with trivial subjective matters that cannot be judged.

Time needs to be released for scholarship and research, but these can only flourish if two other things happen — both of which are also negatively correlated with studio teaching today. The first is that research and teaching are intimately related and, given the lack of theory, ideas and cumulative knowledge in design teaching, that link cannot usually be established. Second, the studio perpetuates the craft tradition of the staff; scholarship and research can only succeed if more academics find their place in schools of architecture.

(Two things are omitted from this simplified argument. First, that there are schools where this is happening, and second, that there is still clearly room for good teachers and researchers.) Thus less emphasis on the studio seems to have major implications for other changes which will improve schools, staff, the profession and our environment.

Some schools pay lip-service to the idea that other things besides design and design studio are important, that there are other kinds of architectural skills and even, possibly, other kinds of architects. But even in schools this is rendered ineffective because what is communicated is very different. It is quite clear to students (and staff) that design and the design studio are central, that most time is allocated to it, that the deadlines of studio projects dominate those of other courses, that resources are allocated very unequally. All these facts indicate a very different picture — that the studio is the navel of the architecture school world. In most cases, of course, there is not even lip-service given to other things. The central importance of the studio is not questioned; its role in defining the identity and uniqueness of architectural education is taken for granted.

In both these cases it is important that a different message be communicated. I would argue that the relative importance and centrality of studio vis-à-vis other things must change. Similarly, what gives way when time is short must change. At the very least equal time and importance must be given to things other than studio. Ideally, much *more* time needs to be given to other things.

Conclusion: Too Much has been Taken for Granted

I have taken an extreme position and stated it in its strongest form. I have questioned the centrality of design and argued for an urgent need to reduce or eliminate the dominance of the studio in architectural education. Consider these to be hypotheses. As such, they may be wrong — but there is only one way of deciding this. But I am unlikely to be wrong about another thing I have been stressing: the need to think about and analyze things that for some time have been taken for granted.

What is really needed is much more thought, analysis and research on how important design is (once we know what it is and what it is supposed to do), how much time it needs and merits, how much of it is to be taught in that way and what is best taught in other ways. This is clearly the first and most urgent task.

Note

1 This essay is reprinted with the permission of the Architects' Journal. The citation of the original can be found in Amos Rapoport's opening statement preceding the essay.

References

Dixon, B. (1983). Say it with words. *New Scientist.* 26.5. 83, p. 572.

Elstein, et al. (1978). *Medical Problem Solving.* Cambridge: Harvard University Press.

Getzels, J. & Csikszentmihalyi. (????). *The Creative Vision.* New York: John Wiley & Sons.

Kostoff, S. (1983). Review of Macmillan Encyclopedia of Architecture in *Design Book Review.* Summer 1983, p. 6.

Mackinder, M. & Marvin, H. (1982). Design decision-making in architectural practice. BRE Information Paper, *IP 11/82*, July 1982, Garston Building Research Station.

Rapoport, A. (1983). Debating architectural alternatives. *RIBA Transactions*, March 1983.

Rapoport, A. (1989). A different view of design. *University of Tennessee Journal of Architecture, Vol.11*, 28-32.

Rapoport, A. (1995a). On the nature of design. *Practices, Vol. 3 & 4*, 32-43.

Rapoport, A. (1995b). Rethinking design (An environment-behavior perspective). In E. Schaur (Ed.), *Building with intelligence (Aspects of a new building culture).* Stuttgart, Germany: University of Stuttgart.

Watson, D. (1982). Sophisticated affirmation of indigenous riches. *AIA Journal*, May 1982, p. 68.

Wilby, P. (1983). Writing cramps engineers' style. *The Times*, 15.5.83.

Zuk, R. (1982). A music lesson. *Journal of Architectural Education*. 36 (3), p. 5.

7 Amos Rapoport: Modernism's Apologist?

Robert M. Beckley

Amos Rapoport has made and continues to make a strong argument for design as a research based "scientific" discipline. His arguments are made, most frequently, citing the inability of modern architecture, contemporary design education and the current design culture to address human needs. Can design be a "scientific" discipline as the founders of the modern movement had hoped and as Amos Rapoport argues? That question is the subject of this paper and is prompted by Rapoport's thoughtful probing of topics that have occupied most of my life: design education, design research and practice.

I love Amos Rapoport dearly. He is like the aunt I remember from my youth who always asked, before greeting me, whether I had combed my hair, brushed my teeth and put on clean underwear. The fact that I had brushed my hair, I thought, should be self evident . But, it never was. That was a question my aunt needed to ask under any circumstance. The teeth — should I smile or grimace? Might one be taken for the other? Ah! A smile. What the heck. She wouldn't notice I hadn't flossed. But, the underwear? How would she ever understand that I didn't wear underwear? My aunt couldn't understand my not wearing underwear because her definition of comfort and hygiene were different from my own. In my aunt's world, brushed hair, clean teeth and underwear were absolute necessities. She could not imagine any other world. But, I loved my aunt and I accepted her world and values, even though sometimes they were a pain.

Amos reminds me of my aunt. He too has created his own world. It is a world which draws us like moths to the flame. Amos asserts, no insists, that architecture, and the fields that support its production, be considered a science: "Design seen as a problem-identifying and problem solving activity must be based on research-based knowledge. In this sense, it is much more like the design of molecules, drugs, and materials than like art" (Rapoport, 1995, p.37). Amos is in good company, though it would aggravate him to no end to be considered alongside others who professed architecture to be a science — the early Modernists such as Gropius and Le Corbusier and countless others who witnessed a revolution in contemporary thinking and wished for the fields of architecture and planning to escape the stylistic whims of their time and embrace design as a science.

Although I applaud Rapoport's contribution to our thinking about people and the environment, I must disagree with him regarding his attitudes about design. I do so out of respect for his intellect and his passion for his position.

I believe it is impossible to exclude the *art* of design from architectural production. Scientific solutions to the architectural problem do not necessarily produce the best solutions in the long run. I've disagreed with Amos on the nature and substance of an architectural education and I must beg to differ with him on this matter as well (Rapoport 1983, reprinted as chapter 6 in this volume; Beckley 1984).

The Architecture Problem

For those of us educated in the post-Bauhaus years after World War Two and before post-modernism, scientific attitudes toward design were very much a part of our education. The aesthetics of a project were derived from solving a problem. And, here is the dilemma. What *is* the nature of the architectural problem?

I recall one of my first design assignments at the University of Cincinnati in the early '50s. We were to design a gas station. First we had to understand gas stations. We all thought we understood gas stations, but we studied them anyway. We observed. We read a few books. (There were very few on gas stations at the time.) Our instructor, a recent Harvard graduate, was convinced there was a better solution to the problem of the gas station than what we saw at highway intersections. But, try as we might, we could not come up with a plan which worked better than the gas station vernacular of the time. It was only later, when I traveled through Europe and saw gas stations tucked inside buildings used for other purposes, that I realized if we had been given the gas station problem within a broader context we might have solved the problem in a different manner. Why? Because the problem would have had other variables than those of accommodating a few pumps, a place for supplies, grease racks and restrooms. Still later it was brought to my attention that functional gas stations had and were being built which were draped in a variety of styles or were simply giant "building-boards" to use the term coined by Bob Venturi and Denise Scott Brown (1977). It was only after my formal schooling that I realized the gas station, a contemporary program necessitated by the invention of the automobile, could be designed as something more than just functional. Their design could also be contextual and/or expressive using artful devices to produce results which were not merely functional but that better fit their context.

Amos' recent pronouncement "...it (environmental design) is much more like the design of molecules, drugs, and materials than art " (Rapoport, 1995, p. 37) sounds very much like that uttered by Adolf Loos: "Am I saying that ...architecture is not to be reckoned among the arts? Indeed I am. Only a very small part of architecture belongs to art — tombstones and monuments. Everything else that serves a particular purpose must be excluded from the realms of art" (in Kruft, 1994, p.366). Walter Gropius was only somewhat more oblique in a statement made in 1923: "We want a clear, organic architecture, whose inner logic will be radiant and naked, unencumbered by lying facades and trickeries; we want an architecture adapted to our world of machines, radios and fast motor cars, an architecture whose function is clearly recognizable in the relation to its form" (Jencks, 1973, p. 109). And, of course, it was Louis Sullivan who is oft quoted as saying "form follows function" before either Loos or Gropius or those to follow.

Architectural ideas of function have mellowed over recent years. Even as the world has become increasingly pragmatic and scientific on the one hand, there is a growing sense that all problems cannot be solved rationally, and architectural problems are no different. Even those concerned with the use of computers as a design tool accept form-making as a part of the architectural designer's role. William Mitchell (1990, p.ix) states "Architects concern themselves professionally with the forms of buildings, with the functions of buildings, and with how to relate the two." Stated another way — the relation of form and function *is* the architectural problem.

Rudolf Arnheim *includes* aesthetics as a functional problem of architecture. He begins his argument by saying, "The aesthetic status of function and functionality in architecture and the other applied arts has been uncertain and uneasy. If an object is designed for a practical purpose, will this intention of the designer and the utility of the object advance or hamper the artistic value of the product? Or is function aesthetically indifferent?" (Arnheim, 1966, p. 193). After articulating the question, Arnheim goes on to elaborate the aesthetic status of function. "Physical function alone will not determine the object. What is more, the reduction of function to physical fitness is quite arbitrary in an object made for human use. The term 'function' in its broadest sense would include all purposes a building or implement is meant to fulfill. It would refer not only to the comfort of the body but also to that of the mind" (Arnheim, 1966, p 195).

If you follow my argument, or should I say "trust my argument," then we can say that aesthetics or the appearance of an object or architecture or any designed thing is as much a function of the designed thing as its operation. Simply put, aesthetics — the (attractive) appearance of an object — is an inherent function of the designed object.

The Problem with Architecture

Amos has a broad definition of design which goes along with his broad condemnation of (current) designers. "I call design any (purposeful) change to the face of the earth" (Rapoport, 1995, p. 35). Can a purposeful change in the earth always be by design? This seems to be a contradiction to Amos' desire to have designers who are *researchers*, *scientists*, experts in what they do. At this time how can one be "expert" in designing every change to the face of the earth? While some of us might like to think we could be, given the opportunity, we designers reside in our little professional niches. Some may be fortunate enough to blur the boundaries. Certainly, we are encouraging students to do that. Interdisciplinary, multi-disciplinary, team approaches, collaboration, etc., are currently buzz words among the design professions. Let us presume Amos is thinking of teams of designers. It is certainly impossible to engage in any significant architectural design commission without engaging a long list of colleagues who think of themselves as "designers." Space planners, programmers, landscape architects, civil, structural, electrical, and mechanical engineers, interior designers, lighting specialists, curtain wall experts, acousticians, and more; all are designing some aspect of the building - changing the face of the earth. Oh, I forgot architects. They are on the team too. They might even have the prime contract, even though they may no longer receive the majority of professional "design" fees involved in the project.

But, lets keep this simple. I think Amos has the biggest problem with architects who he sees as capricious (Rapoport, 1983). When all is said and done it is the architect who puts the facade on a building, and thus determines the building's outward appearance, albeit sometimes with the help of more than one consultant.

Modernism taught us, with the promise of new technologies, that the skin of a building could express its interior. Rapoport goes further, suggesting there should be a direct correlation between a design and "...1) human characteristics: perceptual, cognitive, cultural, lifestyle, etcetera, 2) effects of environment on people, choice, criticality, etcetera, 3) mechanisms linking people and environments, perception, cognition, meaning, instrumental, etcetera" (Rapoport 1994, p.73). There is a close parallel between the modernists' quest for a "scientific" rather than "artistic" view of architectural production and Rapoport's desire to eliminate the willful creative act. Architecture must seek the "truth" and avoid the "facade." Hanna Arendt, however, argues the "facade" has a function. Using the work of the Swiss zoologist and biologist Adolf Portman as a spring board Arendt muses,

> The inside, the functional apparatus of the life process, is covered up by an outside which, as far as the life process is concerned, has only one function, namely, to hide and protect it, to prevent its exposure to the light of an appearing world. If this inside were to appear, we would all look alike...There is, second, the equally impressive evidence for the existence of an innate impulse - no less compelling than the merely functional instinct of preservation - which Portmann calls 'the urge to self-display'. This instinct is entirely gratuitous in terms of life-preservation; it far transcends what may be deemed necessary for

> sexual attraction. These findings suggest that the predominance of outside appearance implies, in addition to the sheer receptivity of our senses, a spontaneous activity: whatever can see wants to be seen, whatever can hear calls out to be heard, whatever can touch presents itself to be touched. It is indeed as though everything that is alive - in addition to the fact that its surface is made for appearance, fit to be seen and meant to appear to others - has an urge to appear, to fit itself into the world of appearances by displaying and showing, not its 'inner self' but itself as an individual" (Arendt, 1978, p. 29).

We can use Arendt's argument to explain the Centre Pompidou in Paris - an incredibly successful urban attraction as a museum, gallery, performance space, archive. An attraction which looks like no other building in Paris and which cannot easily be classified as any other cultural institution, museum, theater, school, library. What it is exactly isn't clear because it has a program like no other. Nonetheless, it is a popular success drawing more people to it than any other Parisian attraction. Why? Certainly not because it tops the list of easily categorized tourist spots. Then why? Because of its program, its location, or because its guts are showing? It's "facade" certainly doesn't give a clue. It is its own thing. In pretending to reveal its interior it conceals the building's multivalent program. It challenges conventional notions of perception, meaning and cognition. Though now, everyone visiting Paris, knows *what* it is.

So we have come to the position that the architectural design problem is complex. That, if you believe Arnheim and Arendt the appearance of an object (architecture) doesn't have to be related to its "inside operation" and yet this appearance has a function.

Now we have the problem of designing this appearance. We've already conceded this to the architect, though the architect here must contend fully with the client. For the building is an avatar of the client. The architectural profession, except for a few superstars who are hired to be the clients' alter ego, is now well disciplined to understand that pleasing the client is important to collecting one's fees and the clients' "opinion" should be listened to because, after all, it is their building. Still, we architects are trained to make aesthetic judgements. Despite Amos views' to the contrary, aesthetics is a teachable subject . I return to Arnheim to help my argument.

> There are...theorists who fully acknowledge the aesthetic aspect of the architect's or designer's task. However, they tend to think of beauty as an additional virtue of the useful object. Fitness is one thing, beauty another. Thus, Leone Battista Alberti maintains that the architect should deserve praise 'both for the wonderful and ravishing beauty of his works and for the necessity, serveableness, and strength of the things which he has invented.' Beauty is defined by Alberti as the harmony of all the parts. In our own century, the architect Walter Gropius tells us that the slogan 'fitness for purpose equals beauty' is only half true. When do we call a human face beautiful? Every face is fit for a purpose in its parts, but only perfect proportions and colors in a well-balanced harmony deserve that title of honor: beautiful (Arnheim, 1966, p. 197).

Arnheim believes in the concept of beauty and is able to describe for us what is beautiful and why. Indeed this may take a bit of connoisseurship and may smell of elitism, but so are other aesthetic pursuits like enjoying an opera or reading poetry with high artistic aspirations.

Of course there is another take on the subject of the facade and here we can't but help comment on the observations of Venturi Scott-Brown and their classification of buildings as "decorated sheds" or "ducks" referring to buildings that advertise what they are by becoming "building-boards" or buildings which are *what* they do (Ducks are sold in the building shaped like a duck.) (Venturi 1977). Their aesthetic manipulation makes us aware of the problems of appearance and authenticity in today's culture where we are bombarded by simulacrums.

Unintentionally we've reduced the architect's role to facadist. An unfortunate circumstance even though it may be true in many circumstances. But, architects don't think of their role in that way. Neither do they think of themselves as designing everything in a building, except perhaps in modest commissions for which non-architects can also qualify. The contemporary building is far too complex to be designed by one individual. Indeed, most building programs are too complex to even begin to grasp all the variables and combinations of possible solutions. The architect thus picks and chooses. If one is designing a church, more than likely the creation of a spiritual quality becomes a driving force. However, we know churches sometimes exist in appropriated store fronts. Here spirituality might have to give way to providing barrier-free access and a security system on a limited budget. The character of a theater, as another example, might be determined by the client mix. A theater board with a strong donor base might demand that an architect spend most of the design time and construction budget on an auspicious entrance, lobby and performance space for the audience. If the theater is represented by strong management, the program emphasis might be on the back of the house and a design that best supports the "production" of theater (Beckley, 1982). Architect Paul Rudolph is quoted by Charles Jencks as saying about building design,

> All problems can never be solved. Indeed it is characteristic of the twentieth century that architects are highly selective in determining which problems they want to solve. Mies (van der Rohe), for instance, makes wonderful buildings only because he ignores many aspects of a building. If he solved more problems, his buildings would be far less potent. This paradox is heightened by the various commitments to functionalism (Jencks, 1973, p. 108).

If Amos is reading this I am certain he has jumped out of his seat by now and is declaring "that is exactly what I'm talking about." I urge him to read on for here we come to a major architectural paradox. Amos uses a medical analogy to frame his argument for a "scientific" architecture, but his premise is faulty. Architectural problems are the most complex of all the problems in the world. Why? Because they are so vague and unfocused. First let me share Amos' analogy:

> The major innovation in these fields (medicine and the life sciences) is their shift from serendipitous or trial and error searches for drugs or materials to more rational procedures based on knowledge, theory, and empirical data. Given a desired end, which needs to be defined explicitly, design is based on the knowledge of the structure of specific molecules, whether of drugs or materials, and the mechanics of their interaction with the medium in which the material is to perform or the biological setting of the drug. Regular reading of scientific journals provides almost weekly examples, all based on achieving predicted results in the given system based on knowledge (Rapoport, 1995, p.37).

First of all, architectural problems are never "defined explicitly." If they are, they are reductionist in nature either by the will of the architect (see Rudolph's reference to Mies above) or by the necessity of the client or budget. Seldom does an architect have the opportunity to optimize a solution. Second, the architect's ability to perform trial and error experiments is limited - we don't have lab animals on which to experiment. Given that we know a great deal more about human behaviors in environments than we did a few decades ago, (and I acknowledge this information is poorly used by architects), still the architect's primary complaint is that this research has focused on what happened not what "might" happen in a given set of circumstances. Why? Humans are not lab animals and their behavior is much too complex to make accurate predictions about specific behaviors (general behaviors, yes.). Finally, the kind of research Amos discusses is referring to specific and very discrete components of the human animal. The medical profession (and medical education) is questioning whether it has over specialized and lost perspective of the whole patient. Architects deal with the whole patient. We are the general practitioners hiring specialists. The medical profession is beginning to embrace the notion of holistic medicine, recognizing that several specialized treatments might make the patient sick because of their negative interaction and sometimes the best treatment is no treatment at all. (I tell my students that the most important analysis an architect can do for a client is to determine whether the solution to the client's problem is actually a building.)

I appreciate Amos' respect for the technical advances in medicine and medical and pharmaceutical innovations and "designs" which are truly amazing. If the same investments were made in architectural research we might have smarter buildings with better circulation systems, fewer cardio-vascular problems, joints that were easily repairable after damage and lower cholesterol. But, these advances in medicine don't make for a better "person." And, it is that quality of "wholeness" which Amos himself wants to test architecture against.

The Science of Architecture as an Art

Along with Amos, I lament the sorry state of research in our field, either design or architecture or any of the other affiliated professions. Materials research, like pharmaceuticals in medicine, is largely done by building materials and component suppliers. Like the pharmaceutical companies we must take them at their word that their new product will do what it is supposed to do without any harmful side effects. Research in the schools is sparse and limited to a handful of schools. The largest research projects (from a financial perspective) are most often the esoteric and least related directly to design decision making. Most of this research is not theoretical but is applied. Computer software applications have sustained research in architectural schools for the last decade. Some schools have taken advantage of federal funding in the health care area, studies of facilities for Alzheimer's patients, etc. That is valuable research but narrow in its application beyond certain building types or certain design operations. Garry Stevens in an article on architectural education points out that

> Research is simply not a "natural" function of the architectural education system of the English-speaking world and never has been...the most important theoretical work — both in architecture and in what others would call building — has always been conducted outside the universities or by individuals only loosely affiliated with universities. (Stevens, 1998, p.163).

He cites theoretical work in "deconstructivist theory" as an example of theoretical exploration moving from the profession to the schools.

Others will argue that "design" as a research topic is not researchable. "Theoretical and empirical studies have shown that creative designing and inventing tap into sources that cannot be predicted in advance. In fact, certain randomness is almost mandatory in a creative search and form combinations are tried out before it is clear what purpose such combinations might fulfill" (Goldschmidt, 1998, p.263). (I feel Amos squirming in his chair again.) What makes some designers better than others? There is obviously a values issue related to this question. However, the design and architectural professions and their critics have ways of identifying "outstanding designers" (and their products) though there is not always agreement on who should be considered such. It is also clear that we don't have a formula for producing outstanding designers. In the medical profession and sciences like physics and molecular biology, the teacher/researcher plays a primary role in mentoring the next generation of teacher/researchers. This very rarely happens in the design profession. Frank Lloyd Wright may have surpassed his mentor Louis Sullivan in pure design talent, but Wright left his apprenticeship early and most often disavowed any influence by his mentor. Certainly none of Wright's own students came close to reaching the acclaim of their master. Apprentices to great designers, with a few exceptions, seldom surpass the talents of their mentors.

The scientific in architecture is illusive. The most fundable research topics are peripheral to the *art* of design. Unlike doctors we don't have an exhaustive array of new technologies to help us advance all aspects of our craft. A new generation of students who arrive at the University already computer literate may change design abilities remarkably. But, these tools will not necessarily create better designs. Neither do the medical professions new tools create better people.

The common cold is to medicine what housing is to architecture. These are familiar problems but subject to only minor search. Why? Perhaps, and this is pure speculation, the common cold has too many variables to be a researchable topic. It is too diffuse a problem type. Whereas, various types of influenza can be isolated and studied and vaccines experimented with until a cure is found.

Many architects have attacked the housing "problem" as though it were a virus, rather than a cold. They have often found cures for this once the variables have been limited. Sometimes they have discovered solutions to problems they did not set out to address in their original hypothesis. Let me use Le Corbusier's ambitious scheme for Pessac, France as an example.

Corbu described the problem he was given this way, paraphrasing his client M. Fruges, an altruistic Bordeaux industrialist... "Pessac should be a laboratory: in short: I ask you to pose the problem of a house plan, of finding a method of standardization, to make use of walls, floors and roofs confirming to the most rigorous requirements for strength and efficiency and lending themselves to true tailor-like methods of mass-production by the use of machines which I shall authorize you to buy" (Le Corbusier, 1967, p.42). An un-ambiguous architectural research program.

But, what about the people who were to occupy Pessac when this experiment in construction was completed. "Instead of installing themselves in their containers, instead of adapting to them and living in them 'passively,' they decided that as far as possible they were going to live 'actively.' In doing so they showed what living in a house really is: an activity (I guess architects do have the equivalent of lab animals to work with). They took what had been offered to them and worked on it, converted it, added to it. What did they add? They built a differentiated social cluster" (Lefebvre, 1979, preface).

Was Pessac a success or a failure? As a research program the project seemed to fulfill Mr. Fruges' objectives. However, the research program changed as the project progressed. Once Corbu and Fruges agreed to the type of housing and its siting, Corbu was able to develop a typology which met Fruges' construction objectives. What wasn't considered were the social implications of their "laboratory" as it was justly called. What was unexpected in this little research project was the facility with which the lab animals adapted their environment to fit their own purposes. As the projects biographer and researcher Philippe Boudon put it "Pessac could only be regarded as a failure if it had failed to satisfy the needs of the occupants. In point of fact, however, it not only allowed the occupants sufficient latitude to satisfy their needs, by doing so it also helped them to realize what those needs were" (Boudon, 1979, p. 164).

Rapoport's book, *House Form and Culture*, defined an entirely new field of architectural research. His admiration for the genius of vernacular architecture was contagious. As his admiration for this form of design grew his suspicion of "self-conscious" architectural design and designers also grew. The conclusion to that book, however, puts the issue of architectural design, design research and design evaluation in a perspective worth revisiting.

> Our era is one of reduced physical constraints. We can do very much more than was possible in the past, and criticality is lower than ever. The result is the problem of excessive choice, the difficulty of selecting or finding constraints which arose naturally in the past and which are

> necessary for the creation of meaningful house form. This great freedom of choice and the fact that house form can be the domain of fashion, suggests the general validity of the concept of criticality, and the primacy of socio-cultural factors, and all that this implies for the understanding of house form, as well as its choice. However, we act as though criticality were high and close fit to physical "function" were essential. I have already commented on the unspecialized nature of vernacular buildings, and their consequent success over time. There may lie the great lesson of vernacular building for our own day - the value of constraints to establish generalized, "loose" frameworks where the interplay of the constant and changeable aspect of man can find expression (Rapoport, 1969. p.135).

By these standards Pessac was great architecture. Corbu's rational system of construction provided the framework, the vernacular, with which people could work to adopt, over time, living arrangements which were personalized to their needs. Was this an accident? It was not a part of the original experiment. If you've found a cure for cancer but your laboratory patient dies of pneumonia is your research invalid? Of course not. In Pessac the patient didn't die. Instead new living habits were devised to adapt to the newly prescribed treatment. The same happened in Levittown, New York twenty years later when a banal architectural model was turned into a living community. Not the intellectual undertaking of Messieurs Corbu and Fruges' but nearly a replication of their earlier experiment. Both produced a generic architecture which was easily adopted by its inhabitants to changing life styles. And, both endeavors were more akin to holistic medical practices than they were to big science cures.

Amos Rapoport is a champion of design research and an articulate spokesman for this cause. For that, and his impassioned plea for us to recognize the legitimacy of unself-conscious design, we can be thankful. But, architectural research cannot be conducted like medical research and the architectural problem is different from the medical problem as currently defined by medical science. Amos was right the first time, in his conclusion after writing *House Form and Culture*, recognizing:

> the value of constraints to establish generalized, "loose" frameworks where the interplay of the constant and changeable aspect of man can find expression (Rapoport, 1969, p.135).

References

Arendt, H. (1978). *The Life of the Mind.* NY: Harcourt Brace Jovanovich, Inc.

Arnheim, R. (1965). *Art and Visual Perception.* Berkeley: University of California Press.

Arnheim, R. (1966). *Toward A Psychology of Art*, Berkeley: University of California Press.

Beckley, R. M. (1982). *Theater Facilities Guidelines and Strategies.* School of Architecture and Urban Planning, Milwaukee: University of Wisconsin-Milwaukee.

Beckley, R. M. (1984). Architects Learn to Make Judgements. *Architectural Record* October 1984. New York, NY: McGraw Hill.

Boudon, P. (1979). *Lived-in Architecture, Le Corbusier's Pessac Revisited*, Cambridge MA, MIT Press.

Goldschmidt, G. (1998). Creative Architectural Design: Reference Versus Precedence *Journal of Architectural and Planning Research* Vol.15 No. 3 Autumn Chicago IL Locke Science Publishing Co. Inc.

Kruft, H. W. (1994). *A History of Architectural Theory from Vitruvius to the Present*, New York, Princeton Architectural Press.

Jencks, C. (1973). *Modern Movements in Architecture*, Garden City NJ Anchor Press.

Le Corbusier (1967). Boesiger W. and Girsberger H. *Le Corbusier 1910-65* NY Frederick A. Praeger, Publishers.

Lefebvre, H. (1979). Boudon, Philippe. *Lived-in Architecture, Le Corbusier's Pessac Revisited*, Cambridge MA, MIT Press.

Mitchell, W. J., (1990). *The Logic of Architecture: Design, Computation and Cognition*, Cambridge MA MIT Press.

Rapoport, A. (1969). *House Form and Culture*, Englewood Cliffs NJ Prentice-Hall Inc.

Rapoport, A. (1984). There is an urgent need to reduce or eliminate the dominance of the studio., *Architectural Record* 10/84, NY NY McGraw Hill Inc.

Rapoport, A. (1994). Bouman, Ole and Van Toorn, Roemer (Eds). *The Invisible in Architecture*, London, Academy Editions p. 73.

Rapoport, A. (1995). *Practices* 3/4 The Nature of Design, Cincinnati OH Center for the Study of the Practice of Architecture, University of Cincinnati.

Stevens, G. (1998). Angst in Academia: Universities, The Architecture Schools and the Profession. *Journal of Architectural and Planning Research* Vol 15 No. 2 Summer p. Chicago IL Locke Science Publishing Co. Inc. p. 163.

Venturi, R., Scott Brown, D. & Izenour, S. (1977). *Learning From Las Vegas*, Cambridge, MA, MIT Press.

8 The Architect as Artist or Scientist?: A Modest Proposal for the Architect-as-Cultivator

Linda N. Groat

Prelude

I well remember, as a newly-minted assistant professor of architecture at UW-M in the early 1980's, feeling somewhat flummoxed and certainly challenged intellectually by Amos Rapoport's rather radical critique of the studio system in architectural education. Not that I considered myself a conservative defender of vested traditions in architecture. Far from it. After 10 years in California — first as a graduate student at the School of Design at California Institute of the Arts (a 1960's inspired alternative to professional education in the design fields), then as a designer for a major San Francisco firm and member of a community activist group in Berkeley named People's Architecture — I certainly thought of myself as representing a more integrative, socially-conscious view of architecture. But banishing studio education was decidedly not part of this view. So I didn't quite get what Amos was on about. And I hotly defended "architectural theory" as worthy of both serious attention and empirical investigation of the sort that I chose to pursue in my research. And implicitly, I suppose I defended the value of studio as well.

I also remember that when Amos' and Bob Beckley's matched pair of Op Ed pieces on studio — Amos con and Bob pro — came out in *Architectural Record* in 1984 (Beckley, 1984; Rapoport, 1984, reprinted as Chapter 6 in this volume), I know I inwardly thought: "Amos has overstated the whole thing once again. Why is he so fierce about this studio thing?"

Now to the present, almost 20 years since I first started teaching at UW-M; and I feel a bit chastened, certainly older, I hope a bit wiser, and much more inclined to see that Amos has diagnosed a lot of things correctly on this architectural education question. In the intervening years, I left UW-M post-tenure to become Associate Dean at Michigan for five years under Bob Beckley's deanship; I began a decade of research on women and minorities in architectural education in collaboration with Prof. Sherry Ahrentzen who I had known at UW-M; and I also got to see and hear about the less benevolent side of architectural education through that research as well as through my service on the ACSA Board and on several accrediting team visits to various schools around the country. I was also able to expand my horizons on pedagogical matters through a variety of interdisciplinary activities at Michigan, among them: biannual seminars on teaching sponsored by the Provost's Office, and a half-time appointment as a faculty associate at U-M's Center for Research on Learning and Teaching.

The end result of these travels through more expansive intellectual terrain is that I have come to value much of Amos' critique of studio education. In many respects, I believe he has hit the proverbial nail on its head. But though his diagnosis may be substantially accurate, I believe his remedy is flawed. I simply don't believe the rest of the architectural world will be convinced by the alternative he offers, nor do I believe it is ultimately desirable.

In Honor of Amos

My goal for this essay, then, is to present an alternative model of the architect and its implications for architectural education. The argument is laid out in four parts. First, I will review and analyze Amos' critique of architectural education, including its studio emphasis, through discussion of his 1984 Op Ed piece in *Architectural Record* as well as his longer essay, "On the Nature of 'Design,'" published in *Practices 3/4* some ten years later (Rapoport, 1995). In the process of summarizing Amos' critique, I will identify many of the points on which I have come to agree with Amos, and will incorporate findings of recent research by myself or others which supports these points of critique. Second, I will identify two key aspects of Amos' proposals for architectural education with which I disagree. In doing so, I will also make use of Bob Beckley's Op Ed piece in *Architectural Record* to represent the typical counterpoint to Amos' argument. (Beckley, 1984). Third, I will then summarize and restate an argument I developed in two articles for *Journal of Architectural Education* (Groat, 1992; 1993) in which I propose an alternative model of the architect — the architect-as-cultivator. Finally, going well beyond the scope of the original argument, I will articulate what the nature of architectural education for a "cultivator" might be like.

Diagnosing the Problems in Architectural Education

Rapoport's[1] critique of architectural education is multi-faceted and defies any simplistic characterization; no thumbnail sketch will do it justice. However, in the segment that follows, I will identify some of the key points in his argument and discuss the extent to which these points have been echoed and/ or substantiated by other researchers and commentators. I will also identify additional points in his argument which I intend to challenge in subsequent segments of this essay.

And so, a few key points to Rapoport's' critique:

1. It is implied in the central position of 'design' in architectural education...that 'design' (however conceived) is the principal thing architects do — and hence should know (Rapoport, 1984, p. 100).

In a 1992 article for *Journal of Architectural and Planning Research* summarizing our study of the status of women faculty for ACSA, Sherry Ahrentzen and I challenged what we called "the design-as-centerpoint" model of architectural education. Although we came to our argument from a very different direction — a combination of findings from the survey we conducted of faculty women and more general theoretical principles from feminist theory — we nevertheless wound up taking a similar stance. Our point was that when design is cast as the centerpoint, all other activities or subject matter become, by definition, peripheral. It is an implicitly hierarchical stance, and as such consistent with patriarchal conventions. Our alternative was to conceptualize all of design education as a tapestry, throughout which the design activity would be woven, but in a way that would enable other ideas/modes of activity to be more integral to the overall model of architectural education.

In a slightly different vein, a string of recent articles in the professional journals and AIA publications have documented a significant trend in the economics of contemporary architectural practice—the increasing proportion of income from expanded, "non-design" services such as strategic planning or facilities management (e.g. Pearson, 1998). Accompanying these statistics, the authors make the point that in the changing context of practice, architects need to be thinking about building long-term relationships with clients whereby they provide a broad range of services; this in contrast to a focus on a per-project basis. Even within the traditional realm of "design" services, Dana Cuff (1991) has clearly demonstrated the extent to which basic skills in negotiating the social dynamics among multiple players can be fundamental to the success of a building project. In sum, "non-design" skills will play an increasingly pivotal role in practice.

2. The studio basically sees design purely as a craft approached subjectively.

Further, the subjective emphasis on personality perpetuates the master-apprentice model. Alternatively, Rapoport argues, the essence of design should stress "ideas, theory, and knowledge." (Rapoport, 1984, p. 100)

The argument that architecture needs to have a more secure foundation in a cumulative body of knowledge is one that a number of other researchers — both before and after Amos' Op Ed piece--have argued. One of the most impassioned is Sharon Sutton (Sutton, 1992). In a 1992 Op Ed piece, she argues that many minorities are not attracted to architecture because it represents such a weak position in society compared to many other professions. Further, it is weak in that it lacks a sufficiently robust body of knowledge as a basis for mounting convincing arguments in the arenas of power. Former *Progressive Architecture* editor Tom Fisher, now Dean at University of Minnesota, takes up this argument and argues that architecture might seek to modify its model of professional practice to be more consistent with either the medical or engineering models, both of which depend heavily on a recognized, established knowledge base (Fisher, 1994).

Similarly, many other commentators have critiqued the apparent dominance of the master-apprentice model. Adopting an explicitly feminist stance, for example, Sherry Ahrentzen and I (Ahrentzen and Groat, 1992) argued that the gendering of the "master" role as almost invariably male was a major impediment to women's progress in the field. On the other hand, in our later survey of architecture students, the results indicated that the vast majority of students are more inclined to consider their studio instructors as "facilitators" than as "masters" (Groat and Ahrentzen, 1996). Unfortunately, since no definitions of these terms were provided or asked for from the students, it remains to be seen how accurate a characterization of studio pedagogy these results reflect.

> 3. In setting explicit objectives for design, criteria are also set for evaluating how successfully goals have been met.... Lacking clear evaluative criteria, there is no way of defining who is a "master," what constitutes mastery, or what one is master of (Rapoport, 1984, p. 100).

The lack of clear evaluative criteria is a common complaint about studio pedagogy, but especially of design juries. Kathryn Anthony's 1991 book, *Design Juries on Trial*, documents important aspects of this problem from the student perspective. More recently, the results of Sherry Ahrentzen's and my survey indicate that when students are asked to evaluate the relative importance of various characteristics of studio, "clearly articulated criteria for evaluation" is one of the most highly ranked of 17 choices. Similarly, in analyzing the results of a similar questionnaire used at the University of Michigan, I found that the greatest discrepancy between the students' *ideal* and *experienced* characteristics of studio occurred on the item "clearly articulated criteria." Indeed, there was a *difference of 65% points* between the number of students who rated "clear criteria" as "essential" for an ideal studio and the number who rated their experience of "clear criteria" as occurring "quite often."

> 4. The studio may be the major mechanism for perpetuating an invalid view of what architects are and what they should do (Rapoport, 1984, p. 103).

Perhaps the best support for Amos' argument on this point is provided by Dana Cuff in her book, *Architecture: A Study of Practice* (Cuff, 1991). In a carefully documented chapter, she compares the two different models of architectural practice promoted by the academy and by the AIA. She then compares both models to her own detailed research on practice. In general, she finds that neither the academic studio nor the AIA are advocating accurate portrayals of the field. Of six characteristics of design in practice, she finds that the academy accurately portrays only one of these: process, which she finds to be "open-ended and curricular" in both the academy and actual practice.[2]

5. [S]tudio is nothing but one method of teaching (and learning) among many others (Rapoport, 1984, p. 103).

Rapoport makes this point primarily to challenge the most common assumptions about the value of studio, i.e. that it is the most effective means of teaching "synthesis" skills. Bob Beckley, in his counterpoint argument (Beckley, 1984, p. 105), takes on this pedagogical format question quite directly by emphasizing the distinction between academic lecture courses which "are expected to teach normative information" on a variety of subject areas and studio where students learn to make the sort of judgments they will encounter in professional practice.

In many ways, recent developments in the pedagogy of higher education have caught up with the point Amos was making. For example, investigations of learning and teaching styles (e.g. Montgomery and Groat, 1998) and developments of teaching strategies for active learning (e.g. Meyers and Jones, 1993) render the sharp distinctions which Beckley charted a moot point. Skilled faculty are, in fact, able to incorporate an array of tactics — such as group learning and in-class problem solving — to make the so-called "lecture" format an active adventure in learning and one that may incorporate many aspects of the typical studio.[3] And the converse is true as well, "research-based" studios may well facilitate in-depth learning in particular subject areas in a way that far surpasses the content learning achieved through lecture modes. In short, there is currently such an expansive investigation of pedagogical modes in higher education that architectural education would be foolish to ignore the potential of a more variegated and carefully orchestrated array of pedagogical formats.

6. [T]he most important decision is *what* to do and *why* to do it rather than *how* it is to be done (which comes later), with which design has traditionally been more concerned (Rapoport, 1984, p. 100).

Although I have long supported traditional EBS arguments for programming and the like, it has only been recently that I have come to appreciate the full measure of Rapoport's critique on this point. No doubt this is because my early research studies entailed empirical assessments of contemporary architectural styles and design principles; in Rapoport's terms, these research questions were about the *how* of, say, designing a particular new building in an historic context, not whether to build it there or not. Subsequently, my research on architectural education got me closer to thinking about how different ethnic or gender groups might tend to value certain *goals* for architecture. However, it wasn't until I joined an interdisciplinary research group involved in organizational research and coincidentally my husband started a facilities planning consulting business that I began to see Rapoport's point much more clearly.

Now I view the *what?* and *why?* questions as THE key questions; ultimately they have more impact on the physical environment than the *how* issues with which "design' is usually associated. The big what and why questions are also the site of a tremendous disciplinary gap. In general, business and organization executives have no training in being able to evaluate how their business goals might be fostered or hindered by particular environmental changes; while architects typically have little or no organizational studies or business training to help sort out how meaningful organizational changes could be appropriately reflected in physical changes. This kind of strategic planning is clearly an area ripe for the 'expanded services' paradigm advocated by Pearson (1998) and others. But it remains to be seen whether architects will be sufficiently capable and astute to make the most of such opportunities. If they are not, there are plenty of management consulting giants ready to fill this potential vacuum.

So far, I have identified six aspects of Rapoport's critique that I believe are accurate and/or well substantiated. To summarize, the points of critique are: a misconceived insistence on the centrality of "design," the lack of a knowledge base, the lack of clear evaluative

Table 8.1 Rapoport's Critique of Studio and Subsequent Research/Commentary

Points of Rapoport's Critique	Supporting Articles
1. *Misconceived Emphasis on Centrality of Design*	Ahrentzen & Groat, 1992 Cuff, 1991 Pearson, 1998
2. *Lack of Knowledge Base*	Sutton, 1992 Fisher, 1994
3. *Lack of Clear Evaluative Criteria*	Anthony, 1991 Ahrentzen & Groat, 1996
4. *Perpetuation of Invalid Model of Architect's Role*	Cuff, 1991
5. *Studio As the Only/ Best Method of Teaching Integration*	Meyers & Jones, 1993 Montgomery & Groat, 1998
6. *Emphasis on 'How' Questions, Rather than 'What & Why'*	Pearson, 1998

Points of Rapoport's Critique	Contested Issues
1. *The Elimination of Studio as an Extreme Position*	Groat, this chapter
2. *The Architect-as-Scientist vs. Architect-as-Artist*	Groat, 1992; 1993

criteria, the studio's perpetuation of an invalid model of what architects do, the misplaced belief in the studio as the only effective way to teach integration, the inappropriate emphasis on the *how* questions rather than the more significant *what* and *why* questions (See Table 8.1).

The Architect-as-Artist vs. The Architect-as-Scientist

Now I would like to turn from the diagnostic aspects of Rapoport's position to the more prescriptive aspects. In this regard, I have two major concerns: the first is about the intentional dichotomization of possible positions, and the second concerns the specific model he advocates, namely the architect-as-scientist.

1) I have taken an extreme position and stated it in its strongest possible form. I have questioned the centrality of design and argued for an urgent need to reduce or eliminate the dominance of the studio in architectural education.... Consider these hypotheses.... What is really needed is much more thought, analysis and research... (Rapoport, 1984, p. 103).

In this concluding passage, Rapoport concedes that he has stated the extreme case against studio to make a point about needing to examine more systematically the taken-for-granted role of studio. Nevertheless, I believe this implicitly dichotomous perspective may have been counter-productive in that it is more likely to force an impassioned defense of studio rather than the careful examination that Rapoport seeks as an outcome.

In fact, Beckley's counterpoint article does precisely that. Not only does he defend the studio as the best and most appropriate mechanism for integration and for learning professional judgement, he also presents a highly dichotomized view of the components of architectural education: academics vs. designers; and academic lecture vs. design studio. For example, in defending the studio's unique role, he states that "[a]n architect is dependent upon rhetorical dialogue to define architectural problems," implicitly assuming that the traditional lecture format can not accommodate such dialogue. As already discussed in an earlier segment of this essay, recent developments in active learning formats for higher education clearly demonstrate that such dichotomization of classroom formats are not only inaccurate but far too limiting.

2) [D]esign needs to be based on a science rather than an art metaphor. Design needs to be seen as a science-based profession, a responsible problem identification and solving activity, not the free play of an artist solving self-set "problems" (Rapoport, 1995, p. 40).

This assertion, quoted from Rapoport's article in *Practices* some ten years after the original Op Ed piece, reveals a level of dichotomization implicit in, but not fully articulated in the earlier piece. Indeed, Rapoport introduces the distinction between "the "sense of design" in art or the "rational design" of molecules, drugs, or materials" in the second paragraph of the article and returns to this theme throughout. A similarly telling passage is the following: "[D]esigners are more like scientists than artists; any creativity must be understood in those terms (Rapoport, 1995, p. 35).

I believe Rapoport has it right when he identifies the designer-as-artist model as problematic; but the designer-as-scientist model which he proposes is, I believe, equally problematic, and from a very practical standpoint, unlikely to be persuasive within the architectural or design professions. It is also unnecessarily oppositional in that it perpetuates the kind of pendulum swing of theoretical models that has occurred throughout 20th century western architecture. This is precisely the point I have argued in an article for *Journal of Architectural Education* titled, "Rescuing Architecture from the Cul-de-Sac" (Groat, 1992) and elaborated in a subsequent article (Groat, 1993). My argument is that the these oppositional models of architecture — the architect-as-artist and the architect-as-technician — as I termed them, have led contemporary architecture to a theoretical and practical cul-de sac. In the following segment of this chapter I will briefly summarize this argument.

The Architect-as-Cultivator

As a foundation for my argument about the pendulum swing between theoretical models of architecture, I draw extensively from contemporary philosophical analyses by such authors as Eugene

Rochberg-Halton, Lawrence Cahoone, and Stephen Toulmin who suggest that modern (post-Renaissance) thought has failed to sustain a viable conceptualization of cultural phenomena (Rochberg-Halton, 1986; Cahoone, 1988; Toulmin, 1990); and I argue that is particularly true of architecture. The common theme in these critiques of modernity is the central role of the "Cartesian dichotomy," with its distinction between, on the one hand, the *mental* "outcomes of reasoning" inherent in human experience and, on the other hand, physical phenomena and natural processes that are *material* (Toulmin, 1990, p. 108). Emphasis on the former is associated with what Cahoone labels as the rationalist position, while an emphasis on the latter is associated with the empiricist perspective.[4]

In architecture, the empiricist perspective has tended to conceive of architecture as an instrumental consequence of powerful physical, social or economic forces. This has led to such 20th century trends as the pseudoscientism of Modernist functionalism and the linguistic model of structuralist analysis. On the other hand, the need to account for the creative spirit of the architect has led the rationalist perspective to conceive of architecture as subjective expression and therefore irrelevant to broader, pressing social concerns. This emphasis on the romantic ideal of the artist has been manifested through such theoretical trends as phenomenology and certain aspects of deconstruction.

These two views of architecture might be termed the "architect-as-technician" model and the "architect-as-artist" model. In their most extreme manifestations, the former suggests a technician observing and navigating the confluence of external social, political, and economic forces, while the latter suggests the notion of the isolated artist working in creative isolation from and above the hubbub of society.

Although these two models of architecture typically function in an oppositional manner, Cahoone has argued that the two underlying philosophical positions — empiricism and rationalism — share an important characteristic: they are both essentially "subjectivist." Both "begin with an analysis of the contents of the individual human mind or consciousness..." (Cahoone, 1988, p.26). Because of this, "neither subject nor object-world is characterized by independent existence, existential integrity, substantiality, or reality" (Cahoone, 1988, p. 85). This, in turn, leads both positions to an inherently anti-culturalist ethos, and results in a contemporary culture that is "hostile to itself" in that it denies the intrinsic value of artifacts, including architecture.

This analysis is the basis for my arguing that Amos' proposal for an architect-as-scientist model is not the appropriate solution to the architect-as-artist model problem he identifies. In my view, the architect-as-scientist, like the architect-as-technician I posited, emerges directly from the empiricist tradition. As such, it represents the opposite point on the pendulum swing from the rationalist architect-as-artist model. Following Cahoone's argument, however, despite their apparently oppositional character, both are implicitly anti-culturalist. Neither is the appropriate model for a profession whose primary role is the stewardship of one of the preeminent categories of cultural artifacts, the built environment.

The alternative to both models, I have argued, is the architect-as-cultivator model. Cahoone's definition of culture forms an important foundation for this concept; he defines culture as: "the totality of a social group's interpretive products, created or inherited, by which the group understands itself and its world," More specifically, Cahoone identifies three primary characteristics of culture: its a priori existence relative to the subject/object world; its communal and communicative nature; and its role as a cumulative and pluralistic product. The first of these characteristics places particular emphasis on the role of meaning by suggesting that cultural artifacts "would not be what they are without their meanings" (Cahoone, 1988, p. 247). The second highlights not only the conversational or dialogical nature of practice, but more important, that individuals derive their essential characters from relations with and among people. In other words, the individual, including the architect, is *constituted* by relations with other people and artifacts. Finally, the third characteristic of culture highlights both the cumulative quality of cultural products as well as their pluralistic and diverse nature. In other words, technical or expert knowledge established by a dominant group is not privileged in comparison to the tacit and practical knowledge of other subgroups. Both combine to form the cumulative product of a culture.

A further layer of understanding is provided by Rochberg-Halton's discussion of the term cultivation. He defines cultivation as "the web of meaning that is the medium for the self and that is not merely a noun, 'culture,' not merely a static, conventional 'system of symbols'.... Indeed, culture considered as cultivation, is itself 'psychic energy,' because it provides the 'moods and motivations,' the ultimate goals to inspire an individual or group to a given course of action" (Rochberg-Halton, 1986, p. 94). Extrapolating from this activated definition of culture to the domain of architecture suggests how the architect-as-cultivator would be more fully engaged in relations with and among people, and benefited by the cumulative and diverse inheritance of the culture.

Whereas the architect-as-technician responds to the power and autonomy of social and physical forces, the cultivator possesses a "personal perspective," animated by transpersonal interaction and motivated to "express and embody in living acts and artifacts a humanized, cosmically rooted intelligence" (Rochberg-Halton, 1986, p. 110). And similarly, whereas the architect-as-artist too often stands apart from or in opposition to society, the cultivator is fully engaged "in an active process of interpretation reciprocally requiring care and inquiry and endowing one in return with the broader perspective of community life" (Rochberg-Halton, 1986, p. 153).

In many ways, I believe that Rapoport's perspective, which is so strongly influenced by anthropology's emphasis on culture, is in many ways inherently sympathetic to elements of the architect-as-cultivator model as I have sketched it out. Certainly, Rapoport's work places the role of meaning on center stage. Moreover, his insistence on developing a cumulative knowledge base would seem consistent with the third characteristic of culture identified by Cahoone. At the same time, I also infer from Rapoport a greater reliance on expert knowledge through scientific inquiry than on the messy reality of diverse and pluralistic voices. Most important, it is Cahoone's second characteristic--the cultural artifact as a communicative, communal, and public phenomenon--where I think the architect-as-scientist model is especially vulnerable to criticism. In emphasizing the need to achieve predictable results and develop explanatory theory (Rapoport, 1995, p. 34), I believe Rapoport is implicitly promoting a model of a detached, expert not unlike the apparently oppositional architect-as-artist model.

In contrast, recent commentators on architectural practice have emphasized (e.g. Cuff, 1991, Pearson, 1998) the way in which the architect must act as a collaborator with client and user organizations. Yes, results of environment-behavior type studies can establish explanatory theory and predict outcomes for design settings (e.g. Newman, 1973; Whyte, 1980), but more often than not the particularities of a given design project will mean that an architect will need to work through the physical implications of organizational goals in a joint exploration. In other words, the relational practices among the people involved, including their tacit knowledge and systematic investigation of the context, will yield a building that becomes the manifestation of — to use Cuff's term — "negotiated hypotheses" (Cuff, 1991, p.97). Or to invoke, again, Rochberg-Halton's concept of cultivation, the architect must be both *attuned* to the 'psychic energy' of all the parties involved in a particular project and *capable of infusing* his/her own psychic energy into the collective conversation.

An Education for the Architect-as-Cultivator

Some years ago in a book chapter entitled "Through the Looking Glass", Dana Cuff analyzed the results of her interviews with seven prominent New York-based architects, including Peter Eisenman, Hugh Hardy, Steven Holl, and others (Cuff, 1989). The focus of her interview was on the image of the people for whom these architects designed. The most telling aspect of her analysis is that, as a whole, the architects focused either on the level of individual (usually spatial and sensory) perception or on the much broader issues of societal or cultural representation. Hardly any of the architects' commentary had anything to say about the group or organizational level of their clients' experiences or behaviors. As Cuff pointedly argues, the architects' lack of attention to these issues stands in stark contradiction to the fact that most of our lived experience in buildings occur within group settings, the physical design implications of which are often documented in the research literature.

I believe that the most glaring lacuna in architectural education has to do with its lack of attention to relational, interactional, and organizational issues. This applies to both: 1) the interpersonal dynamics and processes entailed in architectural education itself; and 2) a substantive focus on the way in which physical design properties foster or hinder organizational goals. The first of these pertains to issues as diverse as faculty governance and student participation, adequate provisions for student counseling, studio workload expectations for students with family responsibilities, the use of less adversarial jury formats, etc. The second has to with helping students learn to be sensitive to the complex dynamics of organizations for which they may be called to design physical environments, including the relational and interactional practice of the building design process itself.

In a recent article titled "Voices for Change in Architectural Education," Sherry Ahrentzen and I analyzed the results of our in-depth interviews with women faculty in architecture (Groat and Ahrentzen, 1997). In it we identified 7 facets of transformation being articulated by these faculty women; and significantly, these facets were consistent with themes from the recent Carnegie study of architectural education (Boyer and Mitgang, 1996) as well as with Robert Reich's recommendations for the education of advanced knowledge workers in his book, *The Work of Nations* (Reich, 1991). In arguing that our women interviewees were articulating a transformational vision of architecture, we do not mean to suggest that male faculty cannot share in such a role. Rather we argue that women faculty can and should play an important role orchestrating the changes in architectural education that are of critical importance, given the changing context of the profession. Most pertinent to this discussion, the 7 facets of transformation suggest ways in which architectural education might begin to support the architect-as-cultivator model. In one way or another, each facet serves to strengthen the cultural foundation of architecture and the process of cultivation.

In summarizing the seven facets (See Table 8.2), the emphasis here will be on their relevance to the architect-as-cultivator model rather than on either the interview material with faculty women or the gendering of educational perspectives.

1) Strengthening the Ideals of a Liberal Education. Many architectural educators have claimed that architectural education, by virtue of its inherently interdisciplinary nature, is itself a "liberal" education. However, the Carnegie study authors flatly reject that notion (Boyer and Mitgang, 1996). Unfortunately, architecture students' exposure to other disciplines is frequently framed by applicability of those disciplines to architecture. Such an instrumental view runs counter to the very principles of liberal education. The political philosopher, Michael Oakeshott, one of the most frequently quoted authorities on the subject, has characterized liberal education as "an adventure in human understanding" that is "liberated from the distracting business of satisfying contingent wants" (Fuller, 1989). In another passage, he states that "we may recognize liberal learning as, above all else, an education in imagination, an initiation in the art of ...conversation" (Fuller, 1989, p. 38-39). Given that Oakeshott considers the conversation among diverse voices to be the essence of culture, a foundation in liberal education would enable architecture graduates to be prepared to be cultivators of the conversations of cultural discourse.

2) Forging Interdisciplinary Connections. Another frequently cited benefit of architectural education is that its inherent interdisciplinarity fosters a natural meeting ground with its allied disciplines. However, the Carnegie study authors question whether this potential is sufficiently realized in many architectural programs: "Making the connections, both within the architectural curriculum and between architecture and other disciplines is...the single most important challenge confronting architectural programs" (Boyer and Mitgang, 1996, p. 85). The authors recommend two types of initiatives: 1) more flexibly organized curricula so that students can pursue architectural specialties that depend on knowledge bases developed in allied disciplines; and 2) increased connections with noted experts in allied disciplines such as engineers, historians, real estate experts, and the like. Similar to item #1, the result of such initiatives would be to enable architecture students to more fully engage the many of the diverse voices who are fundamental to the building development process.

3) Integrating Different Modes of Thought in Studio. This idea directly addresses the chasm between the presentation of "normative information" in lecture courses and the integrative application of knowledge and practical judgments of design in studio which Beckley describes (Beckley, 1994). As has already been noted, however, recent developments in active learning models in higher education render this distinction a false one; many "lecture" courses can be transformed into settings for integrative discourse and problem-solving (Meyers and Jones, 1993; Montgomery and Groat, 1998). On the other hand, while Boyer and Mitgang are enthusiastic about the potential for studio to incorporate multiple modes of thought, they also recognize that many studios do not currently achieve this integrative potential. What is needed is a far more variegated array of course formats, as well as variations of format within courses, such that integration of thinking and learning modes occur across the board. Such an effort would serve to bridge the existing chasm between "design" and other areas of expertise so that graduates would be more flexible and adept in working with all parties in the building design process.

4) Teaching Beginning Design as a Connection to Other Disciplines. Among the four skills that Robert Reich lists as critical to the education of future knowledge workers, he identifies "abstraction"--which he defines as "discovering patterns and meanings"--as the most basic (Reich, 1991). Knowledge workers must be able to reinterpret and rearrange "the chaos of data" through the use of all manner of symbols, including formulas, models, categories, and metaphors. Certainly, in the ideal studio, this is precisely what happens. To the extent, than, that students from a variety of backgrounds and anticipated career trajectories might be introduced to the visual and spatial abstractions of beginning design, architecture programs may provide an essential foundation for knowledge workers in many fields. Again, this sort of convergence of skills and paths for students of architecture and other disciplines would serve to enhance the larger cultural discourse fundamental to the creation of buildings that are truly cultural artifacts.

5) Forging a Communicative Environment. In discussing the prevailing pedagogical practices and milieu in architecture schools, the Carnegie study identifies the quality of communication as a key ingredient. More specifically, the authors express concern about unconstructive and hurtful examples of studio juries and other forms of student evaluations. Although they acknowledge that the worst abuses have probably been eliminated, they also express concern that "only a minority of design faculty are seriously experimenting with changes in or alternatives to the jury format" (Boyer and Mitgang, 1996, p. 95). Among the many improvements they call for are: the use of more explicit, less mysterious evaluative criteria; and an emphasis on process as well as product. Earlier in this chapter, I already mentioned the high priority students in Professor Ahrentzen's and my research placed on clear evaluative criteria (Groat and Ahrentzen, 1996). Secondly, the issue of process I take to mean, not just the designer's individual creative process, but the dialogic process of "negotiated hypotheses" that Cuff identifies (Cuff, 1991). Thus, we come to yet another initiative that would insure that the pedagogical environment provide a better model of the kind of "conversational" process that is central to "cultivating" the creation of a culture's shared artifacts.

6) *Collaboration.* The importance of collaboration in all types of work settings has been the topic of much discussion in various business and professional contexts. For example, in Reich's analysis of the four basic skills for educating knowledge workers, he argues that such people typically work in teams, often in playful ways that facilitate the discovery of problems and solutions unknowable in advance. They also must communicate their working concepts and, just as important, then seek consensus to go forward with the plan. "Instead of individual achievement and competition, the focus [should be] on group learning." Unfortunately, these skills are frequently not emphasized in higher education, including architecture. Although many architecture schools may well have increased the relative amount of team work in studio, discussion of and reflection about how teams work and succeed is largely lacking. And the individual project is still commonly seen as the norm. Again, without sufficient attention to the collaborative process among architects, with other professionals, and in relation to the larger community the conversation that constitutes the culture will remain under-developed.

7) *Fostering the Growth of the Whole Student.* Among the numerous criticisms of the current state of higher education, a significant one is the extent to which faculty and administrators fail to nurture the whole person, or even to address the developing personhood of the undergraduate student (Wilshire, 1990). Similarly, recent developments in the business realm have raised questions about the extent workers are typically discouraged from bringing their whole selves, including their spiritual consciousness, to work (Barrett, 1998). In the realm of architectural education, the Carnegie study also raises similar questions--not only regarding inadequate counseling and lack of attention to non-traditional students (problems that may occur in many disciplines), but especially architecture's peculiar tendency to rely on an "endurance test" model. The Carnegie study asks: "Are

Table 8.2: Transforming Architectural Education in Support of the Architect-as-Cultivator

Transformative Initiatives	**Supporting Articles**
The Architect-As-Cultivator model	Groat, 1992; 1993
7 Facets of Transformation in Architectural Education	Groat & Ahrentzen, 1996; 1997
1. *Strengthening the Ideals of a Liberal Education*	Boyer & Mitgang, 1996 Oakeshott in Fuller, 1989
2. *Forging Interdisciplinary Connections*	Boyer & Mitgang, 1996
3. *Integrating Different Modes of Thought in Studio*	Boyer & Mitgang, 1996 Meyers & Jones, 1993 Montgomery & Groat, 1998
4. *Teaching Design to Connect to Other Disciplines*	Reich, 1991
5. *Forging a Communicative Environment*	Boyer & Mitgang, 1996 Cuff, 1991
6. *Collaboration*	Reich, 1991
7. *Fostering the Growth of the Whole Student*	Barrett, 1998 Wilshire,1990

schools of architecture truly producing 'problem solvers,' ...if students have little time to pause and reflect on the deeper meanings of what they are learning?" (Boyer and Mitgang, p. 106).

The Carnegie study authors go on to emphasize in their concluding chapter the role of education in the development of the whole person, and ultimately of a healthy society: "In the end, education's most essential mission is to develop within each student the capacity not only to build with competence, but to judge wisely in matters of life and conduct. (p. 142.) Expanding that theme to consider the relation of graduate architects to the larger society, they conclude:

> Graduates should be knowledgeable *teachers* and *listeners*, prepared to talk with clarity and understanding to clients and communities about how architecture might contribute to creating not just better buildings, but a more wholesome and happy human condition for present and future generations. Schools of architecture, in other words, should educate students for both *competence* and *caring* — in service to the nation (Boyer and Mitgang, p. 129).

Concluding Remarks: Addressing Rapoport's Points of Critique

In concluding this chapter, I would like to take us back to the beginning of the story: Amos Rapoport's impassioned critique of architectural education. My argument for the architect-as-cultivator model — embodied in the seven points of transformation just outlined — does not respond to the six specific points of Rapoport's critique in a direct one-to-one fashion. This is because the proposed initiatives are based on a different set of premises than either the "traditional" educational model or Rapoport's alternative. Nevertheless, I believe the seven initiatives I've outlined do, in combination, cut across the issues Rapoport raised.

The relationship between Rapoport's points of critique and the seven proposed initiatives are represented schematically in Table 8.3.[5] For example, the centrality of design in 'traditional' architectural education can be effectively countered by substantively incorporating: a more diverse set of insights from allied disciplines, different modes of thought (through more variegated pedagogy), and interdisciplinary teams working in collaboration. Likewise, Rapoport's call for an

Table 8.3 Addressing Rapoport's Critique via the Seven Points of Transformation*

Rapoport Critiques	Points of Transformation						
	Liberal Education	Interdisci-plinary Connection	Different modes of thought	Connection to others	Communicative Environment	Collaboration	Growth of Whole Student
Centrality of design		X	X			X	
Lack of knowledge base	X	X			X		
Lack of evaluative criteria					X		
Perpetuation of invalid model			X		X	X	X
Misplaced belief in studio			X	X		X	X
What & why instead of how	X				X	X	X

*I would like to thank Keith Diaz Moore both for his suggestion that I develop such a matrix and his initiative in formulating of first draft of it.

emphasis on 'why' instead of 'how' could be achieved through: a deeper understanding of values inherent through the process of liberal education, a more communicative environment that emphasizes process, collaboration with client and interdisciplinary teams, and a focus on the whole student whereby personal, group, and community values are reassessed. Although it would be possible to work through the rest of the matrix, this level of detail is not critical to the more general point; Rapoport's critique is indeed addressed through a combination of these seven elements of transformation.

More important, the preceding seven initiatives have been identified as key starting points--not an exhaustive list--for transforming architectural education in ways that would support the architect-as-cultivator model. Indeed, there may well be a variety of other aspects of curricular content and pedagogical principles that could be usefully strengthened or reconsidered. What is crucial is a clearly-articulated emphasis on preparing students to learn the essence of civic engagement, to be prepared for the conversational practice of cultural enhancement.

Notes

1 Because the first segments of this chapter are intended to be personal in honoring Amos Rapoport, I have referred to him by his first name. Since the remainder of the chapter is written in more typical academic style, I have used his surname.

2 The other 5 characteristics which she analyzes are: the role of design, participants, dynamics, product, and stakes. Like the academy, the professional society model is accurate in only one of these, but in this case it is the "stakes" which are "significant to many."

3 Prof. Brian Coppola at University of Michigan has substantially revised the introductory chemistry course to incorporate elements of active learning such that he refers to some aspects of the course as reflecting a "studio" format.

4 Cahoone's choice of terminology for the "rationalist" perspective is a very specific use of the term to refer to the 17th century philosophers such as Descartes, Spinoza, and Leibniz, who believed that the nature of the world could be established by wholly *non-empirical* demonstrative reasoning [A. Bullock and O. Stallybrass (ed.) (1977) *The Fontana Dictionary of Modern Thought*. London: Fontana/Collins]. Rapoport's use of the term "rational" to describe the design of molecules or drugs appears to be a more general usage, synonymous with systematic.

5 I would like to thank Keith Diaz Moore both for his suggestion that I develop such a matrix and his initiative in formulating of first draft of it.

References

Ahrentzen, S. and L. Groat (1992) "Rethinking Architectural Education: Patriarchal Conventions and Alternative Visions from the Perspective of Faculty Women." *Journal of Architectural and Planning Research* 9/2: 95-111.

Anthony, K. (1991) *Design Juries on Trial: The Renaissance of the Design Studio.* New York, NY: Van Nostrand Reinhold.

Barrett, R. (1998) *Liberating the Corporate Soul.* Boston, MA: Butterworth Heinemann.

Beckley, R. (1984) "The studio is where a professional architect learns to make judgments." *Architectural Record* October: 101; 105.

Boyer, E. and L. Mitgang (1996) *Building Community: A New Future for Architecture Education and Practice.* Princeton, NJ: Carnegie Foundation.

Cahoone, L. (1988) *The Dilemma of Modernity: Philosophy, Culture, and Anti-Culture.* Albany, NY: State University of New York Press.

Cuff, D. (1989) "Through the Looking Glass." in R. Ellis and D. Cuff (Eds.) *Architects' People.* New York, NY: Oxford University Press.

Cuff, D. (1991) *Architecture: The Story of Practice.* Cambridge, MA: MIT Press.

Fisher, T. (1994) "Can This Profession Be Saved?" *Progressive Architecture* 2/94: 44-49; 84.

Fuller, T. (Ed.) (1989) *The Voice of Liberal Learning: Michael Oakeshott on Education.* New Haven, CT: Yale University Press.

Groat, L. (1993) "Rescuing Architecture from the Cul-de-Sac." *Journal of Architectural Education* 45/3: 138-146.

Groat, L. (1994) "Architecture's Resistance to Diversity: A Matter of Theory as Much as Practice." *Journal of Architectural Education* 47/1: 3-10.

Groat, L. and Ahrentzen, S. (1996) "Reconceptualizing Architectural Education for a More Diverse Future: Perceptions and Visions of Architectural Students." *Journal of Architectural Education* 49/3: 166-183.

Groat. L. and S. Ahrentzen (1997) "Voices for Change in Architectural Education: Seven Facets of Transformation from the Perspective of Faculty Women." *Journal of Architectural Education* 50/4: 271-285.

Meyers, C. and T. Jones (1993) *Promoting Active Learning: Strategies for the College Classroom.* San Francisco, CA: Jossey-Bass Publishers.

Montgomery, S. and L. Groat (1999) *"Student Learning Styles and Their Implications for Teaching."* CRLT Occasional Papers 10 Ann Arbor, MI: Center for Research on Learning and Teaching, University of Michigan.

Newman, O. (1973) *Defensible Space.* New York, NY: Macmillan.

Pearson, C. (1998) "How to succeed with Expanded Services." *Architectural Record* 1/98: 50-55.

Rapoport, A. (1984) " Architectural education: There is an urgent need to reduce or eliminate the dominance of the studio." *Architectural Record* October: 110; 103.

Rapoport, A. (1995) "The Nature of Design." *Practices* 3/4: 33-43.

Reich. R. (1991) *The Work of Nations.* New York, NY: Alfred A. Knopf.

Rochberg-Halton, E. (1986) *Meaning and Modernity: Social Theory in Pragmatic Attitude.* Chicago, IL: University of Chicago Press.

Sutton, S. (1992) "Power, Knowledge and the Art of Leadership." *Progressive Architecture* 5/92: 65-68.

Toulmin, S. (1990) *Cosmopolis: The Hidden Agenda of Modernity.* New York, NY: Free Press.

Whyte, W. (1980) *The Social Life of Small Urban Spaces.* Washington, DC: The Conservation Foundation.

Wilshire, B. (1990) *The Moral Collapse of the University.* Albany, NY: State University of New York Press.

9 Studious Questions, Studio Responses

Wesley Janz

***Monday, August 24, 1998:* "THIRD YEAR STUDIO MEETS IN 318 IN TEN MINUTES! BE THERE!"**

Day one of the 1998-99 school year at Ball State University. Muncie, Indiana. I conclude a college-wide meeting with the above exhortation.

ARCH(itecture) 301: Third Year Design Studio. The students seem ready. They better be ready — we all know this is the most trying semester of their most taxing year.

Each of my students will design a 75,000-square-foot federal courthouse, courtroom, and bus shelter for downtown Indianapolis. It is, I believe, a good challenge. A courthouse is a civic building filled with symbolism, complicated by circulation concerns. The courts also provide an interdisciplinary lens through which to compare the legal and architectural professions.

The law is everywhere. Grisham alone, bestsells *The Firm, The Pelican Brief, A Time to Kill, The Rainmaker, The Runaway Jury, The Client, The Chamber,* and *The Partner*. Judge Judy rules, and the show's sponsors pay any monetary awards. On MTV, Fiona Apple pleads "What I need is a good defense 'cause I feel just like a criminal." President Clinton is deposed "live." Independent Counsel Starr refers, but does not advocate (he claims), to the U.S. House Judiciary Committee. "The Practice" with hunky Dylan McDermott wins Best Drama Emmy for ABC-TV. This month, Travolta (on *Redbook* cover), Duvall, and Lithgow promote the movie version of Jonathon Harr's *A Civil Action.*

Plus, the law is under construction everywhere. According to the January 1996 issue of *Architecture* magazine, in the next decade 156 new federal courthouses will be constructed across the nation — in Concord, Fargo, Las Vegas, New York City, San Diego, Scranton, Tallahassee and other American cities — at a cost of $8 billion.

Most Americans have opinions about lawyers, have been near a lawsuit, and know something of the law thanks to "Law and Order," "L.A. Law," and "Ally McBeal." The combination of attitude, familiarity, misinformation and construction activity will provide fertile ground for the students.

According to a recent Carnegie Foundation report, the design studio is the *place* where architecture students spend as much as ninety percent of their time and energy, the *product* that is the tangible result of thinking about and making architecture, and the *process* through which elements, possibilities, and constraints of architectural knowledge are integrated (Boyer and Mitgang, 1996).

The studio's fundamental structure is relatively constant: "The instructor poses a problem (site and program established) and then works individually with students as they develop their solutions" (Cuff, 1991, p. 63). Masters model appropriate behavior, values, design strategies, and thought processes--what some scholars have termed "the hidden curriculum"--for their apprentices (Anthony, 1991).

Wednesday, August 26: According to my class, in a good studio, students ask constructive questions and respect other's property, time, space, and ideas. They get work done and do not waste the instructor's time. As their teacher, I should be available, contribute ideas, and know them personally. We discuss design processes, issues, and products. A former student of mine explains his design intentions and related activities.

I add: students identify critical issues, pursue multiple solutions, and make clear recommendations. I present "good" work done by previous students. Architecture, I say, is more than a material act; architects create buildings within social, economic, and political settings. Passion. I want passion. I want them to care deeply about the project, about what they do, say, think, and make.

Studious Questions: Amos Rapoport, in his "Studious Questions" article, attacks the design studio. Too much time is dedicated to *how* something is to be done, not enough time on *what* to do and *why* to do it. No valid theory of design exists. Who can claim mastery in the master-apprentice system? To what extent should one's experience be emphasized? What about other analyses architects do--writing reports, attending meetings--that studios ignore? What of synthesis, setting priorities, trade-offs, and integration? Why not replace the heroic model of the single architect-designer? (Rapoport, 1983).

Rapoport is not alone. "The problem (with the design studio) is its limited focus and unstructured content," writes Louis Sauer, "the student implicitly learns that (courses in professional practice, construction, management and development, or environmental psychology) are not important to design" (Sauer, 1993, p.77).

Thomas Heath goes farther: the student "learns to avoid" the testing of building plans and aesthetic ideas against available methods of construction or information provided by the sciences (Heath, 1984).

Sharon Sutton believes the studio's preeminence affects the quality, workload, and productivity of faculty: long studio hours relegate scholarly work to moonlight status which results in lowered research output and less time and support for research (Sutton 1992).

Friday, August 28: In studio, teams of two students, "Expert Teams," assume semester-long responsibility for a primary courthouse space (judges' chambers, jury deliberation rooms, and the like). We walk the project site, virtually, via on-line camera. Finally, we study strategies for organizing sites and buildings (Ching, 1979).

First year architecture students at Ball State share design studios with landscape architecture and planning students. Year Two features dedicated architecture studios and two semesters of architectural history and structures.

Third year studios are to integrate "all facets of design including design, research, programming, technology, function, human behavior, scheduling, time management, communication, use of materials, and systems" (Ball State University Undergraduate Catalog, 1998, p. 103). What "all facets" means is a question; the definition of design includes design; research is, at best, information-gathering; faculty typically provide building programs; and students are just learning building technology and environmental systems so integration into studio is difficult. But we try.

In Year 4, students work as interns in architectural offices for one-half the calendar year. Fifth year architecture students complete a design thesis that includes a written report documenting their design process and product.

Tuesday, September 1: The department chairman meets with Year Coordinators (like me, for the program's third year) and program directors. "Knowledge" and "skills" are central.

Later, a dictionary:

> Knowledge: the fact or condition of knowing something with familiarity gained through experience or association; the circumstance or condition of apprehending truth or fact. Skill: the ability to use one's knowledge effectively and readily in execution or performance; a learned power of doing something completely. (Mish, F. Ed. 1989, Webster's Ninth New Collegiate Dictionary)

In third year studios, best case scenario, concerns for human beings, technology, and practice issues are integrated, for the first time, with the articulation of a site and building. Is this the "apprehension of truth"? Probably not. The beginning of "doing something completely"? Of using "one's knowledge effectively"? Yes. Of knowing "through experience and association"? Again, yes. We are responsible, still, for basic skills: not only problem setting and information gathering, but drawing techniques, modeling software, model building craft, and more.

Some numbers. 103: number of third year students. 150: percent increase in third year students over each of the past three years. 6: architecture classes for each student this semester (studio, structures, environmental systems, building technology, modern architecture, and portfolio preparation in the fall, internship preparation in the spring). 1: portfolios submitted by each third year student following semester break; this document determines whether students advance toward the professional degree, advance with restrictions, or leave the program with a non-professional degree.

103, 9, 6: third year students, faculty, and teaching assistants I oversee as Year Coordinator. 101: students in the introductory course I teach (with no assistance). 18: students in my studio section. 17: my student contact hours per week. 5: days I teach per week. 4: classes I teach this semester. 4, 3: number of undergraduate and graduate thesis students I advise. 2.5: hours I drive per day. 2: tenure years I have completed. 0: my non teaching days in the past 3.5 school years. 0: hours I am loaded to conduct research this year.

As Sutton suggests, it can be a vicious cycle.

Friday, September 4: In studio, each student will make explicit his or her Project Goals, Project Objectives, and Project Intentions so he or she, and others, can construct appropriate Criteria for Evaluation. Expert Teams review classmates' building and room arrangements.

Wednesday, September 9: 3:00 A.M. wake-up. Five cars to the Cranbrook Educational Community (near Detroit) by noon. We tour Eliel Saarinen's buildings and landscape, and Steven Holl's Institute of Science addition. In Toronto, Ontario hotel at 8.00 P. M.

Studious Questions: "[I]t seems quite clear that the question of *what* to do receives least attention--the initial idea is developed rapidly using little information and research but it also rarely changes much. This fundamental decision is based on the designers' experience which, they believe, is best obtained by *doing* one's own design. Most time is devoted to refinement, minor matters of detail, small changes, choosing materials; in other words, the stress in on the *how*. The teaching of design tends to perpetuate this manner of working" (Rapoport, 1983, p. 56).

Studio Responses: In this studio, students determine what it is they should do, what problems each will set, what intentions he or she will explicitly state. Each will take weeks to make these determinations. The courthouse and courtroom portion of the semester will last thirteen weeks. Students will consider why, what, and how questions; they will explore and discover on their terms, and mine. They will not rush to initial ideas. At the same time, their preconceptions and inspirations can not be ignored and should be encouraged. In point, I will cause them, force them, to reconsider their initial preconceptions, experiences, and intentions.

The conference on courthouse design that we attend provides insights from judges, lawyers, courthouse administrators, technology experts, architectural professors, and architects through which we will consider the law, plaintiffs, defendants, courthouses, and courtrooms. In addition, each student will interview a conference architect-presenter. Note: we are certainly the largest, if not the only, student-faculty group in attendance.

Thursday, September 10: Toronto, Ontario: The Third International Conference on Courthouse Design. Robert Peck, U. S. General Services Administration: "people submit to mediation," experience the "impartial judging of disputes" in courthouses. Robert Rae, former Premier of Ontario: society is becoming less equal, not more; does this impact justice design? Courthouses should offer permanence in a world of change, be places of education, and reflect many forms of mediation.

Mr. Justice Ian Binnie of the Supreme Court of Canada: the defendant about to lose a case must view the process as legitimate. Binnie offers six performance objectives: a courthouse must be practical; reflect the independence of the administration of authority; express the legal process; be a place of peace, quiet, and serenity; demonstrate the legal system's roots; and evidence the fallibility of the architect and the law.

Architect Jack Diamond. Get to the essence. Ask good questions. Study the past. Define clients inclusively, they "drive" design. A project's qualitative aspects are the "real meat." I eat bad Chinese by myself.

Friday, September 11: Professor Larry Wayne Richards of the University of Toronto challenges architects to develop "unique and engaging positions," asks "What are the questions"? and argues that they should be architectural, political, and social. Robert Campbell of *The Boston Globe*: civic architecture must belong to a tradition that it continues into the future.

Saturday, September 12: Back home, again, to Indiana. Along the way, Gehry's addition to the Art Museum of Toledo. I'm in Indianapolis at 8:00 P.M. Exhausted.

Monday, September 14: In studio, we review the courthouse design conference, each student cites: five insights to remember, most important moment, and a key quote. Expert Teams report. Thank you sent to Diamond. I overview centralized, linear, radial, clustered, and grid building schemes (Ching, 1979), show examples; students sketch versions, review other's work, and note promising approaches. Each will construct a "violator" model that challenges five key spatial relations; I want them to question the project's givens, to find their own insights.

This semester, for the first time, I teach ARCH 552: Architectural Research. The class will provide foundational material for next semester's third year studios. Faculty for the spring semester studios agree on several elements. First, each studio section will focus on one large building project to study technological aspects of big volumes. Second, all studio sections will site major projects in downtown Fort Wayne, Indiana to consider the urban condition and the potential to have various studios' projects relate to each other. Third, each studio section will "partner" with an architecture firm in Fort Wayne; practitioners will critique student efforts, share professional insights, and reveal the links between school and offices. Fourth, the final review will engage local organizations and the general community.

Wednesday, September 16: Up at 4:00 A.M., in Fort Wayne with graduate students by 9:00. We walk the downtown, drive in suburbs, convene for lunch at Cindy's Diner, and meet with a practitioner.

Monday, September 21: In studio, "violators." I focus on each violation, the resulting project intentions, and shift discussions to Expert Teams.

Wednesday, September 23: Steel, concrete, and precast concrete structural systems (plans and sections) presented in studio. Later, a Paul Hawken lecture on "Natural Capitalism."

Friday, September 25: In ARCH 301, Nolli's Map of Rome illustrates connections between the city, thresholds and doors, and major interior spaces of buildings.

Tuesday, September 29: A.M.: studio at our house for breakfast. Site visit and federal courthouse tour. P.M.: closing arguments in a murder trial in city-county building; tour of Supreme Court chambers. Four hours to New Harmony, Indiana. It's night, quiet. We climb Meier's Atheneum like it's a giant jungle gym, gather on the roof spontaneously, laughing, whispering. Johnson's Roofless Church; indiscernible building forms and gardens. We stay at the New Harmony Inn, designed by Evans Woollen.

Wednesday, September 30: At 9:30 A.M. we're all over the Atheneum, again, discussing environmental systems, daylighting, purism, Le Corbusier, the Getty Center. Later, the Warrick County Courthouse in Boonville. A half-circle dominates the courtroom: witness and jury at arc ends, judge at midpoint. Judge Hendrickson gives tour of new courthouse under construction. Then, to Paoli. A locked courthouse, but third floor door is ajar. Wild: jury sits beneath judge's bench; all face witness stand and spectators. Almost any courtroom design seems viable; now I can push students' intentions into the courtroom itself.

We've seen five courthouses and courtrooms, notable pieces of architecture, and interviewed a law clerk and judge. Overnight. Indianapolis at 8:30 P.M.

> **Studious Questions:** "Most of us who have gone through years of design studio, and who might have taught it, know how much time is wasted in the studio, how much time is spent chatting and playing cards. Serious thought and research are needed to determine how much time is required to achieve certain objectives which are supposed to be achieved in the studio" (Rapoport, 1983, p.56).
>
> **Studio Responses:** The social aspect of design studios and the design process can not be diminished. I chat with students, all students, but especially those in my studio, seeking to know them as individuals, to help them know me and each other better, to assist them in seeing my passion for knowledge regarding the built environment and the processes that bring it into being. We ride in cars together, play table tennis, debate the relative merits of NASCAR drivers, visit art galleries and eat Chinese food together, all in the pursuit of the best work possible. In this environment, it becomes more difficult to separate work from play.
>
> I initiate chatting, playing, and working. Such support is critical if I am to challenge the students to aspire, take risks, and succeed on terms they never imagined, both in their studies today and careers tomorrow.

Friday, October 2: To Fort Wayne with graduate students. Interviews with a bus company administrator, arts community leader, and parks department staffperson. The Yugoslavian student-couple interviews a coffee shop owner, wait persons, coffee drinkers, and collect eight surveys they sent out earlier. Another student sits in

Cindy's Diner talking to customers, and of course, Cindy. One serves lunch at a homeless shelter, another works at the historical society. I listen to pretrial hearings in the county courthouse, two students and I lunch with the architect who will work with my studio next semester. In Muncie, studio convenes without me.

In the van coming back I ask: Why are you talking with these persons? What are you researching? What voices are credible?

Monday, October 5: Desk crits in studio. I encourage one student to push the design's form; it's too loose, needs rigor. I ask one young woman to integrate technology. Another student has significant health problems, is far behind. A fourth probes differences between objectives and concepts. I suggest a fifth move from sketching to modeling; he's too reliant on drawings. A sixth changed her design after our field trip; I applaud her responsiveness. A seventh re-aligns for the worse; heavy-handedness has replaced precision and subtlety. I move her back to an earlier idea. An eighth can't explain his design, has misplaced his list of intentions, is confused, won't let me teach. I ask a ninth to explore the structural system as an organizing device, that building spaces be placed in relation to the design's massive trusses. That's one-half the class covered in one exhausting studio session.

Friday, October 9: A student's design work is going badly. I do something I've never done before: I ask her to step aside, then take a position at her drafting table and begin drawing as I question her thinking and the work.

Me: *What scale is this?*

Her: 3/32, I think.

Me: *I've never used that scale in my life.*

Her: Well, my plan fits on my trace.

Me: *Buy bigger tracing paper. Use a more conventional scale, 1/8 or 1/4. What's this? A wall? What is a wall? Walls have thickness. Why do you indicate walls with one line?*

Her: I'm just indicating spaces.

Me: *You're designing a building, not a diagram. How is a wall built? . . . Draw walls like this, doors and door swings like this. Why is the courtroom so conventional, so symmetrical?*

Her: I'm showing equality under the law. Everything is centered. ***Me:*** *Okay. Let's draw the spectator benches, the judge's bench, the attorneys' tables, the witness area. Where are they? . . . Here's how to draw them (lots of pencil, parallel rule, and triangle activity) . . . Let's draw a longitudinal section and a main elevation. . . What kind of structure? . . . Where is it? . . . Why that structural system? . . . How will you move conditioned air through the space? . . . Why that way? . . . What about daylighting? Is there any? . . . Why? . . . Where should it shine? . . . Why there? . . . Show a skylight in the reflected ceiling plan. . . Your eraser smears. Get rid of tools that don't work. (I put the eraser in my pocket.)*

I can't tell if I helped or hurt her, or both. I feel like an ogre, but a drastic intervention seemed in order. I'll see.

Saturday, October 10-Tuesday, October 13: Fall Break. I visit two former students in Los Angeles; take a pillow and blanket, sleep on their couch. Projects by Ehrlich, Gehry, HHPA, Isozaki, Morphosis, Moss, Prince, and Serra. The Getty Center by Meier. Watch TV (one is a Michael J. Fox fan). Have dinner with alums working at Morphosis and Gehry offices, and much more. WOW!

Wednesday, October 14: Studio: tour of Alumni Center (Architect: Pei Cobb Freed) led by environmental systems professor. The equipment that conditions air, warms water, and provides electricity is explained, and touched. Later, the instructor discusses Pei Cobb Freed, a firm for whom he worked for eight years. Sixty third year students attend, as do I.

> **Studious Questions:** "I would argue that most studios are not even aware of the range of variables and most of what is taught in other courses is forgotten upon passing the sacred portals of the studio" (Rapoport, 1983, p. 56).
>
> **Studio Responses:** Such content segregation, typically, does not happen in our year level. One professor teaches second semester structures and brings that perspective to her studio. Two instructors

co-teach building technology; their studios feature such concerns. One studio faculty teaches professional practice, another is an adjunct faculty member maintaining an active practice; both integrate professional concerns into their studios. Our six studios meet in one massive room — no walls — so faculty and students overlap, intermingle, question, and learn from each other.

I bring the environmental systems, structures, and history faculty into my studio for desk crits, studio crits, and final reviews. As studio instructor and Year Coordinator, I endeavor to layer, to integrate, so a design studio field trip to a Pei Cobb Freed building is framed as a technology exploration that is given a professional practice twist for these aspiring intern-architects.

In addition, throughout the semester I bring in fourth year students (former third year students of mine) who I assisted in finding internships at the Hodgetts + Fung, Eric Owen Moss, Moore Ruble Yudell, and Killefer Flammang and Purtill architectural offices in Los Angeles. I want this group, one year ahead of my studio, to act as role models, as mentors, as inspirations.

Also, I admit, I want the younger students to see what good things might happen to them if they work hard and do good work in my studio.

Monday, October 19: Architectural Research meets for three hours outside regular class to discuss report. Me: What do we know? What do we need to find out? What studio project ideas do we have? What of the case study reports we critiqued in class?

Tuesday, October 20: The practitioner with whom I will work next semester (a former graduate student of mine) introduces me to his wife, a "teacher of the year" in Fort Wayne. She suggests we present findings to the Leadership Fort Wayne group of which she's a part.

Wednesday, October 21: In 301, each student consults four Expert Teams. During the consultations, each notes two design aspects the Expert Team cites as successfully resolved, two design aspects in need of attention, and what the designer will do in response. I facilitate only. It goes well; a steady dialogue. I ask them about their roles as reviewers and experts, what caused them to better understand some designs than others, and what evidences development from last year to this year.

> **Studious Questions:** "In effect, the studio presupposes that apprentices learn from a master--it perpetuates the archaic master-apprentice system no matter how disguised. This has several problems. Lacking clear evaluation criteria, there is no way of defining who is a 'master,' what constitutes mastery, or what one is master of. This system also nullifies what I think design should be and the essence of university teaching--a stress on ideas, theory and knowledge rather than personality, for example" (Rapoport, 1983, p. 56).
>
> **Studio Responses:** Mastery, as I define it for the students, means that by mid-semester each Expert Team member must know more about his/her area of expertise than I do. It is common for me to ask students to give each other specific input during the semester. They, with me, determine the relative success or failure of the class, their individual projects, and the efforts of their classmates.
>
> Of what am I a master? Others have, and the works of others are, more suitable answers than any I might provide.
>
> I am willing to say of what I am not a master, and that is the "single architect/designer" model "Studious Questions" criticizes: "It is likely we need a whole range of people with different skills--hyphenated architects, as it were: architect-programmers, architect-evaluators, architect-researchers, architect-theoreticians" (Rapoport, 1983, p. 57).

Expert Teams. Attention to architects, lawyers, defendants, and judges. "Violator" challenges to the building program. Information gathering. Problem setting. Beautifully crafted models. Infusion of Form Z modeling software.

I give up single architect "mastery" willingly, and in so doing, share the studio with the students. They see that I often do not know, that I value the knowledge and input of others, that I am passionate about architecture on my terms, not those of a misleading myth. That is the behavior I model.

Thursday, Friday, and Saturday; October 22, 23, and 24: Professor David Rockwood of Pratt Institute teaches three eight-hour Form Z training sessions. Seventy-eight students participate, pay $50 apiece. All year levels. I plan, host, facilitate.

Monday, October 26: Guest critic in another studio. Two, three, sometimes four faculty review student work. While good discussion occurs, we repeat comments, one person talks while others listen, few students attend. Seems inefficient, unproductive. The primary studio faculty member does a lot of talking; at times I wonder why I was invited. I do not meet with my studio.

Wednesday, October 28: Two letters. The first, to Judge Randall Shepard, the Chief Justice of the Indiana Supreme Court, invites him to critique the students' courthouse and courtroom designs. All the students sign the letter; how can he say "No"? The second, to Judge Hendrickson of Boonville, invites him to adjudicate the students' designs.

Thursday, October 29: 3:30 A.M. call. Grad students with me to the University of Michigan (four-hour drive). Discussion with Professor and Dean Emeritus Robert Beckley on University of Michigan master plan articulated by Robert Venturi and Denise Scott Brown; presentation by doctoral student Nancy Wells on research questions, methods, and results, and a lecture by Sheila Kennedy of the Kennedy Violich architectural firm. Home at 1:30 A.M.

Monday, November 2: In studio, time management. Big review in three weeks. What remains to be done? How to be most effective with remaining weeks?

Friday, November 6: Chief Justice Shepard's receptionist: he'll review the student work at 3:00 P.M. in the Indiana State Capitol building on Friday, December 11. Y-E-S!

Monday, November 9: Judge Hendrickson: yes, he wants to review student work and will be in Indianapolis on December 11. Did I know that 162 circuit and superior court judges are meeting in Indianapolis on December 10 and 11? I telephone the Indiana Judicial Center: my students will bring courtroom models to conference hotel for the judges' review.

Wednesday, November 11: I accompany thirty-six third year students to a precast concrete manufacturing plant in Ohio and to the construction site of the Center for 21st Century Science and Industry in Columbus, Ohio as designed by Isozaki. Studio faculty encourage students to attend even though the day-long field trip is held on a studio day.

Friday, November 13: To UW-Milwaukee to deliver the lecture: "My Dinners With Amos: Lessons Learned, Lessons Now Taught." I summarize the "Studious Questions" piece, present studio work from previous semesters, raise criticisms, and conclude with the lessons I learned from Rapoport that I teach my students. Lesson: Ask not only how to build a building, but why a building is to be built, what the building is intended to do, and for whom a building is being built. Lesson: As you ask critical questions of others, encourage others to challenge your work, ideas, key terms, and knowledge. This is the true nature of interdisciplinary work: to question and be questioned. Lesson: While design can be, and should be, a highly personal activity, making buildings, shaping the built environment, is a material and social act. Study and practice negotiation, teamwork, and communication. Lesson: Know as much as you can about your profession and discipline; be responsible. Balance this authoritative position with an open awareness of what you don't know; be curious.

A question: how do my studio students fare in the professional world? My answer, in essence: until the profession values asking critical questions of itself and others, setting intentions clearly, and designing quality environments, well-prepared graduates will encounter working environments marked by avoidance, quick compromise, mediocrity, and little passion. Very simply, the manner in which we educate students of architecture must change AND the ways of the profession must also change. Professors must ask critical questions of students AND practitioners must ask critical questions of themselves regarding why they became architects, what is it they love to do, the sorts of clients with which they should work. Too often, architects, architecture students, and architecture professors avoid the larger social, economic, and political forces that shape both the built environment AND the work of architects.

My students will not "fare in the professional world." In this sense, I am not interested in getting along. My students will change the professional world to represent their engaged, critical, and personal perspectives.

Friday, November 20: Three graduate students to Fort Wayne. They participate in a grade school workshop and speak with a newspaper reporter who has learned of our plans.

Sunday, November 22: I'm at school for ten hours, helping studio students organize their final presentation materials, statements, and last hours. A quick meeting to discuss presentation. I stress THUMP! I want the students to make an emotional connection that flows from the reviewers' hearts to the student's design. Before I leave, they all must leave; I want them to get a full night's sleep.

Studious Questions: "One of the things wrong with most schools of architecture and which affects the profession is the absence of scholarship, research and publication compared to other disciplines. Part of the reason for this is lack of time — what little is done is often in one's own time. One can only do scholarly work if there is uninterrupted time for it — and that can only happen if that most wasteful method of teaching in terms of time — the studio — is reduced. One does not have time to sit around with students, do desk crits, repeat the same thing to each student, go through project after project in juries, again repeating the same things, and deal with trivial subjective matters which cannot be judged" (Rapoport, 1983, p. 57).

Studio Responses: The design studio provides for faculty members "a marvellous [*sic*] way to spend a career, helping young people to develop such [special ways] of thinking" (Broadbent, 1995, p. 23).

I love teaching, love seeing that I can affect students' lives, careers, and world views. Love their ability to change me, what I think, see, and value. It is, as Broadbent purrs, marvelous.

I recently completed a doctoral dissertation (Janz, 1995, University of Michigan). Such a commitment of energy and time represents a complementary love, that of scholarship, research, and publication. This is a love that is denied this school year, and most.

My first four years of teaching experience parallels the worst case scenario profiled in the *Junior Faculty Handbook on Tenure and Promotion:* "Frequently, junior faculty are overly assigned committee duties, heavy student counseling and new course preparation, thereby leaving little time for creative and scholarly activities" (Greenstreet and Malecha, 1995, p. 13).

One does not have time, I do not have time, to do scholarly work, to conduct original research, to publish. If a teacher/scholar's research program does not fit closely with one's studio teaching agenda, as is my situation, then while one "sits around" with studio

> students, concerns for and abilities to conduct research not only recede, they disappear.

Monday, November 23: The final review for ARCH 301. Teams of two to five jurors listen to each student present their work for fifteen minutes, then ask questions and make comments for thirty minutes. Students exhibit work done the previous thirteen weeks: short reports written, early sketches and cardboard models, photographs from the field trip. We occupy two floors of the building's main corridor--hundreds will see this work.

We began at 9:00 A. M. with the first student, finish at 4:45 P. M. with the eighteenth student. I say very little, if anything; the students are on their own. Three faculty members, eight graduate students, and ten undergraduate students (including two from first year) serve as reviewers.

The work is generally well received. The first student begins by explaining her information-gathering, then speaks of her five design intentions: 1) no secrets, 2) the importance of the jury, 3) to create a building with recognizable organization, 4) to feature a procession, and 5) to cause people to feel the weight of the law. She goes on to describe her site, building, and courtroom design. Very nice. Another adds THUMP; he tells of a recent church sermon in which the minister spoke of the aeropagus, the mountain retreat to which wise men withdrew to contemplate life above the crazy marketplace below, and why this metaphor best explains his design intentions. A faculty reviewer summarizes the critique: "This is the courthouse of a new era, a showcase for environmental concerns." WOW! Sixteen others follow.

Three jurists review the work of the student whose desk I briefly occupied earlier in the semester. She created a fine scheme: a classical composition entered via a skylit hall of great columns, centered on an exterior courtyard, beyond which are the four courtrooms. It is a simple diagram with both a classical character and an open, light demeanor. Her final review goes well. Strengths, according to her reviewers, include the daylighting scheme, her thorough design explorations, and the simple, rich scheme. Weaknesses: location of site parking, vulnerability of the judges in a separate building, and an ineffective link to the park.

The semester project was critical to her growth this semester, as were several intensive, somewhat confrontational, working sessions. The extended project forced her to become familiar with the law, the site, and architecture — bringing her closer to the realities of the environmental experience she is designing. Short, intensive discussions questioned her technical abilities and her execution and performance of the design process in general. While difficult, she moves to the next semester evidencing both increased knowledge and advanced skills.

Tuesday, November 24: The interim report for ARCH 552. Most compelling is the "Eight Voices" section, where each student speaks from his or her perspective about an issue or issues of most significance. The coverage here — "the role of the city," "architecture," "social life," "arts and parks," "education and transportation," "the responsibility of the private sector," "preservation," and "social responsibility" — speaks well for the varied backgrounds of the students, their passion for the city and work, and bodes well for next semester's studio effort.

Faculty and graduate students will meet Monday afternoon to discuss the interim report, with special attention given to specific studio project recommendations.

> **Studio Questions:** Schon argues, rightfully so, that studios are the model for education in all the professions. Doctors, business persons, lawyers, and architects have to deal with "complexity, uncertainty, uniqueness and value-conflict." Studio work is "the very prototype . . . a kind of on-the-spot research" that has its own "standards of rigour" however different these may be from the sciences (Schon 1985).
>
> **Studious Responses:** At Ball State, we are discussing refinements, other alternatives, that explore the studio's prototypical qualities. Upon reflection, two of these alternatives share aspects with Rapoport's argument regarding the design studio's relative isolation from other courses resulting in the range of variables addressed in other courses being forgotten upon passing through "the sacred portals of the studio."

One idea redistributes course content into learning modules with technology modules offered early in the semester (and year), only studio offered later in the semester, integrating technical know-how into the what-now and why-now of the studio. An example: the Form Z training session, in eight hours, covered coursework that normally takes twelve weeks of a sixteen-week semester! Suddenly, other challenges arise: Four semesters of structures? Studio every semester? More than one professional practice course? Or none?

A second initiative breaks down boundaries among course content areas. In the first two weeks of spring semester, students will design a small building equipped with heating, ventilating and air conditioning machinery. Each student will then develop a full set of working drawings for this building in the semester-long technology course. Studio faculty will use the smallish building to introduce broader concerns for the larger building that will be the semester's focus. As such, faculty teaching and students working in studio and building technology share, integrate, and benefit. As a studio instructor, I will review student's construction drawings for the smaller building; as a building technology professor, others will critique students' designs for the larger building.

Among Rapoport's "Studious Questions" were a number of queries into the amount of time dedicated to studio teaching. Some of us at Ball State ask similar questions. Why not studio on Monday and Friday afternoons only, with all of Wednesday reserved exclusively for the sort of continuous scholarly pursuits that extended studio and classroom hours will not allow? What is the magic about twelve hours of in-class studio every week?

Friday December 11: Here come the judges. Over one hundred superior, circuit and magistrate judges attending the Indiana Judges Association Annual Meeting review courthouse and courtroom designs. Some judges seem dismayed, others argue over a student's intentions. I corral judges, move them to the students and thank them. Otherwise, students are on their own.

Here comes the judge. To the State Capitol for a review by Chief Justice Shepard. He speaks with each student for 3-4 minutes, focuses on the design intentions of each, and concludes with encouraging words. I knew when I voted for Shepard in November, literally as I pulled the lever, good things would happen.

That evening, students are in my home for a chili dinner, table tennis, and a fireside chat. This full day is my way of saying goodbye—congratulations; be thoughtful; and thank you. Of creating an unforgettable experience of such density and intensity that when called upon in years to come, will release not merely vague memories, but ideas, insights, lessons, tactics, and strategies learned throughout the semester.

Tuesday - Friday, December 15-18: Twenty-minute meetings with each studio student. We discuss the semester, his or her work, next semester, career plans, what I could have done better, what each needs to work on.

The young woman whose desk I occupied agrees with my "B" assessment. She worked very hard, developed appropriate project intentions and stayed with them, completed her presentation requirements, and conducted herself well during final reviews. Yet I am struck by how much learning remains to be done. How significant the challenge is to her teachers. How seemingly unaware she is of how much she must learn and do if she is to attain a professional degree, full-time position, passage of the architectural registration examination, and professional registration.

Postscript

Rapoport's challenge to think closely about why studios exist and what can best be taught there is simple and authoritative. His position demands that we not be mindless, not be satisfied, not be tradition-bound. Instead Rapoport mandates the thoughtful consideration of what it means to be a professional, a teacher of architecture, an architectural scholar securing a body of knowledge, and, implicitly, a student of the architectural discipline and profession.

His self-admitted "extreme position" of 1983 was a bold precursor to discussions about degree nomenclature, the school-office gap, and hyphenated architects (his term) that so dominate architectural discourse today. This, I believe, is a valuable pedagogical position unfortunately and understandably overshadowed by Rapoport's pioneering work in environment-behavior studies.

It is these studious questions, this good thinking, that I am thankful for today and every day when I construct, with my students, our studio responses.

References

Anthony, K. (1991). *Design Juries on Trial.* New York: Van Nostrand Reinhold.

Ball State University (Spring 1998). *Undergraduate Catalog 1998-2000.* Muncie, IN: Ball State University.

Boyer. E., and L. Mitgang (1996). *Building Community: A New Future for Architecture Education and Practice.* Princeton, NJ: Carnegie Foundation for the Advancement of Teaching.

Broadbent. G. (1995). "Architectural Education." In M. Pearce and M. Toy (Eds.) *Educating Architects.* London: Academy Editions.

Ching, F. (1979). *Architecture: Form, Space and Order.* New York: Van Nostrand Reinhold.

Cuff, D. (1991). *Architecture: The Story of Practice.* Cambridge, MA: MIT Press.

Greenstreet, R. and M. Malecha (1995). *Junior Faculty Handbook on Tenure and Promotion.* Washington, DC: Association of Collegiate Schools of Architecture.

Heath. T. (1984). *Method in Architecture.* Chichester: John Wiley & Sons.

Rapoport, A. (1983). "Studious Questions." *The Architects' Journal,* Vol. 178. No. 43 (23 October) pp. 55-57.

Sauer, L. (1993). "The Problem in Studio Education." *Progressive Architecture* (June) pp. 77-78.

Schon, D. (1985). *The Design Studio: an explanation of its traditions and potentials.* London: RIBA Publications.

Sutton. S. (1992). "Power, Knowledge, and the Art of Leadership." *Progressive Architecture* (May) pp. 65-68.

PART III: ARCHITECTURAL ANTHROPOLOGY

10 Culture and Built Form – A Reconsideration

Amos Rapoport

This re-evaluation of the role of culture is a useful point of departure for looking at a few more recent developments that emphasize more specifically *how* culture can be used both in analysis and in problem-solving ('design') (Rapoport 1993a, 1998). As mentioned in Chapter 2, I am currently working on another paper which will be even more specific. This paper first appeared in D. G. Saile (Ed.), (1986). *Architecture in Cultural Change (Essays in Built Form and Culture Research)* Lawrence, School of Architecture, University of Kansas. It was reprinted as Paper 27 in A. Rapoport (1995). *Thirty-three papers in Environment Behavior Research*, pp. 399-436, Urban International Press: Newcastle, UK., and is now reprinted here. – Amos Rapoport.

Introduction

I begin with the observation that this volume and the earlier conference, devoted to culture-environment study are evidence of a growing interest in the subject (to be discussed later). It is also the culmination of a lengthy period of activity. I will not try to trace beginnings, but my own involvement goes back over twenty years. *House Form and Culture* was published fifteen years before this conference.

Given a twenty year history and a major growth of interest, a reexamination of the field seems useful, particularly on the occasion of the first major conference devoted entirely to this topic. Since I am currently trying to reexamine conceptual, philosophical and theoretical bases of Environment-Behavior Research, of which culture-built form research forms parts, it seems important to reconsider some of the basic, often unstated assumptions which inform ongoing work. These assumptions tend to remain unexamined as a field grows: their importance and correctness are rarely assessed. Yet one should, every so often, reexamine what has been done; what has been confirmed; what needs to be rejected; what needs to be changed and how; and what refinements, developments, or redefinitions are needed.

Writing this, I was reminded of the suggestion that complex new problems are typically tackled using a two-stage model. In stage one, a framework or 'anchor' is sought – a concept or image which already exists and seems applicable. In stage two, "adjustments" are made – attempts on the basis of additional information, to arrive at a more fruitful representation of the situation. If the anchor is appropriate initially, the additional, plentiful, and accurate information will not improve this anchor; on the contrary, the additional data may make the situation worse (Tversky and Kahneman, 1974).

It follows that it is important that the anchor itself be reexamined periodically; yet this is rarely done. Rather the major effort tends to be invested in the ongoing development of the adjustments.

The anchor used in our approach to built form was the concept of culture; this is, then, the first thing to reexamine. Even if one were to conclude that this concept is indeed relevant, important, and basically sound, such reexamination may suggest new ideas, new questions, new formulations, new linkages, gaps and problems.

Only a few of the possible topics will be addressed. For example, I will not consider whether there is such a thing as 'culture' (even though that is being asked). I will assume that some such thing exists. Nor will I look at different philosophical approaches to culture. Among questions I could ask are: how have unstated assumptions, once made explicit, stood up? Which assumptions are to be retained, which developed (and how), which modified and which rejected? Is the role of culture as we initially assumed, greater – or less? What is culture and what does it do? Have we asked the right questions and used the right approaches? What mechanisms link culture to built form? What is the role of built form in culture? What seems to be important research questions; hence, where is research urgently needed? What is the relation of culture-built form research to "design"? What *is* design? And so on.

Since all, or even most, of these questions cannot be addressed, I have selected six: (1) Why was culture used in the first place? (2) How can "culture" be conceptualized? (3) How is culture translated into form? (4) How should culture-built form relations be studies? (5) How important is culture in understanding built form? (6) What are the implications for design?

Even these cannot be developed fully, but in tackling them, the necessary reexamination will, at least, begin.

Why "Culture"

To begin at the beginning: Was it reasonable to have used the concept of culture in the first place? I would have to conclude that this was inescapable for several reasons, particularly if one considers culture-built form research to be part of environment-behavior research (EBR). In EBR, one is looking for generalizations about humans in relation to the built environment. In anthropology, from which this anchoring concept comes, it was always accepted that what defines *human* is culture. Even sociobiology agrees that *culture defines our species* although there the origins of culture may be seen differently and its roots pushed further back (Lumsden and Wilson 1981, Bonner, 1980).

Generalizations in EBR require the use of the broadest possible body of evidence. This means that one needs to consider and study all environments – preliterate, vernacular, and popular as well as professionally designed. This in turn means that one must consider the full range of environments through time. Built environments seem to go back almost two million years in their hominid versions (Rapoport 1979a, pp. 5-7; 1979b) and to occur in places and climates where the need for shelter seems minimal, yet immediately after stone tools but before the use of red ochre, fire, art or ritual burial (Tobias 1981, p. 48). Their roots, once again, may go back even further (e.g., Von Frisch 1974). Finally, it is also necessary to consider the full range of environments cross-culturally.

This raises another inevitable question. Why the extraordinary *variety* of cultural landscapes and built forms when human activities, behaviors, and needs are so much fewer in number. *This increasingly seems to be a central question.* The implicit answer seems to be that what makes environments different is that different groups create them – groups which differ in terms of culture.

Thus, in considering our domain, the relation of people and environments, one finds not only that culture makes us human, that is, there would be no built forms (or their study!) without culture. One also finds that culture makes us variable. It is culture which seems to define groups and leads to latent aspects of activities. These vary more than their instrumental aspects (e.g., Rapoport 1982a, 1985) and lead to varied needs, wants and interpretations of 'requirements'. Built environments are *group specific* and culturally variable. Thus, culture seems to play a central role in both these very basic inescapable facts about built form.

Discussions about culture have become more sophisticated relative to both these matters. On the one hand, there has been a revived interest in our communality as humans, all possessing culture, and in possible evolutionary uniformities among cultures and built environments. On the other hand there is also increasing awareness of individual variability among even the most traditional groups. Members of such groups do *not* all act alike; their artists *do* have individuality; there *are* differences among settlements and buildings. The constancy, homogeneity and uniformity among traditional groups, while much more prevalent and striking than in more pluralistic or individualistic societies seems to have been overemphasized. There is also continued awareness that the species was, and continues to be, divided into numerous groups. The differences *among* these groups clearly seems greater than among individuals within them – otherwise one could not talk about such different groups (Rapoport 1980a). Differences among groups are also greater than the similarities of humans across groups – *at least in the shaping of built form.*

The different settings for these different groups, reinforced by what I have called secondary or modifying factors (Rapoport 1969) – site climate, materials, technology, economy and the like – results in specificity and hence the striking variety of built forms. This is one reason for the current interest in this subject, which I will discuss later.

This variety, which in other domains has puzzled and preoccupied anthropologists and linguists, I also find an increasingly challenging question about built environments. One must consider possible reasons for the widely varied settings for these various groups. It has been so ubiquitous a phenomenon that it is likely to be significant; and in some way, culture seems to be involved.

Conceptualizations of Culture

While avoiding questions such as whether culture exists or whether it is generally a useful concept (e.g., Bennett 1982), it is essential to consider the way in which "culture" is conceptualized. This will influence how issues are addressed because generally methods follow from theoretical (ontological and epistemological) considerations.

Using Northrop's (1947) terms: buildings, settlements, dwellings, people and the like, and "intuitional concepts". These can be extremely complex and require conceptual analysis (even the perennial question of "what is human" is still being discussed in EBR: c.f. Downton 1983). They can, however, be seen, touched, and observed. Culture, on the other hand, is a *postulational concept* (a theoretical construct). No one ever has, or ever will, see or observe culture – only its effects and products. In other words, one is making inferences about unobservable entities. There is a tendency frequently to use theoretical constructs such as "culture" as though they were "indirect-observables" that is, "individuals of a larger and more elusive type than usually encountered" (Kaplan 1964, p. 81). In fact, of course, individuals, their properties, relations and products are the indicators and referents for the collective term. "Culture" exists by definition. It is a conceptual summary of human phenomena (Bennett 1982). It was initially use din anthropology, then other social sciences adopted it. In Greek (which is always supposed to have a word for it) there is no such special term – it is the same as "civilization". The concept is also used differently in U.S and English anthropology and archaeology (Binford 1983, pp. 397-401). Given all this, and the continuing and heated discussions about this concept, it seems increasingly important to try and clarify it.

For some time I have used three alternative, very broad definitional classes within which most definitions of culture seemed to fall. These, I have argued, can and should be seen as complementary rather than as in conflict. Briefly, these are: culture as a way of life typical of a group; culture as a system of symbols, meanings and schemata transmitted through symbolic codes; culture as a set of adaptive strategies for survival related to resources and ecology (Rapoport 1980a. p. 9).

Recently there has been a tendency in a variety of fields to argue that in making inferences about unobservable entities, it is more useful to ask not what these entities *are* but rather what they *do*, and then how they do these things – that is, what are the mechanisms involved (as just one example, from cognitive science, see Kosslyn 1983, p.87). Interestingly, some new ways of conceptualizing culture do precisely that: they tend to ask what culture *does* rather than what it is. As an example I will briefly describe three recent answers.

One answer is that cultures may be regarded as *the distinctive means whereby populations maintain their identity*, that is, *cultures are properties of populations* (Rappaport 1979, pp. 60-62). This is clearly intimately related to the discussion above on the variety of environments as a function of group variability so that this variety may be related to identity (Rapoport 1981). However, to say that it is culture that makes groups different is not enough. A major unanswered research question in EBR concerns those characteristics and criteria that define groups which are relevant, valid, useful, or significant for particular problems related to their built environments. I will argue later that by dismantling the concept of culture some answers might be obtained. Moreover, since cultures change, there is also the question of how long a group maintains its identity, that is, remains recognizable both to itself and to others as being distinct since it takes agreement by both parties to maintain group boundaries (e.g., Barth 1969). In this connection, I have suggested that the distinction between the core of culture (which changes little and slowly) and its periphery (which changes quickly) is potentially useful for the analysis and design of built form, particularly in situations of rapid culture change (Rapoport 1983a). These core elements maintain the identity of the group.

A second answer to the question about what culture does is that it can be seen as a *control mechanism* (Geertz 1983). *Culture carries information* and can be thought of as an analogue to DNA or, to use a different metaphor, a blueprint. Thus, culture both directs how behavior and artifacts are to be and transmits information by behavioral means (teaching and behavior itself) and through various artifacts, including built environments (cf. Bonner 1980; Wobst 1977; Rapoport 1982a; Moore 1983; Hodder 1982).

The third answer is that one can conceptualize culture as that structure or framework which gives meaning to particulars (Bruner 1983, p.185). This seems very pertinent in dealing with ecological approaches to culture, since it ensures that due attention is given to availability of information and selectivity. People continue to act in varied ways in response to apparently identical resource situations or demands (e.g. Moore 1983).

These three answers are also complementary rather than conflicting: culture, as the property of groups, exercises control through information and rules; these produce a structure within which elements take on meaning (cf. Hanson 1983). The above discussion also emphasizes the *dynamic and active character of culture,* another emerging theme and one which some of us in culture-environment studies have underemphasized.

Those ways of looking at culture also relate well to some recent ways of looking at environmental meaning such as the idea that the built environment is mnemonic, a form of congealed information reminding people how to behave. They also relate to views about how to behave; views about the role of the built environment in enculturation and habitual behavior; the importance of context and situation and the role of built forms in establishing these; the role of the built environment in maintaining identity, and so on (cf. Rapoport, 1982a). They also fit well my view of EBR more generally and link up with recent work in cognitive science on the role of the schemata, "frames", "scripts" and what has been called "extra knowledge" in language (Johnson-Laird and Wason 1977; Rosch and Lloyd 1978).

Furthermore, "culture: seems far too broad and global a concept to be useful. In a number of fields it has been found useful to clarify excessively broad concepts by "dismantling" them and then classifying and clarifying the component parts. It is not really helpful to say what links numerous studies on diverse environments such as South Nias, the Pueblos of the Southwestern U.S., Indian cities, home furnishings in the U.S., landscaping in Westchester, Australian Aboriginal place definitions and so on is culture. Without specifics, conditions and limits, one is no further advanced. This excessive broadness remains a problem in EBR generally and in culture-built form research specifically.

In this connection, I have argued repeatedly since the 1970s that one needs to "dismantle" the concept of culture. It is not possible to "design for culture" but it may be possible to show that particular parts of the environment are supportive for specific components of culture given some understanding of the mechanisms which link them. I have used a particular sequence of increasing specificity going form culture, through world views, values to lifestyles and activity systems. The specifics of the last, particularly their latent aspects, begin to "explain" the variability of built form. Lifestyle also can reasonably be related to environmental quality since both can be seen in terms of profiles resulting from choice (Rapoport 1985b). But this particular approach is less important than the *principle*: the need to dismantle global concepts.

Similarly, one finds references to "socio-cultural" variables. It can reasonably be asked whether "social" and "cultural" might be different, so that lumping then together is less than helpful. This has, in fact, been argued. One recent suggestion, for example, is that they are best seen as distinct in the sense that *social variables* refer to the actual social behavior and structures, whereas *cultural variables* are ideational, describing the "blueprint" for the social variables (Wallace 1983 and Lawrence in this volume).

This offers another way of dismantling the concept of culture and finding more operational, because potentially observable, units which might be related to form. The social expression of culture includes groups, institutions, social networks, status relations and many others. These often do have physical settings associated with them which can be studied and designed. Hence, starting with these specific concrete social expressions rather than the more ideational concept of culture offers an alternative, or complementary way of dismantling that concept and relating it to built form.

This discussion raises several related questions. Two of these form the next two sections of this paper. First: how is culture translated into form. Second: how culture-built form relations can best be studied.

Translation of Culture into Form

There is a fundamental question of great generality which I think we have failed to address. We have talked about form being related to culture without asking "How does culture get translated into form". In other words, what are the mechanisms involved. Several possible implicit answers have already been briefly mentioned; culture as control mechanism, culture as blueprint, culture as set of rules and instructions. But they need more explicit discussion; as they stand, they are neither specific enough nor do they go beyond analogy (or metaphor).

There is also one implicit assumption in much of the literature on culture-built form relations which seem highly questionable. This is that culture and built form are equivalent units, that is equal in "scale". *They are not.* Culture is a vast domain; built form, a small part of it, a subset of it; moreover it is embedded in the former. This makes the translation process difficult to grasp. Yet it is essential that this be borne in mind when this process is being considered.

There is a need to identify some *mechanism or mechanisms*; explanatory models typically are much more convincing if some mechanisms can be specified. In this connection, for example, the role of mental templates or cognitive schemata, derived from cognitive anthropology, and which I for one have used, have recently been questioned when applied to tools and other artifacts (e.g. Binford, 1983). I believe that they still seem to be useful, particularly at the larger scales of buildings, settlements, and cultural landscapes. In the case of the latter, for example, it provides a possible answer to the puzzling question of how they come to "add up" so that they can be identified although they result from very many apparently independent decisions. But the doubts and the questions still remain about how much schemata are translated into form.

This is similar to the question posed by Miller, Gallanter and Pribram (1960) about how images (discussed by Boulding, 1956), are translated into action. Their suggested answer is that images lead to plans guiding people's rough courses of action. These are tested against various incongruities through what they call the TOTE unit (Test-Operate-Test-Exit). This is not a bad answer, particularly with regard to vernacular design which is the result of a long-term, gradual adjustment process (Alexander 1964; cf. Below, selectionism vs. instructionism).

Another answer which was implied earlier is that culture leads to various social variables and it is these which are then translated into physical form. This corresponds to a translation from the ideational to the actual which, in turn, can more easily be translated into form. This point was made in connection with the more general argument regarding the need to "dismantle" the concept of culture. One does not translate culture into built form. Rather, some aspects of culture (lifestyle, behaviors, social structures, status, power relationships, meanings and so on) are translated into some aspects of built form:

some components of culture are related to some components of environment. This implies that "built environment" also needs to be dismantled (Rapoport 1977a, 1980a) and that the concept of "built form" also needs to be approached in this way and more clearly conceptualized (Rapoport 1980a).

Various components and conceptualizations of "built environment" and "built form" can be proposed. They can be conceptualized as organizations of space, time, meaning, and communication; they represent relationships between people and people, people and things, and things and things; they represent particular systems of settings. I have also reviewed some of the many other proposed ways of conceptualizing these global concepts, although a complete review needs to be done. I have also argued that different settings provide different cues, encode different meanings through fixed, semi-fixed (and even non-fixed) elements to act as mnemonics; that settings are assembled into systems differently – in different sequences, with different linkages or separations, different proximities.

All these successive "dismantlings" and dissections of "culture", "built environment" and "built form" are to enable one to understand better culture-environment (and environment-behavior) relations. They offer the only potentially fruitful approach to "designing for culture" which stated in *that* form, as already pointed out, is an impossible task. Of course, it is also necessary to clarify what is meant by "design" (Rapoport 1972, 1984). Even when so clarified, "design" is too unconstrained – it must be constrained in various ways, at the very least by specifying the specific setting to be designed.

Be all that as it may, once both "culture" and "built form" have been articulated in these ways, two questions can be posed:

1. What gets translated into what? (Which components of one into what specifics of the other?)
2. How does it get translated? (How do the rules, blueprints, schemata, information, and so on, get translated?)

There is also a subsidiary (but most important) question: Why does it get translated? Why not build just "shelter"; why are all these complex informational, mnemonic, meaning, identity, latent and other aspects so important?

There is another way of looking at this in terms of one of the definitions of culture which we have already considered (Rapoport 1979, pp. 59-63). Instead of using *culture*, we could consider a *population* with *culture as its characteristics*. Recall also, as we have already seen when discussing activity systems, that it is people who do things. It is individuals who adapt, succeed, act, behave and compete (as is the case in evolutionary biology for those groups called species). Culture is carried in the minds of people who actively perceive, judge and act. Note that the discussion above of various answers to the question of translation has made this very point, referring to human action. For example, this is the implication of the discussion of how images are translated into action through the plans and TOTE units. People's actions are based on their cognized environments (templates, schemata etc.,) although subjective actions may, of course, have unintended effects in the real ("operational") environment (Rapoport 1979). These cognized models can then be adjusted and revised as need arises. This fits the TOTE model well and also provides a link with the views of ecologically minded archaeologists and anthropologists.

When we ask the question: Who does what, where, when, including whom (and why) which are very useful questions to ask, we are dealing with *people doing things*. Culture is ultimately translated into form through what people do as a result of what is in their heads and within the constraints of their situation (cf. Rapoport 1983a, p. 267, fig. 11). Culture provides the rules, schemata or blueprints about how to behave, how to do things, how to build. Habitual behavior (which is an important aspect of culture) translates culture into form, as in the case of cultural landscapes already mentioned. People may, of course, use these rules and instructions inaccurately – or may even disregard them. Groups identified by their cultures vary in this regard as they do in the degree of sharing of schemata or images. This, however, is another variable which can be studied; the degree of conformity is an empirical question.

Thus it is not the case that culture is translated into built form. Rather culture is translated, through human actions, through a series of intermediate steps, into built form.

In this connection, preference and *choice* play an important role; one can ask who chooses what, where and why (Rapoport 1985). Recall also my argument that design itself is a choice process (Rapoport 1977a, 1983b, 1985). Different people may not only make different choices among the alternatives available (within the rules set by the culture for the group) but the alternatives available also differ. This is not only due to the setting, resources, and other limitations and constraints. It is also due to the previous choices made. People begin with *different repertoires*.

There are also differences in who makes these choices – users, designers, specialists, and speaking metaphorically, individuals or groups. The time scale also differs; in preliterate and traditional societies very long periods of time can occur with gradual adjustments ("selectionism") whereas in contemporary projects the design (i.e. translation) rarely exceeds months ("instructionism"). The criteria used also vary in different groups. All these can be understood as variations in what I have called the choice model of design (Rapoport 1977a, 1983b).

As already emphasized, when one speaks of group choices, one is using a metaphor because the actions are always by *individuals*. What one means is that among some groups there is a very high degree of consensus, so that individual differences are smaller than in other cases. These regularities create group effects. The reason is, of course, that individuals do not act or make decisions in a vacuum. They are enculturated and thus make use of the repertoire mentioned above. The resulting regularity of their actions leads to the intriguing and striking phenomenon of recognizable cultural landscapes already discussed. This is because culture, and hence all its products, are *ordered,* not random. In the case of those products we call built environments, one is dealing with *different orders* rather than with a contrast of order and disorder (chaos). Design, then, is not the ordering of the environment but a re-ordering so as to make a given order more appropriate or acceptable to given users, more preferred by a particular group (Rapoport 1984).

As already pointed out, actions of individuals are constrained not only by group or subgroup membership and resources, but by the previous choices made (Rapoport 1984). These not only limit possible actions, but through the mnemonic function of built form suggest appropriate actions (Rapoport 1982a).

The above discussion not only emphasizes the active role of people in shaping environments. It also suggests another point which, while known, has tended to be underemphasized. This is that *built form is used actively for cultural purposes.* More correctly, it may be so used since it does not have to be since other components of culture, such as song, dance, language, ritual, tattooing, costume, rites and many others are available. However, the point remains that built form is not just a *reflection of culture* or a *container for culture* as, implicitly at least, it often appears.

An analogy seems useful. If we consider what I have called the three questions of EBR then the first question, which characteristics of people lead to particular environments, is the analogue of looking at culture being translated into built form. The second question, the effect of environment on people, is, then the analogue of the role and effect of built form on culture. This then raises the third question – which mechanisms link this two-way process.

We have typically tended to discuss the question of how culture influences (is translated into) built form. Much less attention has been paid to the question of how built form influences culture, *how built form is used for cultural purposes* once built and how it is built for such purposes. One also needs to ask when it is used, under what conditions and by whom (analogously to Rapoport 1983c). This once again, implies an active, adaptive use of built form in culture so that people are active not only in creating it or choosing among alternatives. Built form, like other aspects of culture, is used to transmit information (as already indicated). Information transmission varies as the size, scale and complexity of groups and societies goes up. Hypotheses based on this view should, once again, be researchable questions.

This has been addressed, in a very preliminary way in my discussion of *supportive environments* (Rapoport 1980a, 1983a). this role of built form is at least implied by asking: What is supported? By what is it supported? How is it supported? It also suggests that it may be used directly or indirectly, in which case it supports other social or cultural components which may be more directly used. This is analogue to the distinction between direct and indirect effects of environment on people (Rapoport 1982a). One can also go on to ask how are the various elements of the environment being used so as to be supportive. How used for status, for example, or to maintain social structure, to support roles, to maintain power relations or to preserve important institutions. In this connection, the parallels to the third basic EBR question dealing with mechanisms linking people and environments become useful.

The analogy between the three EBR questions and the relation of culture to environment is also useful because it immediately and intimately relates the concept of culture to any larger theory of the built environment. This requires much research, particularly major *comparative* research. But this topic is best discussed as part of the next section of our reconsideration.

How Should Culture-Environment Relations be Studied

I have already suggested that excessively broad, global, "holistic" concepts and questions must be dismantled or dissected before they can be addressed. Only then can the components of built form and culture be identified, linkages, relations and mechanisms established and studied and the system then reassembled. In this key issue – how one approaches problems – the clarification of concepts through the development of taxonomies is critical. Early agreement among researchers on units to be used and criteria for their definitions seem crucial. For valid comparisons one needs rigorous (even though provisional) definitions, clear taxonomies, clear distinction between theoretical and phenomenal (empirical or intuitive) terms and so on. What one compares, and how, is most important.

In a reconsideration of approaches to culture-environment studies, therefore, it seems that more clarity is an essential requirement; more clarity about the nature of the domain, the taxonomies used to drive units and components and the mechanisms linking components of culture and environment. Also needed is some agreement about ontology and epistemology as well as those methods most likely to be successful once problems have been properly identified. But all these fundamental issues cannot be discussed here.

The existence of an apparent paradox has been pointed out (Jacob 1982, p. 10). By asking very broad questions very limited answers are typically obtained. If, on the contrary, very limited questions are asked, very broad answers often follow. This, of course, implies the need to get rid of the quest for "holism" (e.g., Nagel, 1961, p. 445-446; Efron 1984, p. 52-57; Laudan 1984). Whatever the merits or otherwise of ontological or epistemological reductionism one cannot escape methodological reductionism (e.g., Ayala and Dobzhansky 1974)[1].

One way to understand or verify statements about wholes, such as "culture" or "built form" is thus by observation and study of parts – particularly since one can never observe culture. While views differ on this, *the intelligibility* of the world implies that it is continuous and that one can get from parts (if correctly identified) back to wholes (Kaplan 1964). Even apparently contrary views (e.g., Hanson 1975) do accept this position. The debate is frequently about the nature of the domain and units of analysis.

There is another problem which we face in addressing culture-built form relations. Before one can analyze, it is essential to be able to *describe*. We lack, yet badly need, *descriptive languages* for built environments (in addition to clear taxonomies for them). *Consensibility* must come before *consensuality* (Ziman 1978). In spite of efforts by Gordon Cullen, Philip Thiel and Lawrence Halprin (to name just three), I would argue that we still lack the ability to describe adequately environments, settings and places, their characteristics and ambiences, in such a way that agreement could be reached by different observers, or where such descriptions and qualities could be communicated to others.

Research in a new domain usually begins with a perceived problem or problem situation. Analysis then typically begins with a *natural history stage*, during which one observes, collects, classifies and organizes the "intuitional" empirical concepts; traces patterns and regularities. Only then does one typically move on to the postulational, theoretical stage which results in hypotheses to be tested and other developments. It has even been suggested that this natural history stage is essential and that different approaches are best used at appropriate stages in the development of a field (e.g., Northrop 1947). Often, after a new set of insights resulting from the hypothetical-deductive stage, one may move once again into a more inductive mode. Like design, research is a cyclical and iterative process.

It could be suggested that in studying culture-built form relations the natural history stage was missed, and theoretical terms such as culture were used immediately.[2]

Essentially I have been arguing for greater rigor, clarity and sophistication in terms of domain definition, regarding concepts and units of analysis, in the dissection and reassembly of global concepts. All of that would both raise questions and suggest what filling in is required because of omissions. It is also important that examples and data be used more rigorously. The natural history stage usually leads to great care in data collection and classification. Possibly because that stage was omitted, and theoretical terms and concepts form anthropology used immediately, there has been a tendency to ignore the need for careful data collection and classification, careful definitions and taxonomies as well as of clear exposition of presuppositions and rationale regarding the use of examples and data. We (and I very much plead guilty to this) have tended to adopt a rather "grab-bag" approach to examples, often ignoring chronology and various contexts. The examples have tended to be too "random". Most commonly they have been used as illustrations to support positions rather than as data against which to test propositions.

This use of examples assumes too much; it is essential that the chronological, cultural and contextual characteristics of examples be made clear and explicit, and that the rationale for their use be specified much more carefully.

Given this problematic use of evidence, one might ask as part of our reconsideration: would it be at all useful to go back to a natural history stage? This would imply collecting a large body of data, doing taxonomies, and tracing patterns and regularities. Often, an influx of data can lead to a growth of interpretive questions; more information and data can often help straighten out wrong beliefs. Such data may even force a reconsideration of the anchor. Such data also help in the essential process of clarifying global concepts through refined distinctions which increase in rigor: these, in turn help to discover significant variables and mechanisms.

For example, one might begin to separate "things" (activities, behaviors, cues, meanings, settings) into those that are culture specific and those that are not. One could try to identify situations where culture is important, relevant and useful and those where it does not seem to be.

These distinctions need much more rigorous thought that they have received. I take the position that meaningful translation and understanding of other cultures *is* possible (if it were not, research into culture-built form relations also becomes impossible) and that suitable methods can be derived. It follows that questions such as those above – and those raised throughout this paper – can only be approached through cross-cultural study. This, by definition, is comparative; therefore comparative studies become essential but have been rather neglected.

Comparative work is also necessary for other reasons. For example, in connection with ethnoarchaeology, it has recently been suggested (Kent, 1984, p. 13ff) that its objective (identical to ours) – to link culture, behavior and cultural material can only be done comparatively. Since it is not possible to characterize culture or behavior in absolute terms, the *comparison* of groups is necessary in order that groups can be placed in some general context. Since one cannot measure group characteristics, one can only compare a given group with others in order to see whether any given characteristic is stronger or weaker, greater or lesser, stricter or less strict, more or less present. Usually these comparisons tend to be *implicit*; they need to be made *explicit*. This enables groups to be plotted on a continuum. Without absolute or quantitative characteristics, similarities and differences among groups can only be studied in this way—the position of any one group represents a specific location only in relation to other groups, The basic importance of comparative studies becomes evident.[3]

What is required is comparative study in depth of carefully selected cases, but selected according to explicit criteria form a large body of data covering all history, all environments and all cultures. In this connection, the relevance should become clear of my earlier discussion of the need for more careful specification of the cultural, chronological and contextual characteristics of examples; specification of reasons for their selection (based on clear conceptual criteria) and the need for descriptive languages and taxonomies.

Another major gap in the study of culture-built form relations involves *longitudinal (diachronic) research*, that is, studies over time. To understand the dynamic relation between environment and culture, the study of change sin both is most useful. Currently, such changes are seen most clearly in surviving traditional cultures and in developing countries. We have already missed twenty years; what few studies have been done on culture change *neglect built form*. The neglect of diachronic, as opposed to synchronic, research is part of the general neglect of time. I have emphasized the importance of time as a component of the environment itself. For example, I have argued that temporal cognitive schemata (e.g., linear vs. cyclic), the value of time, the organization of time and how it is used (e.g., for privacy) are important and useful topics. Here, however, I am arguing for a longer range view of time and in a different sense. In this connection longitudinal/diachronic analysis also implies the use of historical data and studies which, in turn, are part of what I call the need to broaden the evidence we use.

Once much more "natural history" material becomes available, comparative studies will be more likely to be successful and useful. It ahs been suggested that such studies would be useful in neuroscience because there already is a body of data accumulated during the past one hundred years so that the descriptive research, which is the equivalent of the "natural history" stage had already been done (Bullock, 1984). In our case, this is still lacking. Before one can even try to explain, a body of adequate data is needed. About ten years ago, I also suggested a minimal set of eight questions that needed to be addressed in all ethnographic research (Rapoport, 1976a, pp. 13-17). Unfortunately no such research has been done either in anthropology or in culture-environment studies.

Having obtained a range (through space and time) of groups, environments and culture-environment relations one could consider differences among related groups and differences within groups. One could also seek to discover the cultural correlates of environmental differences and the environmental correlates of cultural differences (all analogously to Bullock, 1984). This could lead to many more specific questions. Some of these could be about the beginnings of the built environment, for example its origins in relation to human origins and the origins of culture. Others might seek to discover what generalizations can be made about the mutual interaction between culture and built form and what is the range of such generalizations. For this one could consider how components of "culture" and "built environment" covary, hence how these are translated one into the other, the mechanisms that link them and how all these are organized into functioning systems. Regarding design one could consider the insights that can be obtained from such evidence and how useful lessons could be derived (e.g., Rapoport, 1983a, d).

Let me summarize. In this section, I have been arguing for an approach based on two types of developments which need to go hand in hand as part of the iterative research process. On the one hand, I have argued for the need for clear, explicit definitions, concepts and taxonomies and the development of interim models and frameworks. On the other, I have raised the possibility that the "natural history stage" (Northrop, 1947) has not taken place and may be needed. I have discussed at some length what this might imply. I have also argued for the need for careful comparative studies. All this would yield more explicit and testable hypotheses, and even theories, which would not be premature (cf. the analogous argument in Rapoport 1982a).

These various types of research work in tandem, in ways well illustrated by what has been called an "ethological approach" (Chisholm, 1983, pp. 93-94). This is based on a rigorous and often even quantitative natural history approach which makes induction both possible and fruitful (cf. Hinde, 1984). The data collection is informed by the research and theory already available; it is thus based on hypotheses although without too strong a commitment to these so as to minimize preconceptions and allow a form of the "natural history" approach. The goal is to develop further more explicit and testable hypotheses. This approach also encourages casting a wide research net and the use of multiple disciplinary frameworks, and methods. This rather eclectic approach not only makes possible the testing of specific hypotheses but it also encourages the easier generation of new hypotheses from the data being collected. Moreover, this approach, while more explicitly developed in ethology, is also productively used in anthropology (cf. Chisholm, 1983). This, in turn, makes its application to culture-built form research potentially more promising than alternative approaches such as those derived from experimental psychology.

The Importance of Culture

As part of the general reconsideration one needs to ask: How important has the concept of culture proved for an understanding of EBR? More specifically the question is whether, in view of recent adjustments, the anchor holds and if so—whether the role of culture in EBR is more important, as important or less important than assumed initially.

Once again the question needs to be addressed in less global terms. One should really ask: Which parts of culture are how important to whom, when, where, under what (specific) conditions and why?

Some answers follow even when the question is posed globally. Recall the argument that there would be neither built environments, nor study of them, without culture! On the one hand, culture is what makes us human, distinguishes the human from the non-human realm. On the other hand, culture is what leads to the extraordinary variety and variability of groups, lifestyles and their settings – the "pseudo speciation" within a single species. Typically, most work has emphasized the latter; the former has been neglected. Constancy has been studied much less than variability and recent work about the degree of difference between human and non-human, the non-human roots of culture or the built environment, some reviewed briefly above (e.g., Lumsden and Wilson, 1981; Bonner, 1980; Von Frisch, 1974) may redress the balance. The possibility of an evolutionary baseline is also potentially useful.[4]

The emphasis on possible constancy is also found in recent work on cognitive schemata which, I have argued, are central to culture-built form relations. This is because built environments are usefully seen as material expressions of such schemata and their domains. The emphasis in the past has always been on the variability and arbitrariness of cognitive schemata, yet recent work questions this, suggesting much greater consistency and constancy and thus less arbitrariness and variability. This also seems to be the case regarding non-verbal communication (c.f. Review in Rapoport, 1982a). The evidence is not unequivocal, however, since arguments for *greater* cultural variability are also found (Hall, 1984). At this point I am more concerned with *the shift in emphasis*, with its potential links to the idea of evolutionary baselines that with whether the arguments are correct. The very presence of such arguments seems important. This is because it then becomes possible that behind the apparent variability of built environments there are hidden constancies, patterns and regularities imposed by the human mind. This is a difficult but important question which requires much comparative work on large bodies of evidence. There is, however, need for caution, particularly because the new findings tend to be concerned with cognition in the psychological sense (cf. Rapoport, 1976b). When they deal with anthropological cognition, the domain is mainly the *natural* world, for example, color and animal taxonomies. These seem to be much more similar cross-culturally than had been thought, that is, not arbitrary. It seems as though the world is most typically and sensibly divided at certain "natural joints"; the human mind seems pre-programmed to structure the world in certain ways (Johnson-Laird and Wason, 1977; Rosch and Lloyd, 1978).

While the relevance of these findings to *built environments* is as yet unknown, constancy is likely to be less. For example, when dealing with the *meaning* of color rather than its classification, variability and arbitrariness seems greater (Rapoport, 1982a). Variability among schemata is also likely to be more important in built environments than with regard to the natural world.

In this connection the possible distinction between "natural" environments and built environments, which seems to form distinct domains may be significant. *Preference* increasingly seems central in understanding EBR and, in general, cultural variability seems more important in the case of preference than in the case of either perception or cognition (Rapoport, 19977a, 1983c, 1985). The importance of preference can be argued on evolutionary grounds; a position which emphasizes the constancy of landscape preference (Kaplan, 1982). It would follow that landscape preferences should be less variable than preferences for manmade environments (Appleton, 1975; Craik and Zube, 1976, p. 53). Yet at least one test of this prediction found variability of landscape preference to be the case (Lyons, 1983).

To complicate matters further, it has also been suggested recently that aesthetic preferences are less variable and arbitrary, and more similar cross-culturally, than thought both in general (Smets, 1973) and specifically regarding architecture (Purcell, 1984). Similarly, there are findings suggesting both an absence of cultural differences, for example in density preferences between Chinese-Americans and Anglo-Americans, (Loo & Long, 1984), on the other hand major differences between two subgroups in London (Hanson & Hillier, 1982) and Washington, DC (Borchert, 1979).

The question, clearly is not self-evident. It is, however, researchable and urgently needs investigation. I have proposed a possible model for resolving similar disagreements in the domain of environmental meaning (Rapoport, 1982a). Also, in terms of the diagram of evolutionary constancy and cultural variability which I proposed at EDRA 6 (Rapoport, 1975, p. 146) the question can be rephrased in terms of the extent of the constant and variable components. Note, however, that *both* positions are implicitly based on the centrality of the culture, either as primarily non-human or group-specific. Its importance generally is, therefore, difficult to exaggerate.

In considering the role of cultural variables in understanding built form, two different, although related, types of questions can be, and have been asked:

1) The role and utility of "culture" in understanding *particular* environments and situations and responding to specific planning and design problems (e.g., Rapoport, 1980a, 1983a).
2) The role and importance of culture and cultural variables in *ANY theoretical or conceptual framework of EBR in general.*

Clearly, in the present paper the second of these questions is emphasized. In that sense the importance of culture is as great or greater than had been thought initially. The fact that environments seem to vary more than either activities, which are much more constant than schemata for classifying the world, which also seems less arbitrary than thought, gives great importance to culture. This is because latent aspects – imagery and meaning—become central; those seem to be unique to humans. For example, perception, psychological cognition, social interaction and networks can be found among animals. Among humans, however, many of these things seem to vary among different groups, and these variations seem to be greatest in meaning and least in perception, with others intermediate to varying extents. The specific degree of extent of variability, and whether it is real or apparent, needs to be investigated.

Another way of reconsidering the importance of culture is to consider the relative importance of cultural mechanisms vis-à-vis others in understanding how environments are shaped, used and evaluated; how they and people interact. An emphasis on mechanisms is clearly related to the question of what culture *does* (as opposed to what it is); it is also related to the view that without mechanisms, theory and explanation cannot be convincing.

Most of the mechanisms found in the literature, or of which one can think, tend either to be cultural or to have a cultural component, the importance of which in any given case is an empirical question. Consider a few examples:

Activities influence settings more through their latent than their instrumental aspects – and the former are more related to culture.

Communication among people (e.g., the specifics of privacy) varies considerably among cultures.

Social groups, mediating structures such as family, clan, tribe, social networks and social institutions are all highly culture-specific; this specificity in turn influences built form.

Temporal orientations, both short term and those relating to continuity and tradition, are highly culture-specific and greatly influence built environments.

Information flows from the environment, for example the cues that indicate status, identity and other meanings are all culturally variable.

The analysis of such mechanisms can clarify how various parts of the environment are used, for what, by whom, when and why. Such mechanisms link people with settings and systems of settings, and with their various supportive elements, fixed and semi-fixed, at various scales. They also help explain ways in which settings are supportive. For example:

Does an environment communicate and if so, how.

Does an environment reinforce identity and if so, how.

Does an environment communicate status and if so, how.

Are environments used to communicate central core meanings – and how.

In any of these cases, if the answer is negative—why not.

Understanding mechanisms can help suggest what elements may be substituted for others to achieve given goals. Mechanisms indicate ways in which culture is linked to preference and choice; ways in which lifestyle profiles and environmental quality profiles are made congruent (Rapoport, 1985).

The cultural component of mechanisms is thus likely to prove important in explaining the ways in which different parts of different built environments are linked to different components of culture.

Consider yet another way of addressing the question about the importance of culture. A recent proposal is that EBR can be understood in terms of *places, user groups* and *socio-behavioral phenomena* (Moore, Tuttle and Howell 1985, pp. 35-36). Without considering the utility of this approach it is useful to consider the role of culture in each of these elements.

Places: These seem to be culturally defined, and communicated – they appear to be culturally variable. They contain different cues which elicit very different behaviors and different meaning and relative importance is given them. They are assembled into *systems* in ways which are even more variable in terms of sequences, linkages or barriers, proximities, distances and the like (e.g., Rapoport 1982b) – i.e., culture is even more important at this higher level which, in fact, is the most critical since it defines cultural landscape of all sorts.

Groups: These are often culturally defined in the sense that social groups such as family, kin, ethnic, religions, status, caste, occupational, etc. exist and take their meaning within the "blueprint" or framework of culture (Bruner, 1983; Wallace, 1983). Recall also that in at least one formulation culture is precisely what defines groups in the first place (Rapoport, 1979). Moreover, I have argued that the "elderly" or the "urban poor" are not valid user groups, since there seem to be major cultural and other differences within them. Not only is it not self-evident what a valid group might be but most people today are members of nested groups, for example in the U.S. national, sub-group (ethnic, religious, ideological), sub sub-group (e.g., lifestyle), cohort and so on (Rapoport, 1985).

Socio-behavioral Phenomena: I have commented to one of the authors about the lack of "culture", so that the term should, in fact, be social, cultural, and behavioral phenomena. But, given our previous discussion of the link between culture and activities (including their latent aspects) and between culture and social phenomena, both of these can be said to have a cultural component.

I would thus conclude that culture plays some role in all three; how important this role is in general, and in any given case, becomes an empirical question. Finally, among the many concepts which are used, or are found useful, in the study of EBR, consider the following:

The three basic questions of EBR
The four-fold division of functions and activity
The link between activity systems and setting systems
Lifestyle
The link between lifestyle profiles and environmental quality profiles
Privacy as the control of unwanted interaction
Stress
Preference and choice
Cognitive schemata
Environmental complexity
The organization of space, time meaning and communication
The centrality of meaning

As for mechanisms, the question is which of these are mainly cultural, which not at all; to what extent is culture important in which of these? For example, the centrality of *meaning* in the environment is clearly related to culture. Particularly if one accepts the position, certainly not universally accepted, that meaning is culture-specific (Rapoport, 1982a). It is likely that complexity is less related to cultural variables.

It would seem that at least a *prima facie* case has now been made for the following conclusions. It was reasonable to give "culture" a prominent role in studying EBR; it seems at least as important, if not more so, that thought initially. In order to avoid the pitfall of cultural determinism (or reductionism), one needs to examine in much more detail, both generally and in any given case how important which aspects of culture are, to which components of the built environment, to whom, when, where, under what circumstances and why. The kinds of analyses discussed thus far, and those not even mentioned might help determine in which case or circumstances culture is less important, as important, or more important that first assumed. There can be no single answer to this overly broad and global question.

Implications for Design

I begin with a question which logically is also part of the previous section dealing with the importance of culture. This is: why is that "exotic" examples (preliterate, traditional, and vernacular) tend to be used in discussions of culture-built form relations? Could it be that not only are the effects of cultural variables less clear-cut in contemporary situations but that cultural variables are also *less important* today? An argument can at least be made that as other symbolic systems have become more widely available the symbolic role of the built environment has become less important. One tends to assume that the built environment is the critical part of any system. But, as a student pointed out to me almost twenty years ago, the Bororo case described by Levi-Strauss (1955), where by destroying the village the collective memory of the culture was destroyed, is very unlikely to work in the U.S. today. Symbolic information is stored in many other ways and places; in books, journals and other written form; photographs, T. V. and films, computers – what Popper (1972) has called World Three. This may tend to make the built environment less critical or central in culture so that the meanings encoded in the built environment may tend to be more mundane and quotidian, providing cues and mnemonics to facilitate the use of settings, making co-action easier and so on (Rapoport, 1982a). At that level, group differences continue to be important and cultural variables still play a major role.

Should the above argument be correct, it could be predicted that the relation of culture to built form will change. The role of built form in culture would become less important to the extent that literacy and the availability of other forms of symbolic systems goes up (cf. Goody, 1977). This argument has been made regarding Judaism: settlements, dwellings and even synagogue form are all non-specific to the cultural core. That is rather encoded in the written word (Torah and Talmud) with religious laws which regulate most of life, including dress, temporal organization, food habits, behavior and so on. *This* defined the group, gave it identity and contained the essentials (cf. Rapoport 1982f). Many groups today, one could argue, can survive culturally through comparable mechanisms (and others discussed earlier). Built form may no longer be crucial (cf. Rapoport 1981).

This may imply that while culture-built form relations were highly important or even critical in the past, they may be less so now. The corollary may be that culture-built environment relations play a lesser role in analyzing contemporary situations and may explain why contemporary examples are so little used.[5] It would also follow that culture-specific or culturally-responsive design may also be less critical. In this sense, one possible answer about the implications of culture for design, at least in the developing countries, may be that there are few – or none.

This view can, in fact, be found in several guises. The role of cultural variables in design was *implicitly* rejected by the Modern Movement in architecture. One example of an *explicit* rejection is based on the premise that since culture changes continually, and people are adaptive, they can and should adapt to any environment which is instrumentally satisfactory (Sonnenfeld, 1976). This I have explicitly rejected – but again in an "exotic" context of the developing countries (Rapoport 1983a). Even in that context, from the perspective of "modernization", the roles of cultural traditions and traditional environments are often seen as negative because impending progress (e.g., Meier, 1980). This position I have criticized in reviewing the book (Rapoport 1982c). While this position generally has also been trenchantly criticized in a series of writings by Peter L. Berger, an important and troubling question is raised.

Some possible answers to that argument have already been given briefly. Various reasons are possible to the position that people should adapt. 1) One can ask why should people be expected to do so. 2) One can argue that while some adaptations may be positive, or acceptable, others may well have negative consequences. 3) Much depends on the *rate* of adaptation and hence on the need to *modulate* it. 4) *Supportive environments* help modulate rates of change and may be essential where criticality is high (Rapoport 1983c). 5) When change becomes slower, time becomes available for syncretism and creative adaptation. 6) It can be argued that preservation of cultural diversity is important (analogue of preserving genetic diversity in biology; there may be need for a "cultural gene pool"). Recall, however, that built environments do not necessarily play a role in this. 7) There is a an "aesthetic" argument that varied built environments, cultural landscapes and lifestyles are desirable since they make the world richer and more complex; they also increase choice. 8) One could suggest that culture-specific environments work better. But note, once again, that most of these arguments refer to "exotic" and "extreme" situations – mainly traditional cultures undergoing change.

Clearly many of these arguments are partly a matter of values; but once the alternatives are made explicit; research can help – and may even change values. Yet in setting goals and objectives through research one must be prepared for the possibility that such research may contradict one's assumptions (Rapoport 1983b). It is at least possible that cultural variables might be becoming less important.

In the case of developing countries, where culture change is particularly rapid, and more generally regarding possible effects of environments on people (Rapoport, 1983c), I have recently tried to suggest some ways in which research could be used to help decide conditions under which cultural variables remain important. By studying comparative rates of change, one might be able to identify the culture core, the institutions and mechanisms which form part of it – and those physical settings which are supportive (Rapoport 1983a). This often has to do with maintaining group identity. But this, in turn, raises difficult questions: at what point in a process of change is a group no longer what it was but something entirely new? Ever? How could one know? What cultural variables are transmitted? How are they transmitted – what are the processes of enculturation and what is the possible role of the built environment in all this.

For any group to survive (i.e., for the "culture" to survive) there must be continuity at some level. Hence, the *reasons* (the "why") of these processes of transmission become clear and central. *What* continues to be transmitted and *how*, then become important questions. This may or may not be through the built environment, partly through it, or its importance may be decreasing, These are important empirical questions. One also needs to ask which environmental elements are so used and how they are used actively in this transmission process. As argued above, built form is a small part of culture (and architecture an even smaller part), hence, one cannot neglect all the other devices and mechanisms available – language, religion, furnishings, dress, hairstyles, music, art, food habits, festivals, temporal organizations, archives, (books, journals, films) and so on.

Two things should be noted, however. Particular physical elements or environmental units can frequently play a central role in the success of these other mechanisms. One is dealing with the indirect effect of built environments; settings, support institutions which, in turn, maintain identity (Rapoport, 1977, 1981, 1982a, 1983a, 1983c). Secondly, environmental elements may remain important in themselves or new elements may even be invented or created for such reasons. Sensitized to this possibility, for example, by the concept of *defensive structuring* (Siegel, 1970) many examples can be found: the Marae of the Maori in New Zealand; the crosses of the Mayo Indians in Mexico; the new syncretic religion, its rituals and shrines of the Fang in Africa (for these and other examples see Rapoport, 1981). Another example is the use of house decorations by the N'Debele in South Africa which appear to be a fairly recent development used in uprooted conditions.

Built environments, or parts of them, may also regain their importance. This may either lead to preservation, as has been documented in the case of Salzburg (Rowntree and Conkey, 1980) and as may well be the case more generally, or it may come back as part of a search for "roots" or ethnic identity. An example of the latter is the revival of the French-Canadian vernacular housing tradition in the *style neo-quebecois* which is used as a symbol of ethnic identity – although language is clearly more important. Many of these roles of built form (and of many of the other mechanisms) may in turn, be dependent on the maintenance (or creation) of *homogenous areas* (Rapoport 1977, 1980/81, 1981, 1982a) but this is often discouraged or made impossible for ideological or political reasons – a point to which I will return.

The discussion about the possibly reduced role of cultural variables in our situation seems to contradict the observation made at the outset about the growing interest in culture-built form relations, of which the "Built Form and Culture Research" conference is evidence. Additional evidence is easily found. Also in October 1984, the theme of the Northeast Regional ACSA meeting in Montreal was "The Cultural Responsiveness of Architecture". At a number of recent EDRA conferences, sessions on culture-built environment relations have taken place and have drawn large audiences. There is a sizable network on cultural aspects of EBR organized by Setha Low. There is a growing interest in vernacular design which is, I would argue, at least partly related to an interest in cultural aspects of design. For this also varied evidence can be found: sessions at a number of recent EDRA conferences and a large and growing number of conferences, exhibitions and publications about vernacular design, both in the U.S.

and other countries. Suggested topics for invited lectures, and letters from many parts of the world also reflect this interest. Finally, as I argued in a RIBA lecture (Rapoport, 1983b) and reiterated at the Montreal ACSA meeting, "Post Modernism" (as contrasted with the Modern Movement in architecture) seems, *at least in principle*, to show an interest in cultural specificity.[6]

Why there is this current interest is an important question because it might enable is to identify problems in the design disciplines. Typically an interest in a topic results from an important perceived or felt problem – and problem identification and definition can often be more important than problem solving. In any case, the identification of the problem or the problematic situation is, or should be, the start of research.

Many explanations for the interest in culture-built form relations are possible since, clearly, there are many problems. One explanation for the interest in vernacular design is that the place-specificity which often results from clear culture-built form relations (reinforced by climatic, site, material, technological, economic and other variables and constraints) is something which is being sought not only in architecture and urban design but in other domains. The search for "roots", ethnicity, group and other identity, "place" and the like seems world wide. In the domain of the built environment arbitrary criteria do not seem to work; materials, technology, and climatic influences also rarely succeed in meeting these goals. The variety of traditional environments and their specificity is intriguing and often missed. This also helps explain the choice of examples. In addition to some of romantic element, preliterate, vernacular or spontaneous ("squatter") environments, often seem to possess many of the desired qualities. They are also typically seen as reflecting culture. This is why the interest in vernacular design also represents an interest in culture-built form relations and also exemplifies them.

There is another (although related) explanation possible for the growth of interest in this topic. Traditionally (i.e., in preliterate and vernacular situations) built form has always been intimately linked to culture; this is, once again, why most of our examples are drawn from those environments. The clear response of built form to culture, and its role in culture, is also found in so-called "spontaneous" settlement; these do not, of course, happen spontaneously – they are merely designed *differently* (Rapoport 1972, 1984). To a lesser extent, these qualities are also found in popular environments although, in these cases, controls and regulations of various sorts and financing requirements tend to make the results less clear. These conditions, of course, in turn are part of our culture. On the other hand, professionally designed environments tend to be far less successful than any of the above in relating to different lifestyles and neither communicates as clearly nor can be used as effectively for cultural purposes. This lack of success, which is one of the felt problems behind the interest in culture-built form relations, can be attributed to various circumstances. Two new challenges facing designers deserve discussion.

1) In the traditional situation, designers were either the users themselves or designers and clients typically shared the same culture: they were members of the same group. Moreover, clients and users were often the same. At present, neither of these conditions obtains. a) Designers as a sub-culture are very different indeed from clients and, even more, from users (clients are rarely users). b) There are many different user groups which are effectively equivalent to different cultures. This results in "pluralism" and great variability among users as opposed to the much greater homogeneity of traditional situations. 2) Many environments which in the past were vernacular, folk, in a word, "spontaneous" – are now being professionally designed.

This latter point seems particularly interesting and important. Many problems that designers now face are ones they have never faced before simply because *they did not design those environments*. Most of these formed the vernacular matrix within which the high-style, professionally designed architectural or urban elements were located (Rapoport 1980b, 1982d).

In this connection, an analogy from biology is useful. There, Lederberg (cited in Jacob 1982, pp. 15-17) has made a distinction between the processes of *selectionism* and *instructionism*. The former is a process whereby congruence is gradually achieved through selection (e.g., evolution). The latter refers to short term "design", using a model or template and achieved through giving instructions (e.g., the making of proteins by DNA). Preliterate and traditional vernacular design worked through selectionist processes; this was pointed out in the 1960s by Alexander (1964), who called it "unselfconscious design" and myself (1969), although I didn't give it a name (cf. Studer 1982). I prefer the terms selectionism and instructionism to "unselfconscious" and "conscious" design. In current design by professionals, the predominant process is instructionism. It then follows that designers need to "objectify" the knowledge needed in order to be able to give valid instructions; hence the need for EBR research, analysis and so on. Provided one knows why (and how) culture-built form relations worked when the product came about through selectionism, one might be able to achieve comparable results by instructionist means, not by copying but by learning the lessons (Rapoport 1982d, 1983a, 1983d).

One can already propose ways of dissecting "culture" and "built environment" and suggest ways of classifying their components and specifying mechanisms and linkages. One can also discuss dynamics—both temporal dynamics and the active use of built form for cultural purposes. There is also available a sizable body of research which suggests that, at least under some (specifiable) conditions, culture-specific environments are more supportive, communicate better, and are also richer perceptually. One would then expect that design would have begun to change so as to reflect these insights. Yet, this has hardly been the case.

It therefore needs to be asked why the impact on what has been and is being done has been so minimal. As one small example of this, my suggestions about how culture-environment translation might be made today have had no effect, even though some of this work began life as a report to an international agency (Rapoport 1979c, 1980a, 1983d). Assuming that more, and more convincing, research data were available and that we could make better and more convincing arguments, would that influence or change planning or design?

I rather doubt it, for several reasons. Firstly, even among researchers in EBR, cultural variables are still largely ignored. As just one example, note that there is much work on the cultural specificity of environments in India, and criticisms of design work, including new towns (Mukerjee 1961 (1940); Doshi 1969; Grenell 1972; Krishan 1976; Choldin 1976; King 1976; Chandhoke 1977; Payne 1979; to mention a few). Yet, a recent study of Chandigarh (Sarin 1982) totally ignores cultural variables – the term does not even appear in the index. Other researchers seem to need to "rediscover" with apparent surprise, the presence of sub-cultural variability in housing in London, without seeming to know previous work on this topic (e.g., Hanson and Hillier 1982). If this is the case in research then, clearly, the situation in design can be expected to be even worse. Even less can designers be expected to know what is already known – or want to use it. Moreover, if designers were to refer to most mainstream research they would find that suggestions about the possible role of cultural variables in various domains have largely been ignored. That is, they are not even actively rejected after consideration. This has been the case, for example, with suggestions that cultural variables are significant in the study of stress, environmental cognition, environmental meaning and other aspects of the built environment (Rapoport 1978b, 1976b, 1982a).

But there are also other major problems in trying to relate cultural variables to design. I would suggest that generally one has tended to think of the implications of culture in design in terms of effects on *form.* But other kinds of implications may be more important when one addresses the issue of implementation and the use of knowledge. In a somewhat Chinese mode, I think of the problem as *The Three Rejections.*

1) Evidence may be rejected because "facts" alone are rarely enough. They are a necessary but not sufficient condition. One needs to change the way in which one sees things. Recall Bruner's view of culture as that which gives meaning to particulars. In this sense, designers need to change their culture, as I have argued for a long time. Recently, some empirical support for this position has become available. Having done research about the cultures, lifestyle and activities of user groups in an urban park, landscape architecture students and faculty ignored their own research in the design stage of the project, reverting to traditional criteria and objectives (Low 1982). More important than information is a change in the way designers think, how they see the world, see themselves, see problems and designs, and what they consider to be solutions. This involves a drastic set of changes (Rapoport 1983b). In cultural terms the designer culture needs to be changed (Rapoport 1977b) before this first rejection can be eliminated.
2) There is rejection due to ideological and political criteria to which I have already briefly referred. To use only my own very

limited experience, several reports made as a consultant to governments and international agencies on the need for culture-specific design and planning, which imply differential standards and homogeneous areas, were simply not acceptable and not feasible ideologically or politically.

3) There is also rejection of such efforts because users may not want culture-specific design. I have cited several times Ahmed Sifrioni's statement: "I fully appreciate the charm and refinement of our traditional buildings, but I know, like most Moroccans of my generation the absolute necessity of modifying the setting of our life" (cited in Nijst, Priemus, Swets, and Van Ijseren, 1973, p. 1; my translation). I have also given many examples of how such attitudes affect design and lead to rejection. More recently, I have argued that the apparent rejection by the villagers of Hassan Fathy's admirable efforts was due to the negative meanings attached to traditional forms and materials (Rapoport 1982a). I had, however, suggested that often spatial organizations and other core elements may be accepted or even desired (Rapoport 1979c, 1980e, 1983a). I still believe that to be the case but some more recently published evidence suggests that even that may be rejected by users (Martin 1984). It may well be that the rejection of tradition may be even more complete than at least I had expected. Note, however, that this is just one study (i.e., it needs replication), there may be methodological problems, and the specific context (Africa) may well differ from other milieus.

It is thus possible that having criticized the over-romantic and superficial copying of forms, and having tried to approach the problem more analytically, I have still been over-romanticizing the importance of built environments. At the very least the evidence is not unequivocal and more research is needed with much more specific questions and relating to much more specific situations and locales. One also needs to be able to identify needs as opposed to wants and to identify needs behind expressed wants (Rapoport 1985). Then, assuming one is certain that some solutions are, in fact, better, one needs to consider two things. First, are there other, more acceptable, ways of achieving the same goals (cf. Rapoport 1980f), pp. 131-132). Second, can users be convinced of this (Rapoport 1973, 1982e, 1983d). This may then have much more to do with mass communication and the media than with design; it is the obverse of the research and literature on how to get new technology and the like accepted.

Conclusion

Having discussed a range of issues, some summary conclusions need to be made.

I conclude that the enterprise, in principle, was and is well conceived. Without suggesting that it is the only variable, culture seems to be important in analyzing and understanding built environments, possible even more important than one had thought. At the same time, the question was posed early in this paper was too global—and so were the answers. The reconsideration needs to be much more articulated: what aspects of culture are important for what environments, for whom, when, under what conditions and why?

One needs a clear definition of the domain of study, of concepts and mechanisms; explicit dissection and dismantling of global terms, agreed-upon taxonomies and explicit recombination (synthesis). One needs replication of single studies and clarification of conflicting findings. It also follows that examples and data need to be used more rigorously on the basis of explicit selection criteria. Moreover, such data need to be accumulated systematically. There is need for comparative study to answer specific questions and test specific hypotheses. We do have insights and a number of case studies, but not yet a cumulative body of generalizable knowledge: this requires an emphasis on the development of models and on theory-building. We need to convince the rest of EBR, and various social sciences, that culture-built form research is a significant domain. Finally, we need to convince decision-makers, planners and designers—and the problem is not, in the first instance, one of how one translates cultural data into form.

There is a possibility that we may research ourselves out of a job in design; real research is into the unknown, is open-ended and hence "risky". If culture proves not to be critical to design, however, it will still be very important regarding understanding and explanation.

By and large, it seems that we have done relatively well (as has EBR generally, e.g., Rapoport, 1977b). Fifteen or twenty years ago there was no field, only isolated individuals; now there is a large, thriving, and growing field. If I am correct about the current growth of interest, then this is encouraging and provides an opportunity which needs to be grasped.

In general, the importance of culture has been confirmed. In terms of the Tversky and Kahneman model, the adjustments have produced development; the specifics have changed but the anchor had held. The changes have led to more articulation, more qualifications, more elaboration and less simplicity. This has increased the veridicality of the anchor.

Things have become much more complicated, and would appear even more complicated if I had fully developed even the relatively few points addressed. Things do seem less clear-cut than before. But this may be a "good thing", in the sense that we are realizing the presence of new linkages and connections, realizing that the domain (and the world) are rather more complex. The loss of clarity may well be a function of increasing veridicality: this should have positive consequences whether any theory eventually developed is simple or complex. It is possible that, as we continue, we will learn how to simplify at a higher level. It is often assumed that good theories are simple. Pragmatically (or instrumentally) they certainly are, but the inherent epistemic advantage of "simplicity" has never been demonstrated; moreover "simplicity" in this sense is a highly ambiguous criterion. Complexity has at least one big pragmatic advantage—it is a useful corrective to the simplistic nature of much of architecture; so-called "Architecture Theory" (sic) and design.

At the same time, the elaboration, revisions and modifications have raised many questions and some uncertainty; this suggests the fruitfulness of the approach. There seems to be many actual and potential changes in how we address the topic. Some of these I have discussed, especially those which might help the field grow in generalizability, cumulativeness and explanatory power. If we can do that, then even if in the present, the design role of culture proves to be less important than thought (*and this is far from certain*), it will still play a major role in any valid theory of the built environment.

Notes

1 Note that this distinction in itself is an instance of dissecting a global term – in this instance "reductionism".

2 This concept, of course, came from another field—anthropology. In fact, one implication of an emphasis on culture in EBR is that anthropology is a highly relevant discipline. As part of any reconsideration it might even be useful to ask whether this conjunction of disciplines has proved useful and, if so, in what ways and also which specific subfields of anthropology have proved most useful and so on. (e.g., Rapoport, 1980c; this was also discussed at symposia at EDRA 12 and EDRA 13).

3 I find it rather significant that comparative cross-cultural studies were generally lacking at the conference. Most papers were either theoretical with examples or had a case study character.

4 Rapoport 1974, 1979a, b citing work by Lionel Tiger, Robin Fox, David Hamburg, Valerius Geist, Irenaus Eibi-Eibesfeldt and Stephen Boyden among others. The latter has applied this approach most successfully to the analysis of the urban ecology of Hong Kong (Boyden, Miller, Newcombe and O'Neill, 1981).

5 This does not necessarily invalidate my previous argument that contemporary examples are less used because less clear-cut and less striking, particularly since, as argued above, examples have been used illustratively rather than as data they may actually help modernization.

6 I will not discuss here its dismal failure to achieve these goals, nor elaborate reasons for this failure. These reasons, however, have to do with much of what I say in this paper – the need for rigor, analysis. clear definitions, taxonomies, dismantling of excessively broad concepts, study of linkages and mechanisms, the need for research and empirical data.

References

Alexander, C. (1964). *Notes on the Synthesis of Form*. Cambridge, MA: Harvard University Press.

Appleton, J. (1975) *The Experience of Landscape*. London: Wiley.

Ayala, F. J. and T. Dobzhensky (Eds.) (1974). *Studies in the Philosophy of Biology: Reduction and Related Problems*. Berkeley: University of California Press.

Barth, F. (1969). Ethnic Groups and Boundaries. Boston: Little Brown.

Bennett, J. W. (1982). Review of I. Altman and M. M. Chamers, Culture and Environment, in *Environment and Behavior*. vol. 14. pp. 622-624.

Binford, L. R. (1983). *Working at Archaeology*. New York: Academic Press.

Bonner, J. T. (1980). *The Evolution of Culture in Animals*. Princeton, NJ: Princeton University Press.

Borchert, J. (1979). Alley Landscapes of Washington. *Landscape* 23 (3), pp. 3-10.

Boulding, K. E. (1956). *The Image*. Ann Arbor: University of Michigan.

Boyden, S., S. Miller, K. Newcombe and B. O'Neil, (1961). The Ecology of a City and its People (The Case of Hong Kong) Canberra: Australian National University Press.

Bruner, J. (1983). *In Search of Mind.* New York: Harper and Row.

Bullock, T. N. (1984). Comparative Neuroscience Holds Promise for Quiet Revolutions. *Science* vol.225, no. 4661, 3 August, pp. 473-477.

Chandhoke, S. K. (1977). Chaupal - The Men's Community Place in a Jat Village in Haryana. *Urban and Rural Planning Thought,* 20(1), pp. 24-31.

Chisholm, J. C. (1983). *Navajo Infancy: an Ethological Study of Child Development,* New York: Aldine.

Choldin, H. M. (1976). Housing Standards Versus Ecological Forces: Regulating Population Density in Bombay, in A. Rapoport (Ed.) *The Mutual Interaction at People and Their Built Environment,* pp. 287-332, The Hague: Mouton.

Craik, K. M., and E. H. Zube (Eds.) (1976). *Perceiving Environmental Quality.* New York: Plenum.

Doshi, S. L. (1969). Nonclustered Tribal Villages and Village Development. *Human Organization.* 28(4), pp. 247-302.

Downton, P. (1983). On Designing a Human Robot. In D. Joiner, G. Brimilcombe, J. Daish, J. Gray, D. Karnohan (Eds.), *Paper-Conference on People and Physical Environment Research,* p. 49, Wellington, New Zealand.

Etron, E. (1984). *The Apocalyptics (Cancer and the Big Lie).* New York: Simon and Schuster.

Geertz, C. (1983). *Local Knowledge.* Basic Books.

Goody, J. (1977). *The Domestication of the Savage Mind.* Cambridge MA: Cambridge University Press.

Grenell, P. (1972). Planning for Invisible People: Some Consequences of Beaurocratic Values and Practices. In J. F. C.Turner and R. Fichter (Eds.) *Freedom To Build.* pp. 95-121, New York: Macmillan.

Hall, E. T. (1984). *The Dance of Life.* Garden City, NY.

Hanson, F. A. (1975). *Meaning in Culture.* London: Routledge and Kegan Paul.

Hanson, F. A. (1983). When the Map is the Territory: Art in Maori Culture. In D. K. Washburn (Ed.) *Structure and Cognition in Art.* pp.74-89. Cambridge: Cambridge University Press.

Hanson, J. & Hillier, B. (1982). Domesticate Space Organization (Two Contemporary Space-Codes Compared). *Architecture and Behavior.* 2(1). pp. 5-25.

Hinde, R. A. (Ed.) (1984). *Primate Social Relationships (An Integrated Approach).* Sunderland MA: Sinauer.

Hodder, I. (1982). *Symbols in Actions.* Cambridge: Cambridge University Press.

Jacob, F. (1982). *The Possible and the Actual.* New York: Pantheon Books.

Johnson-Laird , P. N. & Wason, P. C. (Ed.) (1977). *Thinking (Readings in Cognitive Science)* Cambridge: Cambridge University Press.

Kaplan, A. (1964). *The Conduct of Inquiry.* New York: Harper and Row.

Kaplan, S. (1982). Where Cognition and Affect Meet: A Theoretical Analysis of Preference in P. Bart, A. Chen and G. Francescato (Eds.) *Knowledge for Design, EDRA 13* pp. 183-185, Washington , DC.

Kent, S. (1984). *Analyzing Activity Areas.* Albuquerque, University of New Mexico Press.

King, A. D. (1976). *Colonial Urban Development.* London: Routledge and Kegan Paul.

Kosslyn, S. M. (1963). *Ghosts in the Mind's Machine.* New York: Norton.

Krishnan, A. (1976). *Housing Design Criteria for School, Cultural and Climatical Conditions of Chandigarh.* M. Arch. Thesis, Dept. of Architecture, University of Washington, Seattle.

Laudan, L. (1984). *Science and Values.* Berkeley: University of California Press.

Levi-Strauss, C. (1955). *Tristes Tropiques.* Paris: Librairie Plon.

Loo, C. & Ong, P. (1984). Growing Perceptions, Attitudes and Consequences Among the Chinese. *Environment and Behavior.* 16 (1), pp. 55-67.

Low, S. M. (1982). *Professional Culture: The Boundary Between Theory and Practice in Design.* Washington DC: U.S. Dept. of NEW, NIE, Educational Resource Information Center (ERIC). No. ED2129290.

Lumsden, C. & Wilson, E. (1981). *Genes, Mind, and Culture: The Coevolutionary Process.* Cambridge, MA.

Lyons, E. (1983). Demographic Correlates of Landscape Preference. *Environment and Behavior.* 15 (4), pp. 487-511.

Martin, R. (1984). Poverty and Professionals. *Journal of the Royal Institute of British Architects.* 91 (7), pp. 17-20.

Meier, R. L. (1980). *Urban Futures Observed in the Asian Third World.* New York: Pergamon Press.

Miller, G. A., Gallanter, E., & Pribram, K. H. (1960). *Plans and The Structure of Behavior.* New York: Rinehart & Winston.

Moore, G. T.. Tuttle, D. P.. & Howell, S. C. (1985). *Environmental Design Research Directions.* New York: Praeger.

Moore, J. A. (1983). The trouble with Know-it-alls: Information as a Social and Ecological Resource. In J. A. Moore & A. S. Keene (Eds.) *Archeological Hammers and Theories.* pp. 173-191. New York: Academic Press.

Murkerjee, R. (1961). Ways of Dwelling in the Communities of India. In G. A. Theodorsonn (Ed.) *Studies in Human Ecology.* pp. 390-401. Evanston, IL: Row, Peterson.

Nagel, E. (1961). *The Structure of Science (Problems in the Logic of Scientific Explanation).* New York: Hacket & Harcourt, Brace & World.

Nijst, A. L. M. T., Priemus, H., Swets, H. L., & Van Ijzeren, J. J. (1973). *Living on the Edge of the Sahara.* The Hague: Government Publishing Office.

Northrop, F. S. C. (1947). *The Logic of the Sciences and the Humanities.* New York: Macmillan.

Payne, G. K. (1979). *Urban Housing in the Third World.* Boston: Routledge and Kegan Paul.

Popper, K. R. (1972). *Objective Knowledge: An Evolutionary Approach.* Oxford: Clarendon Press.

Purcell, T. (1984). Aesthetics, Measurement and Control. *Architecture Australia.* 73 (4), pp.29-38.

Rapoport, A. (1985). Thinking about Home Environments. In I. Altman & C. Werner (Eds.) *Home Environments. Vol. 8 of Human Behavior and Environment.* pp. 255-286.

Rapoport, A. (1969). *House Form and Culture.* Englewood Cliff, NJ: Prentice-Hall.

Rapoport, A. (1972). Environment and People. In A. Rapoport (Ed.) *Australia as Human Setting*. pp. 3-21. Sydney: Angus and Robertson.

Rapoport, A. (1973). The City of Tomorrow, the Problems of Today and the Lessons of the Past. *DMG-DRS Journal*. 7(3), pp.256-259.

Rapoport, A. (1975). An Anthropological Approach to Environmental Design Research. In B. Honikman (Ed.) *Responding to Social Change. EDRA 6.* pp. 145-151. Stroudsburg, PA: Dowden, Hutchinson & Ross.

Rapoport, A. (1977a). *Human Aspects of Urban Form.* Oxford: Pergamon Press.

Rapoport, A. (1977b). The Last (and First) Ten Years. *Man-Environment Systems.* 7(6), pp. 296-299.

Rapoport, A. (1978). Culture and the Subjective Effects of Stress. *Urban Ecology*. 3 (3), pp. 241-261.

Rapoport, A. (1979a). On the Cultural Origins of Architecture. In J. C. Snyder & A. J. Catanese (Eds.) *Introduction to Architecture*, pp. 31-61. New York: McGraw Hill.

Rapoport, A. (1979b). On the Cultural Origins of Settlements. In A. J. Catanese & J. Snyder (Eds.) *Introduction to Urban Planning*, pp. 31-61. New York: McGraw Hill.

Rapoport, A. (1979c). An Approach to Designing Third World Environments. *Third World Planning Review.* 1(1), pp. 23-40.

Rapoport, A. (1980/1981). Neighborhood Heterogeneity or Homogeneity. *Architecture and Behavior.* 1(1), pp.65-77.

Rapoport, A. (1980a). Cross-cultural Aspects of Environmental Design. In I. Altman, A. Rapoport & J. F. Wohlwill (Eds.) *Human Behavior and Environment: Advances in Theory and Research, Vol. 4: Environment and Culture.* pp. 7-46. New York: Plenum Press.

Rapoport, A. (1980b). Vernacular Architecture and the Cultural Determinants of Form. In A. D. King (Ed.) Buildings and Society, pp. 283-305. London: Routledge and Kegan Paul.

Rapoport, A. (1980c). Anthropology and Architecture The Present State of Knowledge. In *Tradition and Identity (Towards an Anthropological Architecture).* pp. 26-35. Proceedings of Symposium at Betelle Institute, July 21-23, Seattle, WA.

Rapoport, A. (1980d). Towards a Cross-Culturally Valid Definition of Housing. In R. R. Stough and A. Wandersman (Eds.) *Optimizing Environments (Research Practice and Policy).* EDRA 11. pp.310-316. Washington DC.

Rapoport, A. (1980e). Culture, Site-Layout and Housing. *Architectural Association Quarterly.* 12(1), pp. 4-7.

Rapoport, A. (1980f). Environmental Preference, Habitat Selection and Urban Housing. *Journal of Social Issues.* 36(3), pp. 118-134.

Rapoport, A. (1981). Identity and Environment: A Cross-Cultural Perspective. In J. S Duncan (Ed.) *Housing and Identity: Cross-Cultural Perspectives.* pp. 6-35. London: Croom Helm.

Rapoport, A. (1982a). *The Meaning of the Built Environment: A Non-verbal Communication Approach.* Beverly Hills, CA: Sage.

Rapoport, A. (1982b). Urban Design and Human Systems – One Way of Relating Buildings to Urban Fabric. In P. Laconte, J, Gibson & A. Rapoport (Eds.) *Human and Energy Factors in Urban Planning: A Systems Approach.* (NATO

Advanced Study Institutes, Series D, Beh. & Soc. Sci. no. 12) pp. 161-184. The Hague: Nijhoff.

Rapoport, A. (1982c). Review of R. L. Meier's Urban Futures Observed. *Urban Ecology*. 7 (1), pp. 73-75.

Rapoport, A. (1982d). An Approach to Vernacular Design. In J. M. Fitch (Ed.) *Shelter: Models of Native Ingenuity*. pp. 43-48. Katonah, NY: Katonah Gallery.

Rapoport, A. (1982e). Design, Development and Man-Environment Studies. *Environments*. 14(2), pp. 1-8.

Rapoport, A. (1982f). Sacred Places, Sacred Occasions, Sacred Environments. *Architecture Design*. 52 (9-10), pp. 75-82.

Rapoport, A. (1983a). Development, Culture Change and Supportive Design. *Habitat International*. 7(5/6), pp. 249-268.

Rapoport, A. (1983b). Debating Architectural Alternatives. *Transactions of the RIBA*. Vol. 3. pp. 105-109.

Rapoport, A. (1983c). The Effect of Environment on Behavior. In J. B. Calhoun (Ed.) *Environment and Population – Problems of Adaptation*. pp. 200-201. New York: Praeger.

Rapoport, A. (1983d). Environmental Quality, Metropolitan Areas and Traditional Settlements. *Habitat International*. 7(3-4), pp. 37-63.

Rapoport, A. (1984). Culture and the Urban Order. In J. Agnew, J. Mercer & D. Sopher (Eds.) *The City in Cultural Context*. pp. 50-75. Boston: Allen and Unwin.

Rapoport, A. (1993a). *Cross-Cultural Studies and Urban Form*. College Park, MD: University of Maryland.

Rapoport, A. (1998). Using culture in housing design. *Housing and Society, 25(1).*

Rappaport, R. A. (1979). *Ecology, Meaning and Religion*. Richmond, CA: North Atlantic Books.

Rosch, E. & Lloyd, B. B. (Eds.) (1978). *Cognition and Categorization*. Hillsdale, NJ: Lawrence Erlbaum.

Rowntree, L. B. & Conkey, M. W. (1980). Symbolism and the Cultural Landscape. *Annals, Association of the American Geographers*. 70(1), pp. 459-474.

Sarin, M. (1982). *Urban Planning in the Third World (The Chandigarh Experience)*. London: Munsell.

Siegel, B. J. (1970). Defensive Structuring and Environmental Stress. *American Journal of Sociology*. Vol. 76, pp. 11-46.

Smets, G. (1973). *Aesthetic Judgement and Arousal*. Leuven: Leuven University Press.

Sonnenfeld, J. (1976). Imposing Environmental Meaning: A Commentary. In G. T. Moore & R. G. Golledge (Ed.) *Environmental Knowing*. pp. 254-257.

Studer, R. G. (1982). Shelter, Behavior and the Unselfconscious Process. In J. M .Fitch (Ed.) *Shelter: Models of Native Ingenuity*. pp. 49-56. Katonah, NY: Katonah Gallery.

Tobias, P. V. (1981). The Emergence of Man. In J. Z. Young, E. M. Jope & K. P. Oakley (Ed.) *The Emergence of Man*. Pp. 44-55. London: Royal Society and British Academy.

Tversky, A. & Kahneman, D. (1974). Judgement under Uncertainty: Heuristics and Biases. *Science*. Vol. 185, pp. 1124-1131.

Von Frisch, K. (1974). *Animal Architecture*. New York: Harcourt Brace Jovanowich.

Wallace, W. L. (1983). *Principles of Scientific Sociology.* New York: Aldine.

Wobst, H. M. (1977). Stylistic Behavior and Information Exchange. In C. E. Cleland (Ed.) *For the Director: Research Essays in Honor of James B. Griffin.* University of Michigan, Museum of Anthropology, Anthropological Papers, Vol. 61, pp. 317-342.

Ziman, J. (1978). *Reliable Knowledge (An Exploration of the Grounds of Belief in Science).* Cambridge: Cambridge University Press.

11 Journey of Self-Discovery: From "Complexity" to "Street Encounters" and Beyond

Yasser Elsheshtawy

Abstract

As a former student of Amos Rapoport this essay will address the impact of his writings in shaping my research interests. Given my interest in the quality of the urban environment and cross-cultural studies, Environment-Behavior Studies offered a means by which this interest could be enhanced and strengthened. Starting from my Master thesis on "Complexity" until my Dissertation on "Street Encounters" this search was modified to be more inclusive and "holistic," reflecting shifts and criticisms found both in the field of EBS research and in Amos's own writing. The essay while using my own work as an overall framework, will discuss these developments while at the same time acknowledging the impact – and importance – of Amos Rapoport's work. At the same time I will address the extent to which I have been able to utilize EBS research within the framework of an architectural curriculum in an Arab university.

Introduction

As a former graduate student who studied and developed his dissertation under the supervision of Amos Rapoport, this essay provides the opportunity to offer a critical account of Amos Rapoport's influence and the extent to which it contributed to my personal, scholarly development. The hypothesis of this paper is that this development is reflective of the various shifts, currents, and directions existing within Environment-Behavior Studies (EBS). The essay will also present some of the problems I encountered as a junior faculty with regard to the use of EBS within a traditional architectural curriculum, especially within the context of an Arab/Moslem culture. The work of Amos Rapoport potential appeal to many in the developing world – including Arab/Moslem countries – as it seems to take on the cause of developing their own identity. Unfortunately, his writings are not very well known – except for those who had the opportunity to study in the United States – since there has been no official translation of his work.

This essay is structured as follows: first, a discussion of my research on complexity within the urban environment and how it was heavily influenced by the work of Amos Rapoport. Second, responding to criticisms I will discuss my interest in the "use and design of urban public spaces" and how that led to my dissertation on pedestrian streets in Cairo. A critical assessment of these developments will lead to the third part in which I will present the extent to which I was able to integrate these issues within a curriculum that is closely tied to a College of Engineering.

Background and Development

My first encounter with EBS came indirectly through the writings of architect/theoretician Christopher Alexander. While still an undergraduate student at Cairo University, struggling with project deadlines and selecting the "right" presentation techniques, I came across a German book in which the author presented various alternative approaches to architecture among them Alexander's pattern language (Gruber, 1987). While not fully equipped to deal with the different aspects of this approach, I found the terminology and the inclusion of humans and their activities as part of the architectural design formula fascinating. The paragraph was relatively small yet the impact was strong. When I began my graduate studies at Pennsylvania State University, my research interests centered on the issue of enhancing the quality of the urban environment – to make it more livable and to search for "patterns," that would enhance this quality. The patterns of Alexander offered an answer, yet seemed vague and difficult to apply. When I first read Amos Rapoport's (1967) paper on complexity, it suggested an alternative approach that is based on science, or a positive approach (e.g. Lang, 1987). Deeply influenced by this study, I began to focus my efforts on developing a tool that would "measure" the complexity of streetscapes (Elsheshtawy, 1997).

The Beginning: Quantifying the Urban Experience

> ...everywhere parallel rows of trees; buildings in rigid lines, low flat structures, long cold perspectives, and the dreary sameness of right angles. No variation in the terrain, not a caprice of architecture, not a wrinkle. Altogether, it was chilly, regular and hideous. Nothing is so stifling as symmetry. Symmetry is boredom, the quintessence of mourning. Despair yawns. There is something more terrible than a hell off suffering – a hell of boredom.
>
> Victor Hugo (1822) in "Les Miserables"

Hugo's quote represented in many respects the issues which I was trying to explore at the time when I began research for my Masters degree at the Pennsylvania State University in 1989. I was intrigued in particular by the link which Victor Hugo saw between the psychological state of a person (the use of such words as "chilly," "stifling," etc.) and the nature of the built environment ("buildings in rigid lines," etc.). Of course, the central question remained unresolved: how could a construct such as complexity be operationalized?

My interest in complexity was primarily motivated by a larger issue: namely, searching for the factors that would make the experience of the urban environment more "pleasurable." This led to a focus on various theories of perception such as the Gestalt theory (e.g. Overy, 1969), Gibson's affordances (e.g. Gibson, 1979), and the work of psychologist Berlyne (1974). The problem posed by these theories is that they were not aimed at issues of concern for architects and urban designers. At the same time, architects who addressed them such as Venturi (1967), in his famous *Complexity and Contradiction in Architecture*, offered a highly personal account about what is considered complex in architecture. Venturi's study is valuable as a heuristic device, but was criticized for its lack of rationale, subjectivity, and pure descriptiveness (e.g. Wohlwill, 1976). A few exceptions existed in the work of Prak (1977) who attempted to incorporate the principles of Gestalt psychology in architecture.

All the above studies were not tied together by a unified framework which would unite findings from various disciplines into one coherent whole and which, in turn, would be of use for architects and planners. In that regard Amos Rapoport's paper written with R. Kantor (1967), *Complexity and Ambiguity in Environmental Design* and his subsequent paper on the perception of urban complexity (Rapoport & Hawkes, 1970) offered a critical response in a number of ways: 1) it made a direct link supported with scientific evidence that there is an association between complexity and levels of preference within the built environment; 2) it discussed how this could be integrated with architectural theory; and 3) it presented an alternative approach within architectural theory that is not based on personal, or normative values but one that is grounded in positive knowledge. In contrast to the sometime ambiguous writings of architects/theoreticians Rapoport's set of papers were written in a language that was clear and seemed to suggest a clear and unequivocal answer to my questions. However one issue remained: how could one measure complexity? The answer was a "tool" — an analytic device — that would quantify such a phenomena. This was the effort of my thesis *Urban Complexity: toward the measurement of the physical complexity of streetscapes* (Elshestawy, 1997).

Briefly stated the tool developed through this study attempted to quantify the complexity of a given streetscape by dividing it into three levels: overall massing; secondary massing; and openings. By counting the number of perceived "groups" within each level (using Gestalt theory) and aggregating these measures, one would be able to reach a "number" representing the complexity level of that particular scene. This number could in turn be used within the urban design guideline process, e.g., by specifying that any new addition, be either above, below, or retain the same, measured complexity level. In order to test this tool, an experiment was conducted in which 33 students were asked to rank ten scenes according to their level of complexity. There was a statistically significant correspondence between the ranking results and the tool measurements (Elsheshtawy, 1997).

This strictly quantitative approach however left many unanswered questions. Could the entire urban experience be reduced to a simple "number?" There were many variables which the tool did not take into consideration and which I argued could perhaps be taken into account in "future" studies dealing with this issue. However, my initial question about the factors that would contribute to the enhancement of the urban experience was only partially answered. Perhaps because of my cultural background, I was particularly concerned with the missing consideration of cultural issues. The tool implied a universality that might not be there in the first place. As I was preparing for the publication of this study I began to address these issues indirectly by incorporating a section entitled "Complexity: Subjective and Objective Approaches" which did not exist in the original study. At the same time the exclusion of many variables — while a valid practice in scientific research — seemed to take away from the holistic nature of an architectural and urban experience. These variables are not simply formal: masses, shapes, colors, materials, etc., but include a building or sites history, people's personal state, the role of myths, novelty value of buildings, and so forth. This was even apparent in some of the results from a test of the tool's validity and reliability. One scene of a "simple" building — according to the tools measurements — exhibited a wide range of responses ranging from those that ranked it as very low to others who gave it a high ranking (i.e. a high complexity value). My only explanation at the time was that this could be attributed to the novelty value of the building, a variable which the tool did not measure, and which contributed to this variation.

It was only when I began my doctoral studies at the University of Wisconsin-Milwaukee (UWM) that I began to see these questions and criticisms as larger issues with which EBS was struggling. It was also at that time that I began to read two books by Amos Rapoport, *House, Form and Culture* (Rapoport, 1969) and *The Meaning of the Built Environment* (Rapoport, 1982). Also, a paper written by Amos entitled *Pedestrian Street Use: Culture and Perception* (Rapoport, 1987) directed me towards the inclusion of cultural factors, which was neglected in the complexity tool, and to expand the boundaries of my research interest to deal with "public spaces" both from a behavioral and formal perspective.

Developments: Street Use and Culture

My interest in the use and design of urban public spaces began during a course taught by Amos Rapoport entitled "Behavioral Factors in Housing Design." Most of my research activity was directed towards street use, or lack thereof, in low-income housing projects. Observing various cities in the United States I was struck by the absence of what one might term a vital street life. I considered the absence of street activities as a negative development. Amos on the other hand argued that street use is a cultural phenomenon, which varies among people based on their socio-economic backgrounds, or life-style. One need not make value judgements about whether the presence of people on the street is good or bad.

To further highlight this point, during many discussions we had on this topic he offered a comparison between his work and that of urban sociologist Richard Sennett. While making similar observations about the use of plazas, streets, etc. the conclusions differed. Sennett calls for a "return" to an age in which there was a vital street life, whereas Amos refrains from making any value judgements (Sennett, 1970; 1974; 1990). Similar criticism was directed at Jane Jacobs (1961) who argued compassionately for having "eyes on the street" to combat crime for example. According to Amos these were all "romantic longings," advocating a return to the past that is simply not possible given peoples life-style changes (car dependence, privacy requirements, etc.). A clear distinction was drawn between a normative or value-driven stance and one grounded in positive knowledge and based on empirical research.

These discussions led me to study pedestrian streets since they offered a perfect example for exploring these issues. The presence of these streets is widespread in Europe. Entire downtown areas have been converted to pedestrian use with a high rate of success. In the United States however the experience has not been positive. In fact many pedestrianized streets were re-opened to car traffic after a drop in commercial revenue generated from car movement, as well as the invitation of such spaces for loiterers, homeless etc. This was taken as proof that street use is primarily culturally based and that one cannot impose on a given population a lifestyle that one deems to be valuable and attractive.

Amos considered this point a "normative" position adopted by many architects who attempt to impose their views — influenced by other cultures — in the United States without studying the characteristics of the population for which they are designing. The question on whether there are some core issues which most people can agree on — such as outdoor street use — was thus not answered since it was relegated to a matter of life style that might be appropriate or not. I was still convinced however that there are many positive qualities behind having an active and vibrant street which might not be apparent to the average user, but which a researcher, educator, and architect need to identify. In order to present a case for such a viewpoint I decided to search for an example for a successful urban setting in my home country — Egypt. This search led to Mohamed Ali street, a street extension passing between two monumental mosques in Cairo. The street was converted to pedestrian use in the eighties and offered residents in Cairo excellent opportunities for enjoying outdoor activities and socializing.

Initially my intention was to present an in-depth case study, an ethnography of the "inner life" of Mohamed Ali's. However, Amos's concern with generalizability and the limitations of a single case study, argued for the inclusion of more than one setting and expanding the boundaries of the case study. At that time his *History and Precedent in Environmental Design* was published and the latter part of the book concerned with the design elements of pedestrian streets offered some interesting ideas (Rapoport, 1990). I was particularly impressed by the systematic categorization of these design elements supported with photographic evidence. One area of criticism however which I perceived was that this was offered as scientific evidence as opposed to the subjective accounts usually presented with regard to this issue. Even though many photographs are offered for each design variable, there is still an element of choice or selection. Thus, one selects those images that may already fit some preconceived notion about what is "good" in street design. Of course underlying the entire discussion is the implicit idea that pedestrian streets are desirable.[1]

I decided to include as part of my research an analysis of traditional streets in Cairo. The study would therefore determine whether design elements proposed by Amos existed in Mohamed Ali street and whether they contributed to the street's success. Also, to enhance the validity of the study I included another street — Dahab — as a comparison. Other issues offered an important and needed context in which the performance of the street could be evaluated; among them, Amos' definition of culture.

Amos Rapoport in numerous writings defines culture as a matter of "life-style," a particular "way of doing things" (Rapoport, 1987). Specifically, he argues that all the definitions of culture can be classified in three classes : (1) culture can be defined as a way of life typical of a group, a particular way of doing things; (2) a system of symbols, meanings, and cognitive schemata; and (3) a set of adaptive strategies for survival related to the ecological setting and its resources. Given the scope and objectives of my study, the first class was adapted as an appropriate starting point in examining the construct of culture. Using this definition in examining the data, I concluded that several elements of Cairo's traditional urban sub-culture are seen as being responsible for the use of *Mohamed Ali* street. They are (1) the concept of *Fos'ha* — enjoying oneself in the outdoors, and (2) outdoor celebration. In addition to these, three more components — while not unique to this sub-culture — are considered as well: (3) the *Qahwa* (sitting on a coffee shop) custom; (4) the changing role of women and gender relationships and (5) the dramaturgical aspect of street life. I argued that in Cairo the ability of Mohamed Ali street to cater to all these components through its unique physical structure has resulted in the heavy use it is subjected to, hence its success (Figure 11.1).

Branching out: Political Dimensions of Research Inquiry

In my original study I offer a detailed description for all these factors (Elshestawy, 1997). In addition the appendix contains an analysis of the morphology of Cairo's traditional streets based on the framework proposed by Rapoport (1989) and the extent to which this relates to Mohamed Ali street. However, the study included another dimension which was markedly different from Amos's writings and my previous research directions. I began to read books by Noam Chomsky and Edward Said and tried to apply their ideas and propositions within my own area of inquiry. In particular Said's analysis of Orientalist scholarship and the extent to which it contributed to western hegemony over Moslem countries and Chomsky's exposure of the dominance of political institutions were of interest (Said, 1979; Chomsky, 1989). Thus, a political dimension was added, making my research inquiry increasingly normative by implicitly offering a strong stance with regard to the desirability of having areas for pedestrian use in addition to how one should deal with tradition and culture within a changing world dominated by "globalization."

It is here where I believe that a radical departure occurred between my work and Rapoport's. Characteristically apolitical in nature, Rapoport refrains from viewing the architect as an agent of change, someone who by the very nature of his education is in a position to change the status quo. Particularly in the Middle East ,where there are many conflicting voices on how one should deal with the inherited heritage while at the same time attempting to join the "universal civilization," it is an architects duty to take a strong, articulated position with regard to what he or she feels is "correct." One should not simply cater to peoples needs or what they express to be important. In developing countries such as Egypt, people are confronted with myriad problems that affect their livelihood and survival; at the same time many are not educated and might not be able to clearly articulate or express their feelings and desires. In Mohamed Ali street for example the execution of the project was a classic "top-down" approach in which an architect and the organization he represents decided to convert a street to pedestrian use; they used design elements and formal configurations that they perceived would "work." The project was a huge success without any direct involvement from the community.

Figure 11.1: Street Life in Mohamed Ali Street

EBS research acknowledges these shortcomings and attempts to overcome them by providing alternative methodologies. Typically qualitative research is offered as a response in that regard. Various techniques such as participant observation, in-depth interviews, indirect observation methods, ethnographies try to extrapolate what people cannot express verbally. Amos Rapoport, was wary — in my view — from overly qualitative research which he deemed too "fuzzy," and "romantic." To address this concern I tried, in my study, to combine both qualitative and quantitative research methods, thus grounding my research findings from indirect methods with concrete numbers and facts.

While our differences on this issue did exist, I found that Amos was accommodating to many viewpoints. In fact he encouraged me to pursue my own interpretation of the data, but asked that I be very explicit about my reasoning and logic that led to a particular conclusion. Overall, his methodic and systematic examination of the data and of my writings, as well as his careful reading of every sentence that I wrote contributed greatly to enhancing my knowledge on the topic and of critically examining my own opinions. It is perhaps this last point which is his most important contribution to my research development.

Environment-Behavior Studies in the Middle East: Future and Prospects

Environment-Behavior studies are slowly finding their way into the curriculum of Arab universities. However, there are no formal courses which deal explicitly with aspects of human behavior and their relation to architecture. This is partly due to the placement of architecture departments within Colleges of Engineering in many Arab countries, such as the United Arab Emirates (UAE). I would like to very briefly address in this final section the contribution of the work of Amos Rapoport as well as EBS research in general towards my teaching and research activities.

First with respect to teaching, I have found Amos's writings particularly helpful in a course entitled "UAE Architectural Heritage." The course deals primarily with vernacular architecture in the UAE, however I have devoted a large part of the course towards an examination of other cultures throughout the world. *House, Form and Culture* (Rapoport, 1969) offered a variety of examples on how people configured their residential environment. Another component of this course deals with the "Emirati Folk House." Students are asked to conduct a research project which deals with aspects of the vernacular house and how it developed over time. The objective is to find the "cultural core" — another Amos invention — through an examination of the elements that changed vs. the ones that persist throughout time. I am using a paper written by Amos as a main theoretical framework to carry out this project (Rapoport, 1983); in addition an assigned book written in Arabic by one of our faculty in the sociology department deals with the same topic and is influenced by Rapoport's approach (El-Aswad, 1996). Overall, students have been very receptive to the course and the research project in particular was carried out with great enthusiasm. Since their primary language is not in English I am forced to offer translations of the text written by Amos since there has been no official Arabic translation of his work.

Another course in which I try to integrate issues from EBS research is the Graduation project which is developed over two semesters (Graduation Project I & II). The first phase is typically a research activity at the end of which students are required to submit a program and 3 preliminary alternatives for their design projects. I try to emphasize during this phase the importance of human behavior and that a building should primarily serve its users. At the same time students should respect their cultural traditions and incorporate these aspects into their design. While many listen to, and are aware of, these concerns, integrating them into the design process does not seem so easy. Unfortunately, as is found in many architectural curricula, students' enculturated main focus seems to be on the end product without realizing the importance of the design process itself. At the same time the influence of western architectural images is very strong, primarily due to the ever present architectural media and the Internet, thus making it increasingly difficult to talk about behavior, culture, and establishing an architectural heritage. Efforts are currently underway to develop a course as a pre-requisite to the Graduation project dealing with "Research Methods in Architecture" thereby emphasizing the importance of research. I anticipate E-B studies

Figure 11.2a Al-Marija District in Sharjah, UAE – A Sightseeing Object within an Existing City

Figure 11.2b Meticulous Preservation without any Traces of Human Activity

and the writings of Rapoport to occupy a large portion of the required readings for this course.

On the research front I am currently engaged in a funded research project entitled "Urban Rehabilitation of Historic Areas in the UAE." The study is guided by a strategy which views rehabilitation projects as a comprehensive effort including both physical upgrading as well as social development. Physical upgrading comprises such traditional notions as preservation/renovation of existing buildings/open areas. Social development encompasses the analysis of existing cultural/behavioral patterns and the extent to which the built environment could be supportive of them. After analyzing existing historic areas in the UAE, I began to focus on one area (AL-Marija, in Sharjah City) to explore these issues in depth. This district has been re-constructed and developed into a sightseeing object within an existing urban community (Figure 11.2). This examination focused on the socio-cultural aspect of preservation -- the extent to which the district is integrated to the city and whether it is responsive to behavioral and cultural patterns characteristic of the area. Based on this analysis suggestions were made for a tighter integration with the surrounding community (Elsheshtawy, 1998).

Conclusion

There is great potential for increased utility of EBS research and the writings of Amos Rapoport among many others which has unfortunately not been realized. This potential stems from four aspects:

1. First, the empathy implied in EBS research towards users of buildings and urban settings which could be of great value for countries facing survival problems such as Egypt. Such issues and the manner in which they are engaged by EBS research could be of real benefit for many residents in the Middle East.
2. Second, the political nature of EBS can be highlighted as it points out the deficiencies existing in current political institutions and the importance of re-examining the traditional role of architect, planners and decision-makers.

3. Third, the emphasis of EBS research, exemplified by the work of Amos Rapoport, on scientific methods in developing architectural theory is of particular importance for researchers and educators practicing within strictly scientific institutions (College of Engineering for example) thus overcoming the image of the architect as artist, or someone whose outlook is not grounded in "reality."
4. Fourth, Amos's concern with cultural issues is of extreme importance for practitioners in the Middle East who are struggling with ways to establish their identity within a world increasingly dominated by western — or to be more specific North American — values.

It is this last theme which could be considered a core issue of extreme importance for Arab educators, researchers and architects. One of the greatest problems facing the Arab/Muslim world is globalization and its opposite, fundamentalism, representing two sides of a similar coin. Both appear to force people into accepting a life-style incompatible with their needs and aspirations and which does not realistically acknowledge changes that have occurred in their societies. It is thus a question of hegemony and exercise of power which can occur externally — through globalization — and internally — through fundamentalism. Being primarily a political construct hegemony has profound cultural and in turn architectural implications. Either through a complete acceptance of western forms and urban models or a rejection of these and a recycling of cliches about what is considered Muslim, Arabic, Oriental. EBS through its implicit, and many times explicit, call for empowerment by providing people with knowledge and by acknowledging their needs and values, offers a general framework in which the problem of hegemony could be more adequately addressed. The application of the question of *how* is partially answered through the work of Amos Rapoport whose central message seems to me that one needs to carefully analyze peoples lifestyles, their culture, and respond to this analysis by designing appropriate environments. It is precisely this message, while appearing amazingly simple, that is ignored everyday in the Middle East.

This leads to two questions:

1. Why is lifestyle ignored?; and
2. How can one address all these concerns expressed above?

With regard to the first, it could be considered to be a socio-political and historical question that needs to be examined in a far different context than in this small essay. With respect to the second, one can take into consideration the following, admittedly obvious means: through educating Arab architects in United States' graduate schools of environmental design, EBS will find its way into the curriculum of Arab universities and simultaneously into the Arab architectural profession. For example, the Department of Architecture at the United Arab Emirates University has among its faculty four who received their doctoral degrees from the University of Michigan and an additional two from the University of Wisconsin-Milwaukee. Also, Arabic translations of classic EBS studies would prove very helpful. Finally various exchange programs among Universities could be yet another way for increasing exposure to the importance of behavioral factors in architectural and urban design.

Taking all of the above into consideration, there is simply no guarantee that there would be actual results as long as lifestyle is not examined in greater detail. There seems to be a trend, no necessarily restricted to the Arab world, of resisting the use of architectural research in professional practice. Yet all Arab architects, whether they desire to or not, confront the issues of culture and lifestyle and their impact on the built environment on a daily basis. The ground is thus fertile for writings by architects who address issues of socio-cultural concern in an empirical fashion, such as the work of Amos Rapoport, and they may yet prove to redress this otherwise sad situation.

Note

1 Interestingly I posed this question during a seminar in 1995 where Amos presented his most recent research activities. He was aware of this criticism but argued that one should make explicit the methodology used in selecting the images to support a certain viewpoint thus minimizing subjectivity -- which can never be completely eliminated.

References

Berlyne, D. (1974). *Studies in the new experimental aesthetics.* Washington, D.C. : Hemisphere Publishing.

Chomsky, N. (1989). *Thought Control in Democratic Societies*. South End Press: Boston, MA.

El-Aswad, S. (1996). *The Folk House: an anthropological study of folk architecture and traditional culture of the Emirates society*. The United Arab Emirates University: Department of Sociology.

Elsheshtawy, Y. (1997). Urban Complexity: toward the measurement of the physical complexity of streetscapes. *Journal of Architectural and Planning Research.* 2:4.

Elsheshtawy, Y. (1998). Understanding Tradition: A socio-cultural analysis of preservation efforts in Al'Marija, Sharjah, UAE. *Proceedings of IASTE: Manufacturing Tradition, Consuming Heritage, Cairo, 1998.* (Berkeley: University of California, Berkeley).

Gibson, J.J. (1979). *An ecological approach to visual perception.* Boston: Houghton Mifflin.

Gruber, R. (1987). *Sichbeschrankungen*. Friedr. Vieweg & Sohn: Braunschweig.

Jacobs, J. (1961). *The death and life of great American Cities*. Random House: New York.

Lang, J. (1987). *Creating Architectural Theory*. Van Nostrand Reinhold: New York.

Overy, P. (1969). *Kandinsky: The language of the eye.* New York: Praeger.

Prak, N. (1977). *The Visual Perception of the Built Environment.* Delft University Press: Delft.

Rapoport, A. & Kantor, R (1967). Complexity and Ambiguity in Environmental Design *Journal of American Institute of Planners* 33:210.

Rapoport, A. (1969). *House, Form and Culture*. Prentice Hall: Engelwood Cliffs New Jersey.

Rapoport A. & Hawkes, R (1970). The Perception of Urban Complexity *Journal of American Institute of Planners* 36:106.

Rapoport, A. (1983). Development, Culture Change and Supportive Design. *Habitat International*. 7:5/6. 249-268.

Rapoport, A. (1987). Pedestrian Street Use: Culture and Perception. In A.V. Moudon (Ed.), *Public Streets for Public Use*, 80-92. Van Nostrand Reinhold: New York.

Rapoport, A. (1990). *History and Precedent in Environmental Design.* Plenum Press: New York.

Ricoeur, P. (1965). *History and Truth.* Northwestern University Press: Evanston.

Said, E. (1979). *Orientalism.* New York.

Sennett, R. (1970). *The Uses of Disorder*. Alfred Knopf: New York.

Sennett, R. (1974). *The Fall of Public Man*. Vintage Books: New York.

Sennett, R. (1990). *The Conscience of the Eye: The Design and Social Life of Cities.* Alfred A. Knopf: New York.

Venturi, R. (1966). *Complexity and Contradiction in Architecture* Museum of Modern Art: New York.

12 Culture, Politics and the Plaza: An Ethnographic Approach to the Study of Urban Public Spaces in Latin America

Setha M. Low

Amos Rapoport has spent much of his career introducing and integrating cultural anthropological concepts such as culture, world view, values, ethos, and activity areas into the lexicon of Environment-Behavior Studies (EBS). He has documented the importance of cross-cultural research as a means of uncovering the relationship of these concepts to built form, and has argued that without understanding culture, we can not create contextually appropriate architecture, much less communicate new meanings (Rapoport, 1969).

Further, Rapoport has developed an explicit analytic model that links culture as a theoretical construct to specific behaviors and activities through the use of the concepts of world view, values, and lifestyle (Rapoport, 1976). These behaviors and activities, he has argued, can be translated into environments that accommodate these functions, as well as produce specifications for an architectural program. His theoretical contribution of linking culture to systems of activities and systems of settings, and then linking activities and settings to cultural meaning, has provided generations of architects, as well as EBS researchers, with a design strategy that incorporates culture as a basic component of any environmental analysis (Rapoport, 1977).

Amos Rapoport's work on culture has gone even farther in his analysis of the role culture plays in how environments produce meaning (Rapoport, 1982). By examining the organization of the four elements of any designed environment--space, meaning, communication, and time--he illuminates how spatial relationships and environmental cues create a culturally meaningful place. These environmental cues in his later work become "fixed" and "non-fixed" furnishings and affordances that are read and interpreted by users. He has argued repeatedly that we must pay particular attention to these furnishings in order to understand and decode environmental meaning. I have found his approach extremely useful in my own work on the Spanish-American plaza in which his admonition to study the non-fixed as well as fixed furnishings provided new data about the changing symbols of political affiliation and class relations (Low, 1996).

Amos Rapoport's body of work on culture and built form has established cultural anthropology as a legitimate concern EBS researchers. He has provided theoretical constructs and analytical models that successfully integrate the key concepts of culture, world view, and values into environmental design. Rapoport generally relied on published ethnographies and monographs to illustrate his theoretical principles. He drew upon a wide range of cross-cultural studies in order to make his conceptual linkages clear and grounded in culturally specific settings. Although he was interested in anthropological fieldwork as a source of data, he did not explore this venue leaving the details of methodology and data generation to others. Therefore, it is in the area of cultural anthropology methodology that I would like to add my tribute to Rapoport's theoretical and synthetic contributions.

As a practicing anthropologist involved in the interdisciplinary study of space and place and cultural aspects of design, I am often asked to develop ethnographic methods to help architects, landscape architects, and urban planners working in cross-cultural settings obtain the data they need for culturally sensitive plans and designs. In response I have evolved a four step approach that complements Rapoport's analytic model linking culture and built form.

This chapter outlines an ethnographic approach to environment-behavior research of the plaza that emphasizes sociocultural processes. The emphasis is on cultural anthropology as a discipline which contributes *methods* as well as concepts for the study of the built environment in cross-cultural situations. This anthropological approach consists of four "ethno" methodological components: the ethnohistorical, the ethnographic, the (ethno) semantic, and the (ethno) proxemic. The "ethno" prefix on each indicates the culture-specific nature of the proposed inquiry and analysis. This meaning-centered and culturally-sensitive methodology provides a sociocultural approach to understanding and designing urban public space that is particularly appropriate for environment-behavior studies where histories of colonialization and exploitation by the United States and other dominant powers make traditional research techniques socio-politically irresponsible or simply not feasible.

The Role of the Outsider Researcher

The researcher faces a number of complications when attempting to undertake environment-behavior studies to understand the local architecture and landscape. It is necessary to know the language, culture and environment as well as the role the researcher plays in the complex arena of international politics and local economics. Colonial and economic imperialism, not just cultural ignorance, have created a situation in which the very act of research is fraught with economic and political overtones. Yet, many of us are interested in questions that can only be answered in cross-cultural contexts, and therefore, must develop collaborative and culturally-sensitive strategies for both gaining entrance and producing information or services that are useful to the host and our research respondents.

When undertaking this kind of research the question arises of whether it is even possible to understand another culture, not just in terms of differences in language or values, but in terms of the gulf between our existential realities. Anthropologists, as perpetual outsiders, have dealt with this criticism by arguing that the descriptions of others that we create are only one interpretation of many, and that these interpretations are to be evaluated by how closely they match the local cultural view or by the insights they provide for other anthropologists and social scientists. This emic/etic, or experience-near/ experience-far, distinction is an attempt to bridge the gulf between these separate worlds. Other anthropologists have responded with dialogic writing in which the voice of the researcher and the voices of respondents are blended in a polyphonic description of the event. Although these strategies do not solve the problem of power inequality in the production of data and knowledge, much less resolve the differences in our perceived worlds, they do provide a partial answer to the concerns of our colleagues and our own sense of social justice and responsibility.

The Plaza in Costa Rica

My ongoing study of Costa Rican plaza provides an example of how this methodology works within a specific cultural setting (Low, 1997). The Spanish- American plaza in Costa Rica was designed as the integrating central space of gridiron plan towns established by the synthetic forces of indigenous and colonial city planning (Low, 1995). Even today these plazas remain the "geographical as well as cultural center of a community, where the evening promenades take place, where the major stores front, adjacent to which, or even in which, will be found the open market. Life seems to swing about these central focal points" (Foster, 1960:48.)

In San José, the capital of Costa Rica, *Parque Central* continues to play this symbolically dominant role of the traditional city center. *Plaza de la Cultura*, a recently designed urban public space just two blocks away, however, is competing for this role by attracting tourists, teen-agers and women with children who represent new constituencies in urban public life. From 1985 to 1997, after having spent almost twenty years as a field worker in Central America, I began a study of the representational significance of these two Costa Rican plazas. Although I will not have the opportunity to provide a full description of the traditional *Parque Central* and the new *Plaza de la Cultura*, the four methodologies that I am reporting, and the examples that I use to illustrate them, are drawn from the data collected and analyses completed on *Parque Central*.

Toward an "Ethno" Methodology

As I previously mentioned, I am arguing that an "ethno" methodology, that is a methodology that is based on the cultural premises of the group(s) studied (their emics) is one possible strategy for culturally-sensitive and responsive research. For outsiders, this approach is particularly important, but it may also be appropriate for training students and members of diverse social classes within countries where the cultural experience of rich and poor, educated and illiterate, may be quite different. When I asked to train graduate social science students in fieldwork methods at the University of Costa Rica, I found that they were afraid to even enter down plazas, and many were totally unfamiliar with urban public life. Therefore, a research perspective that attempts to view a place from the culture's point of view, may include anyone who is not familiar with a place and is therefore in the "outsider" role.

Within this perspective there are four methodologies that provide methods and analytic techniques for the collection and interpretation of data. The ethnohistorical provides a perspective on the history of a place, from the culture's point of view. The ethnographic weaves the details of interviews and observations into a broader fabric of cultural patterns and ideas. The semantic decodes the symbolic and figurative meaning of language; and the proxemic presents the spatial relations of the place in culturally meaningful terms. Each methodology is defined and illustrated in the following sections.

Parque Central: Four Examples

Parque Central is located in the center of San José bordered by the national Cathedral on the east, movie theaters and men's cafes on the north, bars and businesses on the west and movie theaters and banks on the south. It was the *Plaza Principal* (the central governmental plaza) of San José as early as 1751, and in 1869 was adorned with trees, benches and a fountain where residents could first obtain public water. The current kiosk is the last of a series of central pavilions where music is played on Sunday; up until 1995 the bottom of the kiosk was a children's subterranean library. *Parque Central* is a busy center of ambulatory businesses, a men's social club and home away from home; a place where illegal activities can take place next to middle class behavior, and a retreat for the weary, hungry, and tired.

Ethnohistorical Perspective

Ethnohistory offers both a methodology for and an analytic perspective on the cultural history of the plaza. This history often conflicts, or at least questions, the accepted or official history of a place that has been written by the dominant social or cultural group. Ethnohistorical methods include the collection of primary materials — diaries, personal accounts. local records and literary material such as novels, poetry, and essays as well as photographs, paintings, and other pictorial evidence that will cast a light on the diversity of use and contradictions in meanings of public space over time.

Ethnohistorical analysis is the process of reinterpretation of the accepted historical canons with regard to a broader collection of relevant materials and new materials that are undercovered. Let me illustrate this point with an example of a reinterpretation of who the users were at the turn of the century.

History of Parque Central

There is considerable controversy about the history of the users of *Parque Central* and its now absent, upper-class clientele. Historical sources describe the *Parque Central* of the late nineteenth century as a "cultured" place where elite families of San José would stroll and gather. The architectural additions of the Victorian kiosk, the English fountain and impressive gates represent the cultural domination of the coffee elite and their attempt to establish European values as public symbols of their power. Photographs, however, of the *Parque Central* of this period show week-end markets, youths without shoes playing, and workers sitting and eating on park benches. An ethnohistorical analysis, thus, suggests that the park has always had diversity of users, and not just an elite clientele in the past.

Ethnographic Analysis

Ethnography generally is used to mean a cultural description, or a document written by anthropologists that describes a particular culture. Ethnographic methodology, however, varies tremendously in its meanings, ranging from the exclusive use of participant observation in a fieldwork situation to a multiplicity of methods including structured and unstructured interviews, mapping, observation, surveys, and questionnaires used in an effort to obtain a cultural description. In this chapter, I am using the term to refer to a methodology and type of analysis that identifies cultural patterns of meanings and interpretation. The methods involved include all those mentioned above, but what makes it "ethno" graphic is that meanings and interpretations that emerge are those of the cultural group(s.) The analytic task is one of interweaving data collected in one time and place, with all the other, often contradictory, cultural commentary and information available. The strength of long term research is that there will be a broader context and universe to draw upon in this interpretative process.

Religion in Costa Rica. An example of an ethnographic approach to the plaza can be drawn from the analysis of the meaning of religion in the plaza. The Cathedral on the eastern edge of *Parque Central* is the largest, oldest and most important Catholic church in San José where all major civic and religious activities take place. It is visually linked to the *Parque Central* and is a constant reminder of the close relationship between the national Catholic religion and the daily life of Costa Ricans (Figure 12.1).

Josefinos say that the Cathedral is the dominant symbol of Catholicism along with the image of the Virgin of Los Angeles and her Basilica in Cartago. But there are other religious ideas expressed in *Parque Central*. A Christian in animal skins and robes heals passers-by at noon each day on the northwest corner, an evangelical group holds prayer meetings at two in the afternoon under shaded arbor, and religious healers stroll through the *Parque Central* offering to pray and heal as they go (Figure 12.2). The contrast of religious styles, one marked architecturally and the other in the time and space of the daily life of the plaza, suggests that the cultural meaning of religion in Costa Rica is pluralistic and changing; although Catholicism is still the national religion and has architectural dominance, its moral and social control is being challenged by other religious values and norms.

Semantics

Semantics refers to the linguistic analysis of the structure of meaning in a language and culture. Much of semantic work is based on intensively interviewing key informants which produces taxonomies of the cultural world. My use of the term refers to the role that language can play, not as a structure or taxonomic system, but as a metaphoric and symbolic communication about important cultural ideas. Public space is often talked about and talked in, thus creating a perfect setting for a meaning centered analysis of talk. The method for its study is therefore everyday conversation, and the analysis based on decoding of figurative language. The following discussion of the kiosk in *Parque Central* provides an

Figure 12.1 Cathedral at *Parque Central*

Figure 12.2 Evidence of Pluralism at *Parque Central*

excellent example.

The Kiosk. In *Parque Central*, the large, cement kiosk has generated considerable figurative language (Figure 12.3.) One example is the *dicho* (saying) about the cement kiosk when it was first built in 1949 with a nightclub in its base. The saying goes " El kiosko lo construyo Masagosa, debajo el kiosko es donde mas se goza" (the kiosk that Masagosa built is where the pleasure is, or where they are most satisfied in the sexual sense of the word). The saying refers to the fact that the kiosk was built by a wealthy Nicaraguan businessman who was a friend of Samoza and the ambivalence that Costa Ricans feel about Samoza because of current US involvement in Costa Rica and Central American politics. According to conservative Costa Ricans, Nicaragua represents a model of immorality and the tearing down of the Victorian kiosk to put up the cement one was a defilement of Costa Rican and European-linked *cultura* (culture.) However, some Costa Ricans "enjoy," derive pleasure from and exploit the new economic and political relations that the kiosk represents. Ultimately, the night club was replaced by a children's library. The saying, in figurative and metaphoric language, can be analyzed thus as a strategy for expressing conflict about public values and mobilizing change.

Figure 12.3 Cement kiosk at *Parque Central*

Figure 12.4 At North-east Corner of *Parque Central*

Figure 12.5 At South-west Corner of *Parque Central*

Proxemics

By proxemics I mean the cultural meaning of spatial relations, in other words, what a particular spatial configuration means to the cultural group. In some sense, proxemics is an archaeology of spatial behavior or the study of spatial relations as nonverbal communication. The methods used include spatial and behavioral mapping and participant observation, where the participant observation provides information on how spatial relations are interpreted.

Special Corners. An example of proxemics is found in the cultural meaning of spatial relationships of social groups in *Parque Central.* Some zones of the plaza, the northeast corner and the southwest corner are marked as controlled spaces. The northeast corner is associated with the shoeshine men (Figure 12.4), drug dealing and gambling, and their presence changes the meaning of any outsider who may enter their domain. Young women who hang-out on the northeastern corner are considered prostitutes, and tourists, easy prey. If these individuals locate themselves elsewhere in the plaza, their cultural meaning, that is how they are seen and talked about, would not be the same. The southwest corner is dominated by the elderly pensioners who spend their days in the plaza, and the younger men are careful not to sit on their benches (Figure 12.5). Changes do occur in spatial patterns, such as when a group of elderly men moved, after five years in the same spot, to be away from the noise and buses. But over two years of observations, these spatial relationships were basically stable and consistent, and reflect local power and social control that exists through the local interpretations of spatial relations in the plaza.

Conclusion

In this article I have briefly outlined an "ethno" methodology for environment-behavior research comprised of ethnohistorical, ethnographic, semantic, and proxemic methods and analytic techniques. I have focused on the study of urban public space by selecting illustrations and examples from my fieldwork on plazas in San José, Costa Rica. This perspective is proposed for any qualitative study of

Figure 12.6 ***Plaza de Cultura***

sociospatial relations, and it is hoped that insights produced by this methodology can create a more culturally appropriate design. For instance, by understanding the spatial relations of local power and control in the *Parque Central*, the design issues of the new *Plaza de la Cultura* become clearer. The open plan has created new spaces for social groups who had no place in the *Parque Central* such as the tourists and the teenagers (Figure 12.6). Hopefully, the integration of analysis and design will produce a more culturally sensitive methodology that would be particularly important in culturally sensitive settings.

Such a methodology fulfills the dictates of Amos Rapoport's theoretical work linking activities and space through cultural cues. The meaning of these plaza spaces is dependent on a methodology that can elicit the relevant cultural details of fixed and non-fixed features. The use of this four part ethnomethodology generates both verbal and non-verbal data which is consistent with Rapoport's concern with culturally derived environment mnemonics.

Acknowledgments

The research reported in this chapter was funded by the Wenner Gren Foundation for Anthropological Research, a John Simon Guggenheim Fellowship, and a Fulbright Research Fellowship. I would like to thank Elena Danaila for typing this manuscript so it could be submitted for publication.

References

Foster, G. (1960). *Culture and Conquest*. New York: Viking Fund.

Low, S. M. (1995). Indigenous architecture and the Spanish American plaza in Mesoameric and the Caribbean. *American Anthropologist* 97(4):748-762.

Low, S. M. (1996). Spatializing culture: the social production and social construction of public space. *American Ethnologist* 23(4): 861-879.

Low, S. M. (1997). Urban public spaces as representations of culture: the plaza in Costa Rica. *Environment and Behavior* 29(1): 3-33.

Rapoport, A. (1969). *House Form and Culture*. Englewood Cliffs, N.J.: Prentice-Hall.

Rapoport, A. (1976). Sociocultural aspects of man-environment studies. In A. Rapoport (Ed.) *The Mutual Interaction of People and their Built Environment*, pp. 7-35. The Hague: Mouton.

Rapoport, A. (1977). *Human Aspects of Urban Form.* Oxford: Pergamon.

Rapoport, A. (1986). Culture and built form--a reconsideration. In D. Saile, (Ed.) *Architecture in Cultural Change: Essays in Built Form and Culture Research*, pp. 157-75. Lawrence, Kansas: Built Form and Culture Conference.

13 Mnemonic Meanings of the American Capitol

Charles T. Goodsell

In *The Meaning of the Built Environment* (Rapoport, 1982), Amos Rapoport refers to the nonverbal communicative function of the built environment as *mnemonic*. The word means assisting the memory by means of cues. Thus, according to the notion, buildings and other created settings present memory cues to their human occupants and witnesses. By means of these cues, Rapoport believes, behaviors, emotions, and interpretations of the situation are elicited. The resultant responses are not necessarily mandatory, to be sure; cues as opposed to commands, exert their effects in a probabilistic fashion only. Moreover their meanings are interpreted in a subjective and culturally-conditioned way. In Rapoport's (1976) words, the relationship between people and the built environment is mutually interactive.

In a second-edition epilogue to *The Meaning of the Built Environment* (Rapoport, 1990, pp. 221-25), Rapoport argues that the built environment's communicative potential is more complex than a single, global characterization of the mnemonic function might suggest. He develops three subdivisions of mnemonic meaning: high-level; middle-level; and low-level. These may communicate complementary rather than competing types of meaning, and a given environment is capable of exuding meaning at all three levels at once — or, alternatively, at only one or two levels.

Low-level meaning guides behavior on an everyday basis. Simple examples are the curves in the road that tell us where to steer our car or the doors of the building that tell us where to enter the building. Also cues of identification are offered: if a large room in a school has a wooden floor and raised hoops at either end, we know it is a gymnasium. The effects of such cues are immediate, seen as "normal," and a memory assist only in the sense of a prompt or a reminder, often at the subconscious level.

Middle-level meaning in Rapoport's scheme informs us of more subtle realities embedded in the settings we encounter. Particular social mores, structures, or expectations are conveyed. The coach's office leading off the gymnasium denotes the locus of status and authority. Banners on the wall displaying team emblems or recalling past tournament victories communicate institutional symbolism and history. At this level mnemonic memory does much more than prompt — it explains, characterizes, and delineates patterns, as in power relationships.

Finally, high-level meaning produces not simply understanding but an emotive response associated with fundamental framing ideas of our lives, such as cultural schemata or views of the world. Rapoport refers to meanings at this level as cosmological, philosophical, or religious. To continue our illustration of the gymnasium, a crucifix hanging prominently on the wall informs us we are in a Roman Catholic school, but more importantly it constitutes — potentially — a moving symbol for the school children who play there.

The Capitol as a Repository of Mnemonic Meanings

In a brilliant analysis of capital cities around the world, Rapoport (1993), points out that the term "capital" (as well as "capitol") comes from the Latin word for head, *caput*. Hence, in their root meaning, both the seat of government and main legislative building in American political life can be thought of as a *head*quarters of authority.

On the following pages we examine the American capitol as a repository of mnemonic meanings at all three of Rapoport's levels. This particular kind of built environment is useful for a discussion of Rapoport's ideas, for two reasons.

First, it illustrates all three levels of meaning, including at the highest or cosmological level. Rapoport (1990) speculates that meanings at this top level are in decline in the contemporary U.S., with respect to both frequency and importance. In view of the material and secular nature of modern culture he is probably right. Hence to find cosmological examples of meaning we may need to look for architectural anachronisms, so to speak. The capitol as a building type is about 175 years old, hence it is not truly premodern but some of its symbolism can be said to have quite ancient lineage.

Second, as a headquarters of public authority, the capitol is an exceedingly important edifice from a socio-political standpoint. The relationship between official authority and the public is crucial in a democratic society, filled with potentiality for contradictory tensions as well as opportunities for fostering community. A public structure that represents official authority and is the scene of its exercise can affect both the tensions and opportunities. Thus the capitol's mnemonic communications to the citizenry are of innate importance as a topic of study.

I am employing the term "American capitol" to refer to exactly fifty buildings. These are the United States Capitol in Washington and 49 of the state capitol buildings or statehouses. The capitol of Alaska is omitted from the category because it was constructed not as a capitol but a federal territorial office building. Architectural historians Henry-Russell Hitchcock and William Seale (1976) contend that the capitol is a uniquely American contribution to monumental architecture, the only other example being the skyscraper.

Most of these structures were built in the late 19th century and early 20th, with a few having origins from the late 18th century and a few more being products of the mid-20th. Although several exceptions exist, most have six characteristics in common: a dome, rotunda, cruciform plan, low massing, temple front, and parklike grounds. Elsewhere (Goodsell, 1993) I have described these elements as composing a statehouse building type (they are found in the national capitol as well). Facades are generally neoclassical in historical origin, elaborated by the canons of various Revivalist or Renaissance-inspired styles.

There are exceptions to the standard. The Art Deco statehouses of Nebraska, North Dakota and Louisiana are well known for having no dome. Domeless capitols are also found, for a variety of stylistic and practical reasons, in Delaware, New York, Oklahoma, Tennessee and Virginia. "Modern" capitols or legislative buildings are found in Hawaii, New Mexico, Florida, Nevada, and North Carolina; however in the last three states traditional early capitols still stand nearby and receive use.

Low-Level Mnemonic Meanings in the Capitol

Rapoport (1990) says that low-level meanings *must* be present in the built environment if it is to "work" at all, especially for newcomer visitors but also daily users. These meanings show people where to go and how to act. Examples in the American capitol are legion (Figure 13.1).

Figure 13.1 Idaho State Capitol in Boise

From an overall perspective, the distinctive dome catches our attention in the prosaic urbanscape because of its contrasting rounded form. The temple front, with its portico, columns, pediment and massive steps, clearly indicates the location of the main front door. Placement of the building in the middle of an open, parklike setting enhances its visibility and distinctiveness.

Inside the building, the presence of security signifies where one next moves upon entering. Also they show that building security is a serious issue. The open nature of the rotunda, from which various corridors lead without impediment, suggests that once a person has passed the security gates, free roaming in the building is acceptable. Within the legislative chambers, the elaborate rostrum tells us where the front of the room is and where leadership presides. In supreme court chambers, which once existed in the U.S. Capitol and are still found in many state capitols, the high bench shows the position of the justices. Substantial balustrades separating territorial zones in the courtroom floor indicate where the attorneys operate and where the citizens observe.

Over time, certain features of old capitols may change in their communicated meanings. Elaborately decorated water fountains, which in the days before soft drink machines and bottled water provided a valued resource to the public, are now curiosities. A parallel loss of functional purpose occurred for spittoons, ink wells and snuff boxes in the legislative chambers. The porte-cocheres beneath the portico steps, which at one time led the drivers of horse-drawn carriages to their destinations, are now covered entryways to the ground floor. Sturdy vaults in the basement, which once showed how stealing bullion from the state would be most difficult to accomplish, now present themselves as storage closets.

In a temporal reversal, newly added features of the capitol environment convey messages that would have been inconceivable when the building was first built. The computers found in the chambers and nearly every office show everyone where to receive, send, and analyze information. Security cameras in the corridors indicate that scrutiny of one's movements is occurring, while television broadcast cameras positioned in the chambers demonstrate that floor debate is observed by the external public. Electronic vote tally boards on the chamber walls provide the names of individual legislators, and suggest as well that they are accountable for their votes.

Middle-Level Mnemonic Meanings in the Capitol

Rapoport (1990, p.223) believes that middle-level meanings tend to increase in importance in present-day environments. The reason is that, as societies grow in scale and impersonality, each person needs to be told more clearly who is who and what groups are important. The fluid nature of contemporary social relationships requires additional physical cueing as to hierarchical pecking orders, social status, and the loci of power. No longer do garments automatically indicate high office or aristocratic breeding, for instance, although the judges' robes are an exception.

Thinking about capitols in this vein leads us to the initial observation that the capitol building as a whole, the physical headquarters of the sovereign state, sends a strong message regarding status and power. One way this is done is by the monumentality of the building itself, emphasized further by its setback from the street and prominent placement on a hill. Another way is the decoration of interior public spaces. With considerable irony for a house of democracy, these exhibit, in large measure, elitist if not aristocratic cues that convey a sense of high taste, elegant standards, and deep association with the sacred past.

The exterior facade and roofline, for example, often bear pieces of architectural sculpture, depicting mythological figures or charioteers of antiquity. The interior walls of rotundas and other grand spaces are decorated by murals and paintings that portray the heroes and legends of history. Inscriptions of the noble words of ancient philosophers and founding fathers are carved on friezes and entablatures. Ceilings of reception rooms and member lounges can be painted in the Rococco tradition, from which chandeliers of Czechoslovakian crystal hang. Floors are inlaid with teakwood parquet or encaustic tile, or perhaps covered with long-loom rugs from Scotland. On these floors rest antique pieces of European or early American furniture. The unmistakable message received is that this is a most important place, where things occur and people count at a level far above what is experienced in the prosaic world outside.

Within this democratic palace clear status differentiation's are conveyed. The most important physical marker in this regard is an overall vertical hierarchy. The ground floor of the building, clad externally in rusticated stone and given simple doors and windows, houses utilitarian offices and service facilities such as cafeterias and print shops.

The first floor (or second, in the American enumeration) is obviously enhanced over the lower level. The facade is covered by finished stone and penetrated by larger doors and windows. Portico landings are at this level and columns and pilasters commence their reach up the facade. The interior, compared to the story below, has higher ceilings, greater architectural detailing, and the beginnings of mural art. In the state capitols one typically finds at this level the offices of the governor and other elected constitutional officers. In the U.S. Capitol, whose number of floors is fewer than that of many statehouses, this is the level of the House and Senate chambers, Statuary Hall, and the Rotunda floor.

In the state capitols the second floor (often counted third) is where the legislative chambers are usually found, unlike in the District of Columbia. Architecturally this is then the climatic story of the building, with the largest windows, highest ceilings, and most elaborate decoration in the building — a kind of *piano nobile* for the legislative branch. Its superiority is emphasized further by a grand interior stairway that culminates at this level (see Figure 13.2).

Thus, whereas at the national level of government the constitutional separation of powers is expressed architecturally by three separate buildings distributed horizontally on the landscape, in the statehouses the predominant tendency is a vertical distribution by floor. The unmistakable order of priority is to give prime importance to the legislature and to place the chief executive in a second rank. The supreme court, in those instances when it has not moved out of the statehouse to its own building, occupies either the first or second floor or sometimes the third.

Another middle-level mnemonic meaning that derives from the organization of capitol space pertains to bicameralism. Usually the two legislative chambers are arranged in diametric opposition. They are on the same floor of the building, are separated in opposite wings, and their presiding officers face each other across the building, albeit not visually. Moreover the two chambers are given equal weight with respect to floor position and interior decor, even though the smaller senate sometimes requires less space. This confrontation depicts the constitutional

Figure 13.2 Second Floor of Iowa State Capitol

Figure 13.3 Kentucky State Chamber

checking function that bicameralism was meant to provide in our governmental system of separation of powers.

Within the legislative chambers, the built environment of fixed and semi-fixed features possesses aspects that are peculiarly American. In Europe, parliamentary chambers are often characterized by high tribunes in front for the presiding leadership and, for the membership, a series of concentric half-rings of benches that step up in a sharply raked manner. The two sets of structure, rising quite high off the baseline floor, are separated by the remote "well of the house." The several political parties holding seats in the chamber are arranged by ideology around the semi-circle, with Left wing parties seated on the presider's left and Right wing on the right. In Great Britain and some other former members of the Empire the two parties sit in opposing, parallel sets of raked benches, with the "Government" on one side and the "Opposition" on the other. A neutral floor separates the two sides at a distance too far for sword engagement, itself a fine example of a mnemonic cue whose functional importance has been eclipsed by the passage of time.

In U.S. capitols, by contrast, presiding officers stand on relatively low rostra, not high tribunes. Moreover member seating tends to be directly on the horizontal floor or at a slight incline angling downward toward the front. With few exceptions, such as the U.S. House of Representatives, the members do not sit on benches but at individual desks (see Figure 13.3). These are arranged on the floor in a shallow arc, close in to the rostrum. About half the time one political party sits on one side of the center aisle, the other on the other side. Thus the overall topography of the American legislative chamber is flat and intimate. Leaders and membership are closer together, on the same plane, and able to move about the room chamber easily to confer. Also the design supports a two party system as in Britain, but without the government/non-government dichotomy. Individually-assigned desks present each legislator as a significant individual representative of a geographic constituency, not as pawns in fractional party voting.

High-Level Mnemonic Meanings in the Capitol

As indicated, Rapoport does not anticipate that the contemporary built environment, especially in the United States, will display many high-level cosmological meanings. Yet the capitol is not an ordinary building. It is the physical center of the sovereign state. On that score alone it would seem logical that one could expect to find attempts within its design and setting to elicit great ideas and ideals. Furthermore most of America's fifty capitols were built a century ago or more, and as throwbacks to an earlier era of built environment they could reflect a time when sacred symbols were still in fashion and even politically correct.

Outside the building, on the grounds, one inevitably glimpses war memorials. These honor all of the wars of American history, from the Revolutionary War to the Vietnam War. The famous "wall" Vietnam Memorial in Washington has counterparts at many state capitols, as well as realistic depictions of exhausted solders following combat. The Civil War is particularly memorialized, with victory arches and soldiers and sailors monuments popular in the North and Confederate monuments common in the South, some of which romanticize the wartime sacrifices of southern women. More individualized war memorials feature covered shrines, eternal flames, and in Santa Fe a crude but poignant ground memorial to those who perished in the Bataan Death March.

Reminders of the sacrifices and exploits of war are found inside the capitol as well. These include displayed cannon in the lobby, models of naval ships in the rotunda, and old battleship figureheads in the basement. Paintings of historic battles, photographs of returned units, and reliquary-like containers of the names of those who served can be seen. Another common element of capitol interiors is cases of regimental banners. These date especially from the Civil War, and are sealed in glass display cases, protected as precious objects. Several capitols have halls of flags, which are lobbies or corridors dedicated to banner display.

The footprint of the capitol building is typically some variation of the cross. This is, in and of itself, suggestive symbolically. Usually a long major axis bisecting the side wings intersects perpendicularly with a shorter minor axis centered on the front and rear porticos. Countless variations on this pattern exist, including short secondary axes perpendicular to the primary ones, located near their ends, creating a version of the St. Julian cross.

Indeed the capitol as a building type is related to the cathedral, although its sacred heart is not at the proverbial East end but the exact center. This is the rotunda, located at the intersection of the two major axes. On the rotunda floor at this point one often sees the state seal, inlaid in marble or brass. Surrounding it are ropes on standards, to avoid desecration by the human foot. Below the rotunda floor is the basement crypt, used as a room to hold meetings rather bury the saints, as in the cathedral crypt.

Rising above the rotunda floor is the great, circular, open rotunda space, whose height cuts up through all upper floors to an elaborately decorated domical ceiling (see Figure 13.4). Intricate coloring and detailing on this concave surface stems from the ecclesiastic notion that this exalted upper space represents the vault of heaven. Occasionally the center of the ceiling is pierced by an oculus; it may display a round allegorical painting or serve as an opening for a paid-out chain. At the end of the chain is fixed a large chandelier or, at times, a round crystal ball that is internally illuminated. The 19th century ethnographer W.R. Lethaby (1891, 1974) wrote that pendant ostrich eggs have been found hung in domes and tombs in many cultures of the world, presumably symbolizing the origin of life.

Figure 13.4 Oregon State Capitol Rotunda

The external dome itself, rising high above the mass of the building to perhaps 300 feet from the ground, possesses itself great numinous potential. Domes were used by the ancient Romans, surmounted great Renaissance churches such as St. Peter's and St. Paul's, and were built on three early American capitols by Charles Bullfinch--in Massachusetts in 1798, an early version of the U.S. Capitol in 1825, and in Maine in 1832. A tall, pointed dome became an essential feature of scores of state capitols constructed after the Civil War, mounted on a colonnaded drum with its rounded portion or *tholos* ribbed to accentuate the sense of height. Such a dome was completed on the national capitol while the Civil War was still raging; this was done at the insistence of President Lincoln, who saw it as a symbol of the enduring Union.

Baldwin Smith (1950), the leading scholar of domes, maintains that down through the ages the presence of a dome on a building or house conferred importance on the structure. In addition to churches and later capitols, it was employed on temples, tombs, martyria, baptistries, and mosques. One interpretation of its transcendent symbolic meaning for so many cultures and centuries is the cosmic egg, with the lower portion anchored in this world and the rounded upper half aspiring to the higher world. Another view is that it represents the celestial helmut, a sign of royal power; indeed, when seen on the horizon the capitol dome does remind one of the back profile of a giant head wearing an antiquated helmut. When we are reminded that the root meaning of capitol is head, the resemblance gives one pause.

The Value of Applying Rapoport's Ideas

Rapoport proposes that the built environment be thought of as a means of nonverbal communication. He offers three levels at which we can attempt to discern communicated meaning. While one can quibble that the abstraction "communication" is too rationalist and positivist in its connotations to embrace the many social meanings of architecture, Rapoport does not shrink from using it to include subtle and subjective expressions and effects.

By applying his three levels of mnemonic meaning to the American capitol as I have done here, his ideas have revealed their value in two ways. First, clear illustrations are found in this peculiar American "government house," at all three levels of meaning. Second, the three levels of his perspective illuminate the importance of this central edifice in American political life.

The illustration and illumination occur not only at the lower and middle levels of meaning, but also at the highest or cosmological level. This is counter to Rapoport's hypothesis that mnemonic meaning in the deeper symbolic realm is receding with modernism. The capitol building, a throwback to an earlier and more mystery-accepting time, clearly operates at this level, or at least attempts to do so. We are told that Americans are today alienated from government and the political process, as signified by nonparticipation in elections and polling trends that show increased distrust of institutions and alienation from authority.

This kind of commentary would, seemingly, deny much if any importance for accepted cosmic meanings in such merely physical phenomena as: regimental banners that bear the consecrated blood of the young; soaring rotundas that stand at the symbolic centerpoint of lawful authority; and horizon-dominating domes whose rising rounded point repeats an ancient expression of sacred importance. Yet such objects and forms still seem to attract citizens to them, even in this materialistic and information-saturated age. Visitors come from all over the country to walk through the capitols of the states and nation. While there they purchase pictures, books, souvenirs, and three-dimensional likenesses of the building of every description. School children swarm through its public spaces as if on a pilgrimage to a shrine. Political activists organize demonstrations and rallies on the capitol steps at every opportunity. While these buildings are certainly a headquarters for the most cynical acts of political maneuvering — lobbying, logrolling and influence-peddling — they can also attract those who believe in their state and country. These built environments, despite the end of the century's cynicism and anti-government rhetoric, still make hearts beat faster.

Note

The author has recently completed a book on the subject of the American state capitol, *The American Statehouse: Political Analysis of A Building Type* to be published by Kansas University Press.

References

Goodsell, C. T. (1993). "Political Meanings of the American State Capitol," *Journal of Architectural and Planning Research,* vol. 10, no. 4, pp. 294-307.

Hitchcock, H. R., and William S. (1976). *Temples of Democracy: The State Capitols of the U.S.A.* New York: Harcourt Brace Jovanovich.

Lethaby, W.R. (1891, 1974). *Architecture, Mysticism and Myth.* London: Architectural Press.

Rapoport, A. (1976). *Mutual Interaction of People and Their Built Environment: A Cross-Cultural Perspective.* The Hague: Mouton.

Rapoport, A. (1982). *The Meaning of the Built Environment: A Nonverbal Communication Approach.* Beverly Hills: Sage Publications.

Rapoport, A. (1990). *The Meaning of the Built Environment: A Nonverbal Communications Approach,* 2nd ed. Tucson: University of Arizona Press.

Rapoport, A. (1993). "On the Nature of Capitals and Their Physical Expression," in J. Taylor, J. G. Lengelle, and C. Andrew, eds., *Capital Cities: International Perspectives* Ottawa: Carleton University Press, pp. 31-67.

Smith, E. B. (1950). *The Dome: A Study in the History of Ideas.* Princeton: Princeton University Press.

14 The Cultural Revolution in Architecture

Susan Kent

Like others in the turbulent 1960s, Amos Rapoport was a radical, a rebel with a cause. His work eventually transformed the nature of architectural research and, ultimately, the study of the use of space in anthropology. Rapoport created what I refer to as the "Cultural Revolution" in architecture and related studies. Reinventing the field by infusing it with the concept of culture, Rapoport's work — in archaeology, if not elsewhere — was pivotal in revitalizing research of the built environment. Architecture, in many of the social sciences, changed from a static, sterile, descriptive study to a dynamic, insightful, and useful study.

While anthropologists study past and present cultural diversity, they rarely focused on the built environment because they believed that it was not linked to culture. However, Rapoport's book *House Form and Culture* (1969) established the link between, or articulation of, culture and architecture. Now, the built environment became an important facet for many anthropological studies of all kinds (see Low, this volume). By the 1970s, ethnographers and archaeologists were beginning to apply Rapoport's idea that culture shaped the use of space and architecture, rather than the reverse (e.g., Bourdieu 1973; Cunningham 1973; Glassie 1975; Hugh-Jones 1979; Plimpton and Hassan 1978; Watson 1979; Yellen 1977; and others). Today, it is almost taken for granted by ethnographers and archaeologists that culture influences the built environment.

Rapoport's ideas can be incorporated within anthropology because the study of the past relies on models from the present; models, which are then evaluated with archaeological data and either, accepted or rejected. However, prior to the late 1960s, architecture was usually only *described* by anthropologists while the use of space was often ignored. When anthropologists, and particularly archaeologists, did conduct spatial patterning studies, they often inappropriately applied biased Western-centric models to non-Western societies. In the late 1970s and early 1980s, however, archaeologists read Rapoport's publications and discovered that architecture is a significant part of a group's material culture. Consequently, understanding the use of space by prehistoric inhabitants became an essential part of many archaeological studies.

The sometimes-subtle relationship between architecture and culture has been a focus of Rapoport's research for 30 years. What specifically makes his work preeminent compared to others is his perspective of culture as being a socially constructed abstraction that is expressed in the concrete realm of architecture and behavior. Therefore, the interpretation and meaning of the built environment differs for each culture, just as the language or political system varies. This view mandates cross-cultural studies. Such studies are imperative for learning about the architecture of any single society. Cross-cultural research thus, is critically important for understanding both the use of space and the meaning of architecture in the past.

Before Rapoport's research, many archaeologists thought that the built environment was primarily influenced by the physical environment alone (e.g., Binford 1983). Although often simplistic, it was generally thought that climate, available building materials, and local topography were the most influential factors shaping architecture. Instrumental in challenging this deterministic and non-cultural view of the built environment, Rapoport demonstrated that people were not passive slaves to their environment. Instead, humans used culture and architecture to modify their physical environment, rather than the other way around. Skeptical materialist-oriented archaeologists had assumed that the physical context determined architecture and the use of space. They never conceived that something as abstract as culture could be the primary factor influencing the built environment. However, Rapoport was able to demonstrate that abstract concepts such as worldview, sociopolitical complexity, and ways of thinking *did* structure a society's built environment. This, in my opinion, is Rapoport's greatest contribution to archaeology.

Cross-Cultural Studies of the Built Environment

One revolutionary aspect of Rapoport's work is his cross-cultural perspective of the built environment. This aspect is crucial to ethnographers and archaeologists who often do not study Western societies. Prior to Rapoport's research, archaeologists unintentionally assumed that all societies used space and architecture in the same ways and with the same meanings as Westerners. Such a culture-specific view led to many biased and often incorrect interpretations of the built environment, both past and present. For example, paleoanthropologists occasionally used analogies from modern hunter-gatherer peoples, such as the Basarwa (Bushmen or San as they are also known), to recreate how *Australopithecus africanus*, one of the earliest human ancestors living two or more million years ago, used space (e.g., Isaac 1978 and elsewhere). These small-brained australopithecines probably had no language as modern humans do. Their very rudimentary culture consisted primarily of simple lithic chopping tools that had a few stone flakes removed. Anthropologists never questioned applying the modern Basarwa's use of space to the australopithecines' because they as yet did not realize that the use of space is shaped by a group's culture. If the use of space was not cultural, then it would not matter which group served as an analog or that the australopithecines had nothing remotely similar to modern human culture. Rapoport's research demonstrated that the use of space was culturally prescribed.

Because the built environment was thought not to be a product of culture, it did not occur to the researchers to ask their informants about their use of space or to think that it differed significantly from Western society. Instead, the researchers projected their own culture's usage. Therefore, archaeologists often interpreted a prehistoric group's houses as segregated by gender and activity function as is common in Western houses, even though segregation does not occur in all societies. Archaeologists felt no need to prove that space was separated by gender and activity function because they assumed that such behavior was isomorphic across societies and time periods. This assumption justified and reinforced the Western pattern of discrete and often partitioned activity areas which were separated by function and/or gender.

As a graduate student, I was puzzled why archaeologists always assumed gender-specific work areas and the presence of function-specific loci at archaeological sites. Participant-observation among several Western and non-Western groups demonstrated that Rapoport was correct — culture *is* responsible for the nature and meaning of the built environment. By this I do not mean to suggest that climate, geography, behavior, or ecology are irrelevant, but the manner in which they are engaged is mediated through culture. That is, they are given cultural meanings that are expressed in the built environment. For example, I found that Navajo Indian architecture and use of space differed distinctly from Westerners'. While hogan dwelling space was gendered, no where else was space divided by gender (Kent 1982, 1984). The Navajo also varied their use of space and architecture seasonally. Other differences existed between more traditional and less traditional Navajos. Only Navajo culture, not environmental conditions themselves, provided the explanations for the variability in their architecture and use of space (Kent 1990a).

Learning from the Navajo

Space inside the circular, one-room Navajo dwellings (hogans) was divided into male and female areas. Without the presence of any physical barriers or partitions, men used one half almost exclusively while women primarily used the other half of the hogan. However, the space located outside the hogan was not similarly divided by gender. Even more interesting, rectangular one-room ramadas, inhabited during the summer were not partitioned by gender. Why would the use of space be strictly segregated by gender only in the hogan and no where else at Navajo camps? Now that Navajos are sedentary, hogans and ramadas are sometimes located at the same camp only a few meters apart, but their very different use of space, despite being functionally the same, persists. This apparent enigma can only be explained by understanding Navajo culture, specifically the Navajo religion and worldview.

At the heart of Navajo culture is the cosmos, which combines the *Blessingway* (a ritual and prayer), harmony, and complementariness between the genders. One of the core Navajo beliefs — that harmony always must be maintained — extended to that between individuals and nature (Reichard 1974). A breach in individual or group harmony would result in illness, death, misfortune, or other unwanted consequences. When such an event occurred, the *Blessingway* ritual had to be performed to restore the all important harmony.

The cosmos imbues harmony in Navajo every day life through

architecture and the use of space. The four cardinal directions facing the four sacred mountains mark the border of the cosmos, which itself is round and divided in half by gender (Reichard 1974). Throughout the *Blessingway* prayer, the hogan is described as a physical representation of the cosmos. To be a hogan, the structure (by definition) must be round and the entrance must face east. As in the cosmos, north in the hogan is reserved for special guests (visiting shamans, etc.). Ceremonies can only occur in a hogan and never inside a rectangular ramada or Euroamerican-style house because the latter do not represent the cosmos. In fact, some semi-traditional Navajos living in Bureau of Land Management, Euroamerican-style, rectangular housing built hogans next to their houses that were primarily used for ceremonies. Less traditional Navajos living in hogans did not separate space by gender because they no longer adhered to the Navajo religion and therefore no longer saw the hogan as a representation of the cosmos (Kent 1982, 1984). They did not segregate space by gender or task anywhere. As the culture has evolved, the meaning of the built environment has changed and thus so has the use of space.

This latent meaning of the hogan is reinforced when one contrasts it with other spaces. For traditional Navajos the space outside the hogan was not segregated by gender because neither outdoor space nor the rectangular ramada were representations of the cosmos. Thus, the general use of space in Navajo society was not partitioned by gender *except* inside a hogan. The anomalous use of space in the hogan differed from elsewhere because the hogan was conceptualized as a sacred dwelling, a physical manifestation of the cosmos. To maintain the harmony of the Navajo world, one must not disrupt the universal or cosmological harmony which means the hogan must be spatially patterned as the cosmos, including the partition or segregation of genders. Certainly there are no environmental reasons for the difference in the use of the hogan and the ramada, since, for the past 50 to 100 years, they often occur at the same camps. There also is nothing inherent in the structural form or material construction of the buildings that explains the differential use of space. However, there are extremely important and persistent cultural reasons for why the use of space inside a hogan differs so conspicuously (at least to a non-Navajo Westerner) from that inside a ramada or from that inside a Euroamerican house.

The Importance of the Cultural Context

Because not all societies conceive of or use space in similar ways, architects, ethnographers, archaeologists, and others studying non-Western peoples need to learn the cultural context for the particular society which they are attempting to understand. This also means that cross-cultural research is essential for all built environment research. Even those studying architecture within Western society need to recognize and understand variability in contexts. For example, the upper class elites in North America segregate their home space with more rooms and function specific activity areas than the lowest lower class families. In contrast, Basarwa eat at the same locus at which they sleep, entertain, work, and perform other tasks, even though it is quite feasible for them to partition space by activity or gender. The Navajo and other cross-cultural studies implicate culture as the most influential (although not sole) variable that structures and explains the built environment, regardless of the society, time period, or ecology of the region (Kent 1990b).

The critical need for everyone studying architecture to test the validity of their ideas with cross-cultural data is clear from Hillier and Hanson's (1984) statement that the reason British houses are segregated into gender specific rooms is because of a strong British taboo against incest. This simply is not valid. Navajo Indians, for instance, have many more severe sanctions against incest, but all live and sleep in a one-room dwelling. Cross-cultural research needs to be a part of all architectural research in order to understand the context of a built environment.

Culturally-bound Variability: The Impact of Meaning on the Built Environment

What causes the diversity in architecture and use of space around the world? A literature review of over 80 different cultures revealed that the sociopolitical organization or complexity of a society is the most influential variable impacting a society's built environment (Kent 1990a,b). Economics — such as hunting and gathering, farming, pastoralism, wage-labor, and others — appear to be important but only because economic pursuits are often correlated with a group's sociopolitical organization. For example, most historically known hunter-gatherers were band or tribal-level in their sociopolitical complexity. Yet hunter-gatherers who were more socio-politically complex also exist. The link between economics and sociopolitical complexity does not always hold in the cases where societies have the same economy but different sociopolitical complexities (i.e., band-level, tribal, chiefdom, etc.). It is the complexity of a society that influences the organization of space and architecture. Small-scale, band level, hunter-gatherers use space and architecture similarly to small-scale, band level horticulturists. Conversely, complex chiefdom level hunter-gatherers (such as the Northwest Coast Indians and the Ainu of northern Japan) use architecture and activity areas more similar to complex chiefdom-level farmers or pastoralists than to the non-complex band-level hunter-gatherers (Kent 1990b).

Spatial Differentiation

Many scholars assume the physical environment is extremely influential in determining architecture. However, we can see that within North America with its diverse environments, climate and similar variables play a much smaller role in domestic architecture and use of space than culture. Regardless of the geographic region, be it Hawaii, Arizona, Alaska, or New Jersey, houses are partitioned into separate activity areas or rooms and the number of rooms is partially dependent on the sociopolitical class of the owners. Houses of the upper class tend to have more function-specific rooms than the lower classes. My research demonstrates that the number of rooms per person in a house is not simplistically related to the size of a house. Irrespective of geographic region, houses are segregated by function-specific or limited rooms and occasionally gender-specific rooms/areas. Some lower class families choose to close off extra rooms while some middle class families choose to add partitions to create more rooms in their houses. The reason is not because of climate or geography. Societies use architecture to mediate between human needs and climate, yet how that mediation is achieved is completely cultural. Houses inhabited by the middle and upper classes accentuate and reinforce the notion of hierarchies in Western society while those occupied by the lower classes minimize them because, I suggest, they are disadvantaged being at the bottom of these hierarchies. This is visible in the number of rooms per person among each of the three classes.

Houses in tribal societies tend to be less partitioned than any in North America (with certain minorities maintaining traditional architecture, such as the Navajo Indians, as exceptions). Why walls in one society and not others segregate space is cultural. Western society not only segregates its space, but also its wealthy from disadvantaged minorities through zoning regulations. In the same way, Western society also stratifies its sociopolitical organization into classes, its political organization into hierarchies, its religion into specialized practitioners (e.g., nuns, monks, priests, bishops), and so on (Kent 1990a,b). A complex society is one in which there are many pieces to the whole, and these pieces are ordered in hierarchies. Using Rapoport's ideas that architecture and the use of space are a reflection of culture, cross-cultural comparisons show that societies that segment or segregate activities and/or gender in their architecture (i.e. with different rooms or use areas), also segregate their social organization into different classes, and their political organization into hierarchies (e.g. president/king, lesser governing officials, etc.; Kent 1990b).

A band-level society, such as the Basarwa, does not segregate its social or political organization, so why would Basarwa segregate their use of space or architecture? There is no reason not to partition their space and architecture, but they do not. I posit that societies organize space in the same way they organize their social and political organization (Kent 1990b). If no segregation occurs in their culture, it will not occur in the built environment.

Cross-cultural research shows that less socially-politically complex societies do not partition their houses physically or conceptually. Thus, the differential use of space cross-culturally, I suggest, reflects each culture's hierarchical (or lack of hierarchical) social status, wealth, political authority, age, gender roles and interactions. The G/wi and G//ana (Central Kalahari Basarwa) with whom I have worked do not have social stratification, occupational specialization, or political hierarchies. As a band-level society, the G/wi and G//ana neither stratify their gender categories, hierarchically evaluate the genders (e.g., men are not considered to be more important, moral, intelligent and resourceful then women), nor specialize tasks by gender (Kent 1999). In traditional highly egalitarian hunting and gathering societies, men usually hunt and women collect wild plants. What Westerners do not often realize is that hunting is not perceived by men or women as either better or worse, superior or inferior, exciting or dull. Basarwa men achieve no more respect or status for being hunters than women achieve by being gatherers (Kent 1996). Whereas Western observers, including some anthropologists, attribute more importance to one subsistence activity than another, the Basarwa do not. Men, for example, do not resent women for not hunting, and women are not jealous of men for hunting (e.g., Lee 1979). Furthermore, G/wi and G//ana women hunt and trap small animals and men gather approximately 40% of the wild plants used.

In other words, egalitarianism in small-scale hunter-gatherer societies extends to the conception of gender equality with very flexible gender roles wherein men and women perform activities that are gender-separate in other societies. Among the G/wi or G//ana, there is no gender-segregated space or architecture anywhere at any time (except immediately after a woman gives birth). There is too much overlap in activities and an absence of elevated status or importance between men and women for the G/wi or G//ana to conceive of separate male and female activity areas.

Once researchers understand the cultures of different groups, it becomes evident why band-level hunter-gatherers do not generally segregate space by gender. Egalitarian societies which have, by definition, no stratification, specialization, or hierarchies in their political or social organization will not have stratification, specialization, or hierarchies in their built environment. In other words, activity areas and architecture are partitioned by function and/or gender of the users only in societies that partition the rest of their culture, including (1) social differentiation or stratification (i.e., partitioning of the social organization), (2) political hierarchies (i.e., ranked stratifications), and (3) task specialization (i.e., categorizing and/or separating activities by the gender of a user or by the function of a task performed).

Rapoport (1982, 1990a) noted that architecture is a mnemonic device to remind participants of the structure of their culture. A society that has segregation in its culture (i.e., stratification, etc.) will have segregation in its architecture or use of space. My cross-cultural participant observation research and the cross-cultural literature consistently demonstrate the reliability of this relationship between culture and the built environment (Kent 1990). That is, material culture, such as architecture, and behavior, such as the use of space, are a direct consequence of culture and how it is organized — this is the way in which architecture and the use of space act as mnemonic devices. That Western architecture reflects differential power, status, and wealth is an excellent reminder of the discrepancies that exist in our society. Anomalies that exist in traditional societies, as in the Navajo example previously described, can usually be explained by idiosyncratic cultural themes that happen to run through the built environment. For this reason, the culture of a society must be well understood in order to understand its built environment.

Expectations and the Built Environment

A final example illustrating the fallacy that all cultures use built environments the same way comes from ethnographic research with the G/wi and G//ana, who inhabit a recently sedentary community near the Central Kalahari Game Reserve, Botswana (Kent 1996). Archaeologists around the world have assumed that the longer a site is occupied, the more artifacts will be deposited and the more substantial the architecture will be, etc. Though this makes sense to Westerners, it did not necessarily make sense to non-Westerners. After a decade of field seasons observing and interviewing G/wi and G//ana and inventorying and drawing their camps, I was surprised to discover that this seemingly commonsense proposition about material culture occurs in many disparate societies. Asking Basarwa occupants how long they had planned to inhabit a camp when they first established it as compared to how long they actually had lived there at the time of my interviews revealed that the length of time people *anticipate* staying at a camp explains the size of huts and the camp, the permanence of their dwellings, and their absolute number of objects located at a camp. Usually anticipation and actual occupation length of time coincide, but when they do not, the planned time length and not the actual time of camp inhabitation is the determining factor in the size of their huts, the overall size of camp, and the number of objects at a camp. I tested whether this was influenced by other factors, such as the number of site occupants at a camp; however, the only consistently significant factor was the anticipated length of habitation.

Was this counter-intuitive proposition valid in Western society? Interestingly, the G/wi and G//ana pattern held (as it does with subsequent cross-cultural analyses). An anecdotal example illustrates the influence of the number of items located at North American residences by anticipated length of occupation in contrast to the actual length of occupation. A family who was transferred to a new city for what was supposed to be a short time, but ended up being a much longer stay than anticipated, took very few possessions. They put most items in short-term storage until they moved to a new, more permanent location. When for various reasons their short-term stay turned into a long-term occupation, the family, still believing that they would be moving soon, slept on mattresses on the floor, lived out of boxes, and ate on a picnic table in their rented apartment. Only when they re-evaluated the situation several years later did they change their plans and anticipate a long-term occupation. At that time, they shipped the contents in storage to their supposedly temporary location. This is an example of expectations failing reality, but the expectations still influence the people's behavior and material culture despite the empirical facts. Another example comes from research in which I inventoried all objects located in middle-class Euroamerican houses, including the contents of dressers and closets. Once again people who planned to occupy a residence for a relatively short period had fewer objects at their house because they brought fewer with them. They did not purchase more because they continued to think they would move soon. In contrast, the possessions were much more numerous in a middle-class Euroamerican family who planned to occupy their house for a long period (over five or ten years). This principle, first recognized among the Basarwa hunter-gatherers of the Kalahari Desert, Botswana, is, as far as the individual societies I have examined, consistent across cultures (although what is considered to be long or short periods of time is specific to a particular society).

Conclusions

Sometimes the public questions the validity or utility of examining distant, exotic societies such as the Basarwa if they are mostly interested in their own Western society. However, Rapoport's research shows that culture structures the built environment and that it is useful to examine dissimilar cultures in order to understand one's own culture. Rapoport also demonstrated that the reasons for the variability of the built environment across different societies are a product of how each society organizes its specific culture. Rapoport, encouraging interdisciplinary research through example, documented that neither interdisciplinary nor cross-cultural research need be superficial.

Without the notion of culture structuring architecture and the use of space, archaeologists had no reason to focus on the built environment as they are ultimately interested in culture. The cultural revolution in architectural and use of space research that began with and was promoted by Rapoport changed the study of the built environment. Now architectural and spatial studies in archaeology are relatively common. My cross-cultural research shows that state-level, highly complex societies segregate their social and political organization by gender and task function (by using prestige, wealth, ethnicity, age, or other variables to stratify the social or political organization). Such societies also segregate their behavior into function-specific and/or gender-specific activity areas. As a mnemonic device, highly complex societies partition their architecture to remind users of their segregated behavior and complex culture. Thus, British and other Westerners partition their architecture more than many groups, not because of incest taboos (which almost every culture has in one form or another), but because Western society is highly complex and has numerous divisions, based on the stratification that occurs throughout the culture, behavior, and built environment.

It seems ironic that Rapoport's ideas had a greater impact on studies of the built environment in anthropology/archaeology, his adopted discipline, than in architecture. I suggest a number of reasons why this may have happened. One is that archaeologists excavate non-Western buildings. We can empirically see that the use of space and architecture were both variable in the past. Different societies have different percepts about architecture and the use of space. Many architects are taught architecture within a Western cultural framework. They do not realize or understand that architecture is completely cultural in every aspect, from the building and the building materials, to its use and peoples' conceptions about it. Second, archaeologists are anthropologists and although most have not conducted their own ethnographic field research as I have, all read ethnographies to understand the range of variation there is in material culture including architecture, in behavior including the use of space, and in culture. Most academic architects do not study non-Western societies *in depth*. Architectural education encourages the belief that the only important ideas, designs, use of space, customs, and so forth are Western ones. Therefore, many architects do not see any need or usefulness in studying specifically how culture shapes their ideas about the built environment.

An anecdote illustrates the above. An international architecture student planning to work in her own country had a very difficult time with her committee in the United States because the committee continually rejected her designs. They demanded that she design a building that conformed with Western notions of the built environment. Other faculty would only accept designs that adhered to concepts they as Westerners had about her African culture. These concepts were based on ideas that often were misconceptions or stereotypes. The committee thought that features which are considered aesthetic or functional in Western society should also be so in Non-Western societies. A third reason architects have not embraced Rapoport's ideas to the same extent that anthropologists have is because they do not understand (or believe) that architecture is a cultural expression. Instead, many see architecture as an art form emanating from their creative inner core. Their idea of beauty, just as their idea of functional, does not necessarily coincide with that of others.

How can architects design culturally sensitive buildings that will better conform to the society in which it will be built and used? This would require much more research and education; more than I think most architects would be interested in spending. They would have to learn what culture is, how and why culture varies across societies, and how the built environment articulates with a society's culture. The question really is not about how — they could take anthropology courses. The more important question is, will they? I do not think so. I do not think that most architects will ever feel that a solid knowledge of culture is a necessity to be a good architect. This is particularly true for those architects who divorce culture from architecture.

How could architects miss this most important and influential concept regarding architecture — culture? One reason is because architects often do not live in or use the buildings they design. Their job is finished when the construction is completed. They seldom test their ideas. For example, architects do not ask long-term occupants of their designs what worked, what did not, and why. They assume that if they as the designer like the building, so will everyone. This attitude might stem from the tendency of some architects to see themselves as artists, not as culturally sensitive designers of habitats. As part of a study to understand the diversity of architecture and peoples' use of it by sociopolitical and economic class in the United States, I noted how often home owners felt the need to change the design of the building in order to make it more compatible (i.e. comfortable) with their beliefs and lifestyles. If architects surveyed the occupants of the buildings they designed, many would be very disappointed to learn how common it is to drastically alter the design of one of their buildings.

Culture is what humans use to modify the physical environment through their architecture. In other words, the built environment is merely a concrete manifestation of culture. Thus, when Rapoport elucidated the link between culture and architecture, many archaeologists had no difficulty in accepting his ideas because the concept not only fit their data and theories, but it also fit the ethnographic data. However, Rapoport's ideas were not as enthusiastically embraced by architects because most were not aware of the role culture plays in their own lives and ideas, or in those of people adhering to a different set of beliefs. Rapoport's position challenged deeply held assumptions regarding the architect as artist. The change would have to be momentous for the discipline of architecture to turn from this paradigm and embrace culture as influencing built form and the variability in the use of space. At the moment many architects see the discipline as part of the arts: art, dance, creative writing, and the like. Instead, I suggest architecture needs to be seen as a social discipline — one that focuses on people and culture and regards some empirical assessment of individuals' ideas.

Every revolution has to have a platform from which it embarks. In regard to Rapoport's "revolution," archaeology had one — the knowledge of culture. For architects however, the concept of culture influencing their designs creates such cognitive dissonance, the revolution has been easier to dismiss than engage. In archaeology we have a saying: "Archaeology is anthropology or it is nothing." This means that the two cannot be separated. Archaeology today exists within an anthropological framework, as it must. I suggest architecture needs a similar saying: "Architecture is culture or it is nothing." Architecture exists within a cultural framework (see Groat, this volume). Architects of the twenty-first century need to incorporate the study of culture and cross-cultural inquiry in all facets of their research. This is more true today than ever before as the growth of a global economy means designing building that are culturally-sensitive and functional -- functional defined and designed as understood within a particular culture. I have no doubt that Rapoport's contributions will continue to inspire archaeologists. I hope they will begin to inspire more architects more into the twenty-first century.

Acknowledgements

It is no exaggeration to state that many of the ideas presented in this chapter and elsewhere would not have been conceived if it were not for Amos Rapoport. He is one of the rare, truly great scholars who also is deferential, kind, and encouraging. By changing the course of study in architecture, Rapoport opened up a new perspective to see and understand the past and for that I am most grateful.

I would also like to thank Keith Diaz Moore for inviting me to participate in this collection. There are too many people and groups to thank individually for allowing me to work with them and to understand their view of the world. Nonetheless, I am grateful to each. I thank Judy Mercer for her editorial suggestions. No one except myself is to be blamed for any inaccuracies or shortcomings that may still remain in this chapter.

References

Binford, L. (1983). *In Pursuit of the past: Decoding the Archaeological Record.* London: Thames and Hudson.

Bourdieu, P. (1973). The Berber house. In *Rules and Meanings: The Anthropology of Everyday Knowledge*, edited by Mary Douglas, pp. 98-110. Harmondsworth: Penguin Books.

Cunningham, C. (1973). Order in the Atoni house. In *Right and Left: Essays on Dual Symbolic Classification*, edited by Rodney Needham, pp. 204-238. Chicago: University of Chicago Press.

Hillier, W. & Hanson, J. (1984). *The Social Logic of Space*. Cambridge: Cambridge University Press.

Isaac, G. (1978). The food-sharing behavior of protohuman hominids. *Scientific American* 238:90-108.

Glassie, H. (1975). *Folk Housing in Middle Virginia*. Knoxville: University of Tennessee Press.

Hugh-Jones, C. (1979). *From the Milk River: Spatial and Temporal Processes in Northwest Amazonia*. Cambridge: Cambridge University Press.

Kent, S. (1982). Hogans, sacred circles, and symbols -- The Navajo use of space. In D. Brugge & C. Frisbie (Eds.) *Navajo Religion and Culture: Selected Views*, pp. 128-137. Museum of New Mexico Press, Santa Fe.

Kent, S. (1984). *Analyzing Activity Areas: An Ethnoarchaeological Study of the Use of Space*. Albuquerque: University of New Mexico Press.

Kent, S. (1990a). Activity areas and architecture: An interdisciplinary view of the relationship between use of space and domestic built environments. In S. Kent (Ed.) *Domestic Architecture and the Use of Space — An Interdisciplinary Cross-Cultural Study*, pp. 1-8. Cambridge: Cambridge University Press. (Reprinted in paperback 1993)

Kent, S. (1990b). A cross-cultural study of segmentation, architecture, and the use of space. In S. Kent (Ed.) *Domestic Architecture and the Use of Space--An Interdisciplinary Cross-Cultural Study*. pp. 127-152. Cambridge: Cambridge University Press.

Kent, S. (1996b). Cultural diversity among African foragers. In S. Kent (Ed.) *Cultural Diversity Among Twentieth Century Foragers: An African Perspective*, pp. 1-18. Cambridge: Cambridge University Press.

Kent, S. (1996b). Hunting variation in a recently sedentary Kalahari community. In S. Kent (Ed.) *Cultural Diversity Among Twentieth Century Foragers: An African Perspective*, pp. 125-156. Cambridge: Cambridge University Press.

Kent, S. (1998). Invisible Gender — Invisible Foragers: Late Stone Age southern African Hunter-Gatherer Prehistory and the Archaeological Record. In S. Kent (Ed.) Gender in African Prehistory, pp. 39-67. Walnut Creek, CA: Altamira Press.

Kent, S. (1999). Egalitarianism, equality, and equitable power. In T. Sweeley (Ed.) *Manifesting Power: Gender and Interpretation of Power in Archaeology*, pp. 30 - 48. London: Routledge Publishers.

Kent, S. (submitted). How egalitarian are highly egalitarian societies — Variation among Kalahari foragers. Manuscript submitted to journal for review.

Lee, R. (1979). *The !Kung San: Men, Women, and Work in a Foraging Society*. Cambridge: Cambridge University.

Plimpton, C. L. and Fekri H. (1978). Social space: A determinant of house architecture. *Environment and Planning B*. 14:439-449.

Rapoport, A. (1969). *House Form and Culture*. Englewood Cliffs NJ: Prentice Hall.

Rapoport, A. (1976). Sociocultural aspects of man-environment studies. In A. Rapoport, (Ed.) *The Mutual Interaction of People and Their Built Environment*, pp. 7-35. Paris: Mouton Publishers.

Rapoport, A. (1977). *Human Aspects of Urban Form*. Oxford: Pergamon.

Rapoport, A. (1982). *The Meaning of the Built Environment*. Beverly Hills: Sage Publications.

Rapoport, A. (1985). Thinking about home environments: A conceptual framework. In I. Altman & C. Werner, (Eds.) *Home Environments*, pp. 255-286. New York: Plenum Press.

Rapoport, A. (1990a). Systems of activities and systems of settings. In S. Kent (Ed.) *Domestic Architecture and the Use of Space — An Interdisciplinary, Cross-cultural Study*, pp. Cambridge: Cambridge University Press.

Rapoport, A. (1990b). *History and Precedent in Environmental Design*. New York: Plenum Press.

Reichard, G. (1974). *Navaho Religion: A Study of Symbolism*. Princeton: Princeton University Press.

Watson, P. J. (1979). *Archaeological Ethnography in Western Iran*. Viking Fund Publications in Anthropology, No. 57.

Yellen, J. (1977). *Archaeological Approaches to the Present*. New York: Academic Press.

